LYNDALL URWICK, MANAGEMENT PIONEER:
A BIOGRAPHY

Lyndall Urwick, by Karsh of Ottawa.

Lyndall Urwick, Management Pioneer: A Biography

EDWARD BRECH, ANDREW THOMSON,
AND JOHN F. WILSON

OXFORD
UNIVERSITY PRESS

OXFORD
UNIVERSITY PRESS

Great Clarendon Street, Oxford, OX2 6DP,
United Kingdom

Oxford University Press is a department of the University of Oxford.
It furthers the University's objective of excellence in research, scholarship,
and education by publishing worldwide. Oxford is a registered trade mark of
Oxford University Press in the UK and in certain other countries

Published in the United States of America by Oxford University Press
198 Madison Avenue, New York, NY 10016, United States of America

British Library Cataloguing in Publication Data

Data available

ISBN 978-0-19-954196-6

Preface

There are different types of biographies. This one follows Thomas Carlyle's view that biography is a part of history, and that the lives of great human beings are essential to our understanding of society and its institutions. This is appropriate because our subject, Lyndall Urwick, 'urged the study of great men and women of the past—management heroes—because he believed that the study of the methods of those who had been successful would inspire others' (Witzel 2002: 59). It is therefore not a family history or an autobiography, although it contains some elements of Urwick's own partial autobiographies; nor is it a psychological exploration of personality or part of the modern vogue for a debunking biography or a treatise on his writings on management and administration, a topic to which we cannot do full justice in the available space. It is written primarily as a contribution to the study of management history and the role of people within it, of which Urwick himself was one of the first and most influential exponents. And management history in turn is an important component of the study of management, the most critical component of modern economic organization.

Most biographies in management are of people who lead great companies, important in their particular industry but rarely influencing the wider industrial and commercial scene. Urwick did indeed lead an influential company, but beyond that was one of those people whose wider-ranging vision in both thought and action shaped the culture of his time and more importantly the future. His writings covered a wide range of management activities from scientific and systematic modes of management decision-making to the theory of organizations to leadership to the histories of the originators of management thought and action. His actions included directing the first international management organization, creating what was for several decades the most influential management consultancy in Britain, and leading the attempts to professionalize managers through organization and education. These taken together tell us a great deal about the state of management in Britain and internationally during his lifetime.

Because Urwick's importance can be divided reasonably clearly between his thoughts and his actions, the chapter structure of the book, while also being conventionally chronological, follows this division. We have a short Introduction to the man himself. Chapters 1 and 2 take us through his upbringing, education, experiences in the First World War, and employment until leaving Rowntree's in 1928. Chapter 3 is about his time at the International

Management Institute (IMI). Chapter 4 discusses his writings up to the Second World War. Chapter 5 deals with his consultancy company, Urwick Orr and Partners (UOP). Chapter 6 is a relatively short chapter about his activities during the Second World War. Chapter 7 deals with his activities in relation to various British institutions of management and management development. Chapter 8 is about his 'mission at large' in Britain and abroad, while Chapter 9 covers his writings from the 1940s. Finally, Chapter 10 evaluates Urwick's contribution to management in its various aspects.

The background to the writing of this book needs some explanation. It was initiated by Edward Brech, who had been Personal Assistant to Urwick at Urwick Orr and co-author of several books, to say nothing of being an author of considerable distinction in his own right. But Edward did not start work on this biography until spring 2003, after the 2002 publication by the Thoemmes Press of his monumental five volumes of management history, *The Evolution of Modern Management*. Sadly, he died in September 2006 aged 97, leaving a large manuscript for which he was seeking a publisher. The manuscript and copyright were left to the Worshipful Company of Management Consultants, with whom Edward had an honorary role as Archivist. It was, however, at some 205,000 words, too long to be considered by a commercial publisher.

At this point, John Wilson and Andrew Thomson, who had been very closely associated with Edward as successive secretaries of the Management History Research Group, and had also just finished a book, *The Making of Modern Management: British Management in Historical Perspective* (2006), which covers much of the same time period and subject matter, volunteered to take the manuscript forward to publication. With the assistance of Allan Williams and Edward's son, Robert, this was arranged with the Worshipful Company, and a contract was negotiated with Oxford University Press.

Working with the manuscript has inevitably meant very substantial editing, indeed a reduction by more than half in length, and some considerable rewriting to bring it to its present form. The rewriting has taken two forms: firstly, to add perspectives from outside the Urwick papers and Edward's own knowledge; and secondly, to provide a final chapter evaluating Urwick in his numerous contributions to management. References have also been affected by the dual approach to writing. Material taken from the Urwick records is not referenced because Edward did not do this, and this includes references to articles and books; however, material which we have used and not taken from this source is referenced. For similar reasons, not to mention a lack of space, we have not attempted to provide a total bibliography of Urwick's works, although note is made of an interim one which was produced by UOP in 1958.

Urwick had a substantial library even from a relatively young age, and kept his papers in good order, for which the authors of this biography are truly grateful. The great majority of the material is taken from the Urwick records at the library at Henley Management College, where Edward Brech is fondly remembered and worked indefatigably for several years. There is a huge amount of material covering almost every paper Urwick wrote between 1910 and his death, including a great deal of correspondence, especially with other figures in the management movement. Indeed, one cannot help but be amazed at the sheer amount of material and that one man should have initiated all this, much of it while he was also an active manager at Fownes Brothers, Rowntree's, the IMI, or UOP. Urwick also wrote two partial auto-biographies and plans were made for another, to be entitled 'Management Pilgrimage', with external assistance, notably from Jackie Smyth, VC. However, none of these was ever brought to fruition.

We are extremely grateful to the staff at Henley for their help to Edward and our own visits more recently; without their cooperation the book would not have been possible. The Lyndall Fownes Urwick archive, Henley Business School, and the University of Reading kindly provided a number of the photographs in the book. The Open University Library, where Edward Brech's documents have been archived, the Management Information Centre at the Chartered Management Institute at Corby, which inherited the Urwick-originated Management Library, and the Paihia Library have also been very helpful in making relevant material available. There are others who must be thanked. Sir Alan Urwick, Lyndall's son, has been extremely supportive in a number of ways, not least in his provision of several of the key photographs in the book. David Musson has gone well beyond the formal requirements of his role as editor for Oxford University Press, making valuable points and giving encouragement and support, and Matthew Derbyshire has also been most helpful. We would also like to thank the three referees for Oxford University Press, not only for their recommendations that the book should be supported, but also for their interesting and helpful advice. Amongst our academic colleagues, we would like to pay a special note of gratitude to John Child and John Quail for their valuable comments after having read an advance draft. On a personal basis, we would like to thank our wives for their forbearance. And last but not least, we as the junior authors would like to pay tribute to Edward as the senior author not just for his massive contribution to this book, but also for his leadership in the whole area of management history.

Andrew Thomson
John F. Wilson

Contents

Abbreviations

AACP	Anglo-American Council on Productivity
AGM	Annual General Meeting
AMA	American Management Association
ASC	Administrative Staff College
BA	Bachelor of Arts
BBC	British Broadcasting Council
BIM	British Institute of Management
BMC	British Management Council
BPC	British Productivity Council
BPR	business process re-engineering
CIME	Council of Industry for Management Education
CIOS	International Committee for Scientific Management (Conseil Internationale de l'Organisation Scientifique)
DNB	*Dictionary of National Biography*
DSO	Distinguished Service Order
ENSA	Entertainments National Service Association
FBI	Federation of British Industries
FME	Foundation for Management Education
HMSO	Her Majesty's Stationery Office
IAM	International Academy of Management
IIA	Institute of Industrial Administration
ILM	Institute of Labour Management
ILO	International Labour Organization
IMI	International Management Institute
IPM	Institute of Personnel Management
LSE	London School of Economics
Lt. Col.	Lieutenant Colonel
MA	Master of Arts
MBA	Master of Business Administration
MBO	Management by Objectives
MC	Military Cross

MRG	Management Research Group
NAAFI	Navy, Army and Air Force Institute
NASC	National Administrative Staff College
NEDO	National Economic Development Office
NIIP	National Institute of Industrial Psychology
OBE	Officer of the Order of the British Empire
OTC	Officer Training Corps
PA	Personnel Administration
PE	Production Engineering
REFA	Reichsausschuss fur Arbeitszeitermittlung (National Committee for Work Time Determination)
TVA	Tennessee Valley Authority
UOP	Urwick Orr and Partners

Introduction

Lyndall Urwick was never known by his first name during his lifetime; it was always 'Lyn', or when referring to him in the third person, 'L. U.'. Nevertheless, we will use the more formal name in this biography. It was said of Lyndall Urwick in his obituary in *The Times* that he had as many careers in his life as he had sides to his character. He had a military background based on his experiences in the First World War, and a continuing bent towards using military examples in his management career. He worked in business, especially with Rowntree's, at that time the leader in Britain in new thinking about management. He was an international and national civil servant in his role as the Director of the International Management Institute and later during the Second World War. He founded his own management consultancy, which rapidly rose to be the leading firm of its type in Britain. He was an educationalist, concerned with bringing education to managers. And, perhaps above all, he was a gifted and prolific writer and speaker, using these abilities to pursue the cause of 'modern' management around the world until his death. Through all these roles, he can be seen not only as a pioneer, but also as arguably the most outstanding figure in the history of British management, not least because he has been the only one to achieve genuine international recognition. It is these different facets of his career with which we will be concerned for most of this biography, before trying to pull them together, alongside the different sides to his character, in Chapter 10.

But before moving on, it will be helpful to understand the kind of man about whom we are writing. In this context, it is fortunate that an affectionate pen-portrait was compiled about him in 1960, at a high point of his career, by Mrs Dorothy Rowe who had served as his Personal Assistant in his 'missionary' programme for nearly a decade. This provides a generous and sympathetic starting point in evaluating his character, and so we present it here:

'Colonel Urwick', a 'retired old gentleman' as he puts it, is in his late sixties, something above middle height, spare of build, grey-haired and with regular features. He has the military bearing his title would lead one to expect. His gaze is direct, his manner and stride energetic as he advances from his antique leather-topped desk, pipe in mouth and hand outstretched, to welcome the visitor. Once settled in congenial conversation, however, he will sit oblivious of time for hours, speaking slowly and listening with deep concentration. He prefers to deal with one subject thoroughly and at length, rather than to rush through several in the course of a business day. A preference for military things occurs fairly often among men like Col. Urwick who have seen some action in war, but have never been regular soldiers in peacetime. But this is unusual in a man whose reputation has been made in the world of business and whom the *Daily Express* nicknamed 'Mr. Efficiency'. The visitor, aware that this doyen of management consultants is Chairman of one of the largest British firms in the profession, that he holds the highest international award for contributions to the science of management, finds with surprise that the conversation soon turns to the excellent organisation patterns of the British Army, or the contribution of Nelson to the art of leadership in great undertakings. Col. Urwick is unrepentant in his prejudice. Viewed in the light of his practical achievements, it can hardly be dismissed as irrelevant.

In his personal leadership of his employees, he is anything but the traditional army disciplinarian. Complete informality is the rule. 'L.U.' is on first names terms with all from the most senior man to the typist and the charlady. At social Company functions, of which there are many, it is the newest recruit to the firm, at whatever level, who is placed next to him at table. His informality does not, nevertheless, detract from a natural dignity which wins respect. He is an able platform speaker, with a resonant and pleasing voice. He trusts his colleagues and those lower down the line of authority. His own absorbing interest is in board policy, in choosing and promoting staff, and in public relations. Apart from these activities he leaves individuals to carry out their responsibilities with very great freedom from control.

He is materially generous. After the Second War he transferred his ownership rights over his Company to a profit-sharing trust on which he is a single member only. He is impetuous and does not suffer fools gladly. Emotionally drawn towards public service and tireless in his contributions to it, he has lacked the moderation and the skill in compromise which would have brought its full successes and rewards. An O.B.E. and an M.C. both earned for military service before he was twenty-eight are poor recognition of a world-wide reputation in the science of management.

His humour is the pleasure of his friends and the anathema of his ill-wishers. Reporting to American top executives on the need to train future business leaders young, he said 'Hollywood learned your lesson long ago, that one cannot groom elderly spinsters for stardom'. It was witty, but the elderly spinsters were not all amused.

He has always been an innovator, although his favourite claim is to have originated no new thinking but merely to have drawn the public's attention to the great thinking of others. A writer and researcher of boundless industry with some 280 titles of books and articles to his credit, he has seized and launched a number of ideas a decade before they were ripe for public acceptance – the creation of an administrative staff college, of a national institute of management, the recognition of the work of F.W. Taylor, Henri Fayol and Mary Follett, to mention only a few examples. His colleagues still think him 'a crazy loon' today. But they remember that the business he began in a back room in Bloomsbury has grown in twenty-five years to operate in a number of countries.

He is solitary in his tastes. His thinking is based less on conversation than on reading and reflection in a comfortable study in his Dorset manor house, a room into which even his family do not intrude uninvited. His hobby is genealogy, pursued either at home, or in the quiet of the Reform Club Library. As he grows older, he no longer seeks out with such zeal for battle those who quarrel with his views, but confines his social life to the circle of his friends and disciples. Among his favourite pastimes nowadays are his numerous informal talks to managers, particularly younger managers, who meet in various professional groups, most of which he was instrumental in founding, where they discuss topics about which he wrote books thirty years ago. In the obvious enthusiasm of these younger men for causes which he still has at heart but for which he is no longer so ready to lose sleep and leisure, Colonel Urwick finds his most satisfying reward for four decades of endeavour.

1

Early Life, the First World War, and Glove-Making

Sustaining the theme that Lyndall Urwick had as many careers in his life as he had sides to his character, it is fascinating to delve into his early life, given its exciting and diverse nature. We shall see that after an extensive education and a brief period with his father's company, Fownes of Worcester, he was then pitched into the First World War, a mighty challenge for one so young. His military experiences were, however, part of the crucial formative influences that helped to fashion a range of influences and skills. We shall also see in this chapter that after another short spell with Fownes, which was ended prematurely by a major row with the other partners, Urwick was obliged to endure a period of unemployment. It was during this difficult year that he first came into contact with Seebohm Rowntree, precipitating yet another phase in his life that will be charted in Chapter 2.

ANTECEDENTS AND BIRTH

Lyndall Fownes Urwick was born on 3 March 1891 at Northwood, North Malvern, Worcestershire, the son of Henry and Annis Urwick. All of his three names are unusual and relate to his antecedents. The Urwick name had Saxon origins in the rural north-west of England, while Lyndall came from earlier generations of his mother's family, including his grandfather, Lyndall Whitby of Yeovil. Of the three, however, the Fownes name was in some respects the most important for the situation into which Lyndall Urwick was born. Lyndall's great-grandmother was a Fownes, a name that had Norman origins, again in England's north-west. Annis Fownes was the daughter of the founder of the family glove-making business. The origins of the business seem to have lain with John Fownes, known to have been a fur, leather, and glove merchant in London in 1777, with some references to a well-established glove-making unit in Worcester, based on outworking (Coopey 2003). When he died in

1827, the business was taken over by his two sons, Thomas and Edward, hence the name of the company, Fownes Brothers. They took their nephew, Lyndall's grandfather Samuel John Urwick, into partnership in the company in 1856. Thomas was childless, but Edward had two daughters, one of whom married William Gardiner Rigden in 1869, and he was immediately also taken into a similar partnership in the Fownes Company. Thus, the two families, the Urwicks and the Rigdens, came in succeeding generations to control the company, a development which was to have considerable importance for Lyndall's own career.

Samuel John Urwick had four sons and four daughters, of whom the eldest son Henry, born in 1859, was Lyndall's father. Henry was also taken into the business, a few years later becoming general manager of the new Fownes factory in Worcester, with one of the younger Rigdens to support him as assistant manager. In 1889, Henry married Annis Whitby, the daughter of Elias Lyndall Whitby of Yeovil, who was the head of another glove-making company. Indeed, the two met when Henry was engaged in trading activities in the West Country (Figures 1.1a and 1.1b).

At this time, glove-making was a medium-sized industry, with its own Livery Company. It was enjoying increasing demand as the middle stratum of

Figure 1.1a Urwick's father, Sir Henry Urwick.

Figure 1.1b Urwick's mother, Lady Annis Urwick, née Whitby.

the national population grew throughout the nineteenth century, alongside considerable export opportunities (Coopey 2003). The Fownes Company had operations not only in England but also overseas, notably in the United States and Germany, while the Whitby company was also a flourishing organization. Since Henry was earning a reasonable income as general manager of the Worcester factory, and both he and his wife were earning dividends from their respective companies, the family were financially very well established and able to maintain a comfortable lifestyle, as well as being held in high esteem by the Urwicks and in social and business circles in Worcester. It was into this stable and comfortable ambience that Lyndall was born. As Lyndall later wrote: 'I consider that I was exceptionally fortunate in my parents.'

UPBRINGING AND SCHOOLDAYS

Unusually for the period, Lyndall was an only child, due to a medically complex birth that prevented his mother from having further children. Clearly intelligent, he was nurtured by his parents, with the expectation that he would succeed his father as general manager. At the age of 3, he began attending a local kindergarten catering for both boys and girls. Three years later he was transferred to a local private co-educational boarding school, at which Lyndall was a day-pupil, where he apparently excelled in amateur dramatics, a hobby copied from his father. Four years later, when he was 11, his parents decided that boarding school would be more appropriate in order to prepare him for one of the great public schools. The Boxgrove School in Guildford, Surrey, was chosen for this purpose; it gave him a love for reading, a solid command of the English language, a readiness to study, and an excellent facility in composition, coupled with an enjoyment of writing, capacities and skills which were to serve him well later in life (Figure 1.1c).

Success in the Common Entrance Examinations in 1904–5 brought the need for a choice of school; consultations by his parents among local friends resulted in the choice of Repton School in Derbyshire, which accepted Lyndall in September 1905. The useful local information had designated The Priory as the first choice of 'House', because the master in charge (Henry Vassall) was known to be dedicated to the boys, a 'born schoolmaster'. Lyndall always

Figure 1.1c Lyndall Urwick, aged seven.

looked back on him with high admiration and warm personal regard, as well as declaring his Repton years as 'very happy'. They were also scholastically very successful, because his examination results firstly placed him in the Remove (between the fourths and the fifths) and then the Upper Fifth. Going to Repton had also focused attention on an important family issue: while the parental expectation was a career within Fownes, they refrained from pressuring him, making it clear to Lyndall that the choice was his, and his alone. With both parents steeped in a background of business activity, there must have been a good deal of informal domestic discussion on business management and finance matters, giving the young Lyndall a broad under-standing of these issues. On the other hand, his own inclination was towards developing a preference for a military career, in part prompted by his reading, as well as by an affection for his uncle, Frank Davidson Urwick, his father's younger brother who was already well established as a professional soldier. Certainly, even as a young boy Lyndall enjoyed playing with toy soldiers.

While without being seen as a 'swot', his scholastic progress at Repton was manifest. There were also further activities adding to the enjoyment, particu-larly writing and especially poetry. His ability in this field came to light through the misfortune of an attack of measles during the Easter vacation of 1907, when his father encouraged him in whiling away the time to enter for the British Schools Annual Competition in poetic composition. His entry was a set of twelve sonnets which 'to his own astonishment as much as to everybody else's' gained a prize. He was also contributing occasional articles and poems for publication in the school magazine, *The Reptonian*, the editor of which he became for three years. He also entered for a number of the existing Repton School and wider Public School Essay Competitions, gaining several prizes in successive years: the Howe (four times), the Navy League (three times), the Repton School Essay (twice), and the school's Modern History Prize (twice). While these amounted to substantial achievements in themselves, what he regarded as his greatest triumph came in his last year at school, responding to his father's special wish by entering for the recently inaugurated Duke of Devonshire Public Schools Essay Competition. This required an essay on 'The Organisation of the Defence of the Empire', a highly ambitious project for a schoolboy of 18. It involved knowledge, amongst other subjects, of the recent Colonial Conference and Haldane's Army Reform programme, as well as recognizing differences of opinion in Britain on these issues. His essay was selected by the Headmaster as the Repton submission and it gained the 1910 prize, resulting in his first publication, in *The British Empire Review*.

Those scholastic and literary accomplishments undoubtedly were features promoting his appointment as House Prefect in 1908, as School Prefect in

1909, as well as Head Boy in The Priory in that year. Personality factors must also have played a part, indicating that he displayed leadership qualities, as well as social skills. School sports did not interest him much, because he recognized his limited prowess in both cricket and football. His own pre-dilections lay with boxing and long-distance running, in both of which he was able to display some ability. In the former, the school's Sergeant Instructor encouraged him in two successive years to enter the Public Schools Champi-onship trials (held annually in Aldershot) as a featherweight. The strongest attraction for him within the school, however, lay with the Combined Cadet Force into which he enrolled from entrance, gaining thereby a practical environment for pursuit of his already long-standing interest in soldiering. Under the Haldane reforms of 1906, the Combined Cadet Forces within schools and universities were transformed into an 'Officer Training Corps' (OTC), with specific facilities for studies and training geared towards gaining a Special Reserve Commission as a junior officer in the Territorial Army. Lyndall Urwick was strongly attracted to this route, encouraging him to involve himself actively in the School Corps training unit, to the point where he was promoted to Colour Sergeant for his last year in the School Corps, the highest rank open to boy-soldiers.

Upon entering his last year of schooling in the autumn of 1909, the question of a future career came under consideration. Although attendance at Oxford University was taken for granted, it was important to choose the most appro-priate curriculum. During the previous couple of years, Lyndall himself had steadily veered towards accepting employment within the family firm, given the excellent prospects of advancement that were clearly open to him. The interest in active military matters remained, but was already partially assuaged by the years of OTC involvement. Lyndall's own inclination was to respond positively to his father's wish that he should join the firm, because he was very fond of, and closely attached to, his father, leading to the clear outcome that Lyndall should enter for the University Scholarship Examination.

In December 1909, Lyndall Urwick sat for the Scholarships and Exhibitions Examinations for the Balliol and New College group at Oxford, with Modern History as his selected area, gaining an Exhibition at New College for the following October. It was characteristic of Henry Urwick that he decided against acceptance of the funding accompanying the award of the Exhibition, so that it could be used for the benefit of another young student. This person turned out to be none other than Harold Laski, one of the most eminent political and economic theorists of his generation. By that time, Lyndall was also revealing a keen interest in contemporary affairs: he had acquired *What to Read on Social and Economic Subjects*, compiled by the Fabian Society, which he annotated copiously. An important family arrangement was also confirmed consequent upon Lyndall's clear decision to commence his career with the Fownes Company after graduation. His father had secured agreement from the Rigden family partners that upon attaining the age of 25 in 1916, Lyndall would become accredited as a share-owning junior partner.

OXFORD UNIVERSITY

Prior to going up to New College, Oxford, in October 1910, Lyndall Urwick spent some weeks in Karlsruhe, with a family headed by a German professor, reflecting a desire to prepare thoroughly for the opportunities awaiting him. He was especially keen to develop as a proficient public speaker, by gaining membership of the Oxford Union and participating in the many debates and discussion meetings. In addition, he read extensively about national politics, though never with a view to taking an active role. Unlike his father, who had aspired to be a Member of Parliament, Lyndall was content to educate himself in the subject, perhaps because the Rigden partners within the Fownes Company were all staunch Conservatives, whereas Henry Urwick was a member of the Liberal Party. Nevertheless, in deference to his father, he became active with a group of fellow undergraduates in establishing the Liberal Party within the University. To some extent the Union debates also had a political orientation, and since Lyndall showed himself to be proficient at public speaking, this meant being regularly invited to participate. All this came to a head in his third term, upon being selected as the University's spokesman in a debate on 'Welsh Disestablishment', the subject being an issue currently active in Parliament. In the opening speech by a distinguished Parliamentary visitor, Lyndall found himself 'being massacred', as he later described it, instead of receiving what he had expected, a kindly treatment for a young undergraduate not yet experienced in public life, even if he recognized the humour with which the massacre was laced. In courtesy to a Union visitor, his own subsequent reply had perforce to be appropriately polite. The episode ended any direct interest he had in politics, as well as curtailing active participation in debates. Nevertheless, he did achieve the significant recognition of becoming Secretary of the Union, at a time when he had some famous contemporaries such as Harold Macmillan, Walter Monckton, and A. P. Herbert. Sadly, though, many more of his contemporaries were to die in the First World War.

With specific regard to his Oxford studies, as the Modern History School required candidates to take up a special subject, Lyndall chose Economics, in the hope that it would equip him for his intended business career. However, he soon found that the subject matter lay primarily in 'Currency and Banking' and 'Public Finance', topics which disillusioned him in the following two years. Moreover, there was no tutorial instruction available for him in Economics, so the acquisition of knowledge was dependent upon a very sizeable range of recommended reading, little of which was relevant to the business world. Indeed, 'business' had no place in British academia at this time; it was still rare for sons of family firms to pursue a university education. Fortuitously in those latter two years, Lyndall had a sympathetic tutor, albeit one with no knowledge of the business world. Discussing the problem with Lyndall in the best way he could manage, the tutor stressed the continuing development of intellectual discipline that stemmed from a systematic programme of studies, irrespective of the field. Lyndall could do little else but accept that viewpoint, although perhaps his dedication was less intense than a different context might have engendered. Consequently, although as an Exhibitioner Scholar he would have been expected to gain a First-Class Honours BA in Modern History, in fact he finished with only a Second Class. Later in life he was apt to express 'dissatisfaction' with his years at Oxford, although to most people his time there would have been more than satisfactory. Maybe that failure to gain the First Class influenced the dissatisfaction, although he himself had the rather strange explanation that it was 'partly due to the fact that my father had not been an Oxford man'.

There were, however, various other factors contributing to the lower outcome. One lay in the way he spent his vacations, given that his tutors expected him to complete reading assignments not covered during term, while his father wanted him to develop foreign language proficiency, again unusual for businessmen at that time. As a consequence, he spent long spells in Hanover during summer vacations, while Easters were spent mostly in France. His father having presented Lyndall with a motorcycle, he also enjoyed a cross-country riding holiday in France, accompanied by a couple of English friends (Figure 1.2). His competence in French gave him ample opportunity for practice, because his friends relied on him to deal with all travel and accommodation issues. Moreover, during the terms he participated in a number of social and leisure pursuits, particularly amateur dramatics (playing Julius Caesar in an Oxford University Dramatic Society production), long-distance running, though not competitively, and he was part of a group which founded the Camelot Club, which survived as a dining club known as 'The Circus'. Another distraction stemmed from his enjoyment of writing, with the university magazine *Isis* providing the medium. Early items were two articles in 1911 issues on battels (the system of charging for accommodation, food, and other services), which served to demonstrate some analytical skill in diagnosing weaknesses in method, organization, and practice. Furthermore,

Figure 1.2 Oxford student trip to France, 1912.

his predisposition for poetry came into play during 1912, with seven poems accepted for publication in issues of *Isis*, revealing both imaginative flair and an interesting competence in their differentiation of structure and style.

Another significant diversion from studies was membership of the OTC, an involvement which Lyndall took very seriously. Having achieved Certificate A standard at Repton, he was able to spend a probationary year in the Oxford Unit in order to proceed towards Certificate B in the second year, spending some eight weeks of the 1911 summer vacation on military service in the OTC Camp. Soon after enrolling, he successfully applied to the Adjutant of the Third Battalion, the Worcestershire Regiment, to seek a commission in the Special Reserve, conditional upon success in gaining Certificate B. He entered into the programme earnestly, including membership of the Oxford University War Games Club, where he was able for several evenings each month to enjoy the fascination of mock military exercises. Additionally, he had a syllabus of military studies to pursue, ending with the award of Certificate B in 1912, resulting in promotion to Special Reserve Second Lieutenant.

It is perhaps no surprise, then, that Lyndall Urwick did not achieve a First-Class degree, given his extensive extra-curricular activities. Nevertheless, convinced that he should continue to study, he sought advice from two of the leading figures of that era, Sidney and Beatrice Webb, already well known in the social-economics domain and both holding tutorial roles in London University. They readily understood his unease at the transition that he was about to face, particularly the loss of the intellectual stimulus of university life. To bridge the gulf, they recommended him to register as an External Student at the London School of Economics, within the Economics Faculty (which included a historical slant), where he might gain a Higher Degree through research, possibly on the glove industry. They even offered to tutor him, resulting in some preparatory reading on the subject. However, because his father insisted on a further trip to Germany, this time to Berlin, Lyndall never registered for the research degree. One can only wonder whether taking up the Webbs' offer would have converted him into a full-time academic scholar, diverting him away from the world of practice that he was soon to enter.

With his final examinations completed, Lyndall Urwick came down from Oxford in June 1913. After his summer activities in Berlin, he went to live in his parents' home in Great Malvern and entered the family business. Fownes had always favoured sons of the partners coming into the business, albeit at the operational level to learn the basics of glove-making, in order to provide the necessary continuity of management style. Lyndall recognized that he could be no exception, despite his graduate status. While he continued to read widely on a series of subjects, inevitably conversation within the family must have often focused on the factory, bringing to the surface aspects of method, of operational planning, of supervision, and of factory management that would soon become his *raison d'être*.

THE FIRST WORLD WAR

In the summer of 1914, while Urwick was bedding himself into Fownes, fate intervened. During July, he was serving at his TA Camp, stationed at Tidworth on Salisbury Plain, when the Battalion Colonel regretted having to inform him and all the others with him that the War Office had declared a 'Precautionary Period', meaning that Urwick was not free to withdraw from service and return to civilian life. The unit was sent to Weymouth and two weeks later, on 4 August 1914, war with Germany was declared. Urwick's battalion then almost immediately sailed from Southampton to Le Havre,

Figure 1.3 The trenches in World War I.

to become part of the assembling British Expeditionary Force of some 60,000 (Figure 1.3).

The base camp for assembly of British troops in France was established near the port of St Nazaire, from which point units were dispersed to battle areas. The German army had invaded and crossed Belgium, thrusting westwards towards north-east France and south-west towards Paris. The French forces opposed the latter, while the British Army battalions were hurried across country to the frontier with Belgium, meeting the advancing German forces in the area of Mons, where heavy fighting continued for a couple of weeks in August. During the remaining months of 1914 and early 1915, the major battle areas for British forces in action were Mons, Le Cateau, the Marne valley, and the Aisne valley; in all of those Urwick's unit was constantly engaged in serious fighting, entailing very high levels of casualties on both sides. Urwick's command of French enabled him to keep his platoon of soldiers informed of progress elsewhere from the published French bulletins and despatches. He was also careful about informing his men as to objectives and actions, as well as giving them praise for their accomplishments, indicating that he had an excellent grasp of human relations strategy.

As the Mons onslaught by the Germans was extremely heavy, having been mounted by far superior manpower and artillery, the British command at base headquarters decided quietly to pull back so as to conserve manpower for a better-placed attack. In the ensuing confusion, while Urwick's platoon did not receive the order to retreat, he was able through personal initiative in local reconnoitring activities to work out what was happening, displaying commendable skill in piloting his own and the neighbouring platoons quietly back to base during the night. In later life, he always looked back with a sense of pride on the Mons battles, valuing his 'Mons Star' among his most treasured possessions.

As 1914 progressed, the British units regrouped in the area of Le Cateau, alongside the French forces from the south, to block the German thrust towards Paris. For Lieutenant Urwick those weeks were a severe test of his man-management command skills, with heavy casualties necessitating constant inflows of new recruits to his platoon. Within the platoon, he also had to face fatigue to the point of exhaustion amongst the men, shortages of food rations, heading off demoralization resulting from the death or injury of comrades, and maintaining morale to endure the relentless battles with all their complexities of shifting locations as ground was gained or lost. His own morale remained high in sharing those terrible conditions with his men, never taking advantage of any situation whereby rank would give him an advantage. In November, he paid the price; utterly exhausted and underfed, he collapsed into a slit trench full length and fell instantly asleep, not aware that he had fallen into mud and lain in inches of water. Upon awakening after a couple of hours, he had both fever and a severe attack of enteritis. The Company Captain ordered him to the First Aid station behind the lines, in order that the Medical Officer could apply some immediate short-term relief, but on the M.O.'s inspecting the forlorn body Urwick was transferred immediately to the Field Hospital. Half-an-hour later, an unexpected heavy German artillery attack killed a number of his men; he himself would undoubtedly have been among them had he still been in that command station.

While a short spell in Base Hospital away from the battle arena overcame the fever element in his malady, the enteritis persisted severely. Nevertheless, he was keen to return to his fighting unit. The Commanding Officer was uneasy about that, as was a consequent Medical Board, which eventually decided to post him for a four-month tour of duty at the Base Assembly Camp (by now moved to the Rouen region) to assist the Adjutant. On meeting him, Urwick wrote in his partial autobiography:

His dress was irregular – a sky-blue pullover, tartan trews and thigh-high gum boots. On another chair was a glengarry bearing the badge of the 42nd Highlanders, the Black

Watch. 'Hullo', he said, 'I'm Walker'. He examined my papers and said 'three months base duty. There's nothing whatever for you in one of these Base Depots. You'll be bored to suicide'.... I little knew, however, at that moment, that in that brief meeting with the then Captain James Douglas Walker DSO, subsequently Lt Col J.D. Walker DSO, OBE, I had, so to speak, met my fate. The six months I was to spend under his command as Assistant Adjutant... were to prove the most formative experience of my life, and, as it turned out, to determine the whole direction of my future.... Walker had some physical disability which prevented him from serving in the line. But he was big in body, bigger still in generosity of mind and temper, and a born organiser.

As the Camp was where new recruits arriving from England were temporarily housed while being appropriately equipped and assessed for attachment to relevant units at the front, these exercises entailed a major managerial operation. In addition to the physical logistics of housing men in tents and providing meals, there was also a responsibility for handling, storing, and subsequently despatching military equipment and supplies of all kinds. In his memoirs, Urwick estimated that some 250,000 men passed through the Camp during the months of his attachment there, as well as innumerable thousand items of hardware and foodstuffs. In all this, Urwick's innate systematic mode of thinking and concern for method made him an invaluable assistant to the Adjutant. He also brought usefully to bear his command of the French language in dealing with port authorities, railway staff, and transport services generally.

Despite their difference in military ranking and age levels, Walker and Urwick enjoyed each other's company. Additionally, Captain Walker came quite early to recognize Urwick's mental capabilities and decided to take practical advantage of them. As he had long been ill-at-ease with the cumbersome and bureaucratic administrative documentation and procedures at the Camp, Walker invited Urwick to join him in a review of the established system. Urwick readily accepted and was able to contribute new lines of approach from his own analytical thinking, oriented primarily towards simplification and streamlining. Eventually, a comprehensive revision was accomplished and documented, forming what a later generation would call 'standard practice instructions', and later, after yet another generation and amidst another war, would emerge as 'organization and method studies'. As part of his contribution, Urwick compiled all the revised documents, routines, procedures, and methods into a manual which was easy to handle and use, reducing the administration required of officers at the front or in bases. Another benefit was improving the unloading of hardware and supplies from ships at the ports, greatly shortening the turnaround time of the ships in a situation when shortage of capacity was acute.

In parallel with the review of procedures, Walker raised another three special tasks based particularly on Urwick's competence in the French language and involving their shared concern for the well-being of the men assembled under their care. Periods of waiting for these men at the Base necessarily varied and there was virtually nothing for the men to do, apart from drills and exercises. Even buying a beer in the evening became a problem, given the difficulties of reaching nearby villages. Walker found the remedy, which Urwick carried into effect: find the main brewers in Rouen, discuss possibilities, and select a couple willing to participate in a major sales enterprise. This was a great prospect for the brewers, given that there were thousands of potential customers, while the Base provided large marquees as canteens which the brewers would staff for specifically established hours of opening. Urwick raised volunteers to support him in supervising at the Base, while facilities such as chairs and tables were also supplied, so that the men could write their letters. Eventually, foodstuffs and cigarettes also went on sale. Pricing arrangements were agreed with the brewers, giving the soldier-customers the lowest practicable prices, as well as a small margin for the Base Camp to spend on 'welfare' services. In later life, Urwick recalled that once fully established sales were running at over £1,000 per week, gradually building the 'welfare fund' to over £3,000. Indeed, so successful was the operation that in 1916 the War Office sent a working party of businessmen to report on the venture. It could be argued that this was the forerunner of the Navy, Army and Air Force Institute (NAAFI) so beloved of later generations of servicemen.

It was inevitable that the rising success of the 'canteen' initiative led to plans for more entertainment, Captain Walker coming forward with another bright idea for Urwick to implement. As Walker understood France to be a country favouring the circus, he made enquiries and was successful in securing a circus-master capable of establishing facilities for seating an audience of some 2,000 men. Urwick's assistance was required in the discussion and negotiations, while he also masterminded the programmes that started in spring 1915. Through family contacts in Britain, Urwick was even able to secure the presence among the recurrent programmes of a 'British entertainment party', headed by Seymour Hicks, then a famous contemporary actor, and including Gladys Cooper, an equally famous actress. This initiative in turn was something of a predecessor of the Entertainments National Service Association (ENSA). Another, rather more limited, activity was the establishment of a local boot-repair operation, saving shipping space by stopping the regular practice of sending all footwear back to England for repair and then bringing it back to France. Although local cobblers proved willing to cooperate in this venture, however, and the operation proved highly successful, Walker was later reprimanded for departing from regular army practice.

There can be no doubt that Urwick enjoyed his convalescence at the Rouen Camp, because these special tasks proved both interesting and organizationally challenging, as well as providing a camaraderie with Walker to which he often referred in later life. One other incident during his stay that was of great significance for Urwick occurred when Walker remarked to him (citing Urwick's own version of what was said):

Urwick, if you come through this junketing still alive to return to your family's business, there's a book I'd like to recommend to you that I feel sure you would enjoy. I came across it a couple of years ago shortly after its publication: written by a fellow named Taylor, an American. He can't write for nuts but the content is most interesting, quite remarkable. It carries the strange title of *Shop Management* and you could well find it useful.

It is interesting to speculate on how Walker came to hear of what to many is regarded as one of the most important management texts ever produced, which was certainly not normal reading for Regular Army officers. Indeed, taking account of Walker's other initiatives noted earlier, not to mention his rank and status, it is clear that he was a remarkable man. Expressing his appreciation for the recommendation, Urwick's next letter home asked his parents to obtain a copy for him, using assistance from the company's associate in the United States. Inevitably, it took quite a while for that to be achieved, with Urwick well back into the trenches and the fighting before he could start to read it. Moreover, Taylor's book was not the only managerial tome Urwick read in the War. His mother noted in 1916 the publication of a book by William Trotter, carrying the unusual title *Instincts of the Herd in Peace and War*, which she sent to Lyndall, rightly realizing that he would find it interesting. It was his first foray into social psychology.

After the initial worries, the calmer situation and regular supply of food at the Base had diminished Urwick's attacks of enteritis and dysentery. On the other hand, in head and heart he was still strongly 'the soldier', itching to return to what he felt was his rightful place at the front. Late in April 1915, the Medical Board cleared him for his return to the Third Worcestershire Battalion in May, by which time they were active in the Ypres salient in fierce fighting. Through the following months, Lieutenant Urwick and his platoon were continuously in the thick of the battles across north-east France. It was during this phase that Urwick read Taylor's *Shop Management* by candlelight, while he was sheltering in some shattered stables of the chateau at Hooge on the Menin Road. As he recalled later: 'That was it! It answered the problem which had worried me at Oxford, how to reconcile a business career with being useful to society. It made of management "an intelligent occupation". I determined then and there that if I survived I would devote my life to management.'

In August 1915, he was promoted to Acting Captain, a post that was formally confirmed in October. Two months later he was again promoted, albeit not in rank, to Staff Captain for the 75th Infantry Brigade within the 25th Division, resulting in his withdrawal from direct command of a fighting unit. His performance must have been highly commendable, because a year later he was awarded the Military Cross, while in November 1916 he was made Brigade Major. This promotion also resulted in him being transferred to responsibilities in England, because the senior commanders deemed that his gruelling two years in the front line had resulted in both grave health worries and possible impairments to his judgement. For the ensuing six months, he was consequently in command of the Eighth Training Reserve Brigade, based in Dorset, although still only 25 years of age. Earlier in the year, he had also been inducted as an owning partner and general manager in Fownes, in accordance with the agreement negotiated by his father with the Rigdens. It was to be another two years, however, before he was able to take up these responsibilities.

April 1917 found Urwick back in France, as a Brigade Staff Major (Figure 1.4), initially to serve with the Tenth Division, but shortly afterwards transferred to

Figure 1.4 Urwick as a staff officer in World War I.

the Eleventh Division as Assistant Adjutant and Quartermaster General in charge of all administrative activities. Clearly, his superiors were becoming aware of his administrative capabilities. He remained in that role and with his rank of Staff Major until after the Armistice was signed on 11 November 1918. For the remaining weeks of that year, he had a far more pleasant task to plan, direct, and supervise: the release and repatriation of British and Allied soldiers held in German prison camps. The retreating German forces had apparently opened the camp gates, leaving the inmates to fend for themselves and providing the British and Allied command with a complex rescue situation. Within the areas under the command of the Eleventh Division, Urwick set up 'reception stations' on the main roads, with facilities to provide ex-prisoners with an identity record, a bath, an immediate meal, and overnight accommodation. Within a day, they would also be transported to a Base, where a new uniform would be available and arrangements made for repatriation to Britain. This was an enjoyable process to command and successfully accomplish, a fitting swansong to years of gruelling warfare. Finally, on compassionate family grounds primarily resulting from his father's faltering health, Urwick obtained early release (although not yet demobilization) at the end of December 1918.

Although promotions of the sort Urwick achieved were by no means unknown, he undoubtedly had a 'good war'. During his years of service, in addition to the Mons Star Medal (with Bar) and Military Cross, he had three times been 'Mentioned in Despatches', while in the month after demobilization news of an Officer of the Order of the British Empire (OBE, Military Division) was received. However, it was not only his fighting prowess that was noteworthy. The Army taught him to be self-reliant and to appreciate the importance of training. He learnt especially the value of staff work behind the scenes as a support for the men in the front line. He saw leadership in action. His thinking about military organization, manifested in his reading of writers such as Haldane and Hamilton, his recognition of the importance of human relations even within the war context, his grasp of organizational problems in his work with Captain Walker, and his immediate recognition of the importance of the work of Frederick Winslow Taylor, all boded well for success in a business context. By the end of the war, he had formed the strong viewpoint that the directors and managers of the nation's industrial enterprises could learn a lot from the experiences of military commanders. One should note, however, that the common picture of military organizations as subject to command and control systems with strict hierarchies was not what Urwick had in mind here; he saw military activities as much more complex and flexible, pointing out that successful military communication does not adhere to the dictates of a rigid organization chart (Mutch 2006). Clearly there is a need for initiative at lower levels, and for private soldiers to win high medals for pursuing it, while what Walker and Urwick did at the Base Camp at Rouen were classic examples of successful middle-level initiatives. And at the higher levels, Urwick's references to military analogies often related to the use of staff to support the top commanders.

THE BREAK WITH THE FOWNES COMPANY

As a partner in Fownes Brothers & Co., civilian life would mean immediate employment for Urwick. There were, however, two events which ruined his reasonable expectations of a smooth career, both connected with the joint owners of Fownes, the Rigden family. During the War, Urwick's father, Henry (Sir Henry by the War's end, as a result of being knighted for services to the Liberal Party), operated the factory in Worcester with the assistance of one of the Rigden sons, while the Rigden father and two other sons were in charge of the London merchanting office. While superficially this arrangement worked smoothly, there was nevertheless some tension between the families. Lyndall Urwick always felt that the Rigdens regarded the Urwicks as 'poor relations', even though Lyndall's grandfather had been accepted into partnership in the firm in 1856, thirteen years before the first Rigden joined the firm. Over the next generation, however, the Rigdens had three sons taken into partnership, giving them a majority position over the two Urwicks.

The first event that stirred the deep-seated tension between Urwicks and Rigdens occurred in the autumn of 1917, when the three London Rigdens were charged with trading with the enemy, one of the most serious wartime crimes a firm could commit. The basis of the charge was that when war broke out Fownes Brothers had a German manufacturing factory, as well as a large American merchanting and manufacturing business. In August 1914, the American business had a large order of German-made ladies' gloves awaiting shipment from Amsterdam to the United States, which was still a neutral country. The American manager, Smellie, who was technically an employee of the British partnership, asked the London office if the gloves could be sent to the United States, but without payment, so that the firm would not have aided the German war economy. Urwick's father, aware of this request, had advised the younger William Rigden in London that the correct course was to consult the Crown Solicitor's office about the proposed action. Rigden failed to take this advice. More than two years later, the London offices of Fownes Brothers were raided by Scotland Yard and Whitehall officials, resulting in the correspondence with the American company being seized and used as evidence. In the ensuing court case, the Rigdens were not unnaturally frightened and confused and made bad witnesses, while their defending counsel, who had been hastily briefed only a week in advance, advised them to plead guilty after only one day of the hearing. The elder Rigden was fined and the two sons sent to prison, one for three and the other for eight months. Lyndall Urwick later wrote a note entitled 'A Miscarriage of Justice', arguing that it was a 'put-up job' to enable Whitehall officials to meet the prevailing public criticism of weak attempts to prevent trading with Germany by prosecuting a high-profile case. The net result of this case was that Sir Henry Urwick was burdened with overall managerial responsibility, largely without immediate senior-level support, with the publicity undermining his otherwise sound physical and mental physique. It was this that led to Lyndall's early release from the Army.

The beginnings of a second issue involving the Rigdens related again to the American subsidiary. In the autumn of 1919, Sir Henry was feeling sufficiently restored in health and strength to undertake Lyndall's introduction to the American company, which with three factories and several merchanting branches had become a large enterprise. In Sir Henry's personal view, it was too large and successful to continue as the privately owned subsidiary of a smaller British family business. Among his objectives in arranging the visit, Sir Henry hoped to explore the possibility of selling shares to the American directors and managers, while retaining some of the ownership in British hands. As the idea was well received by the American participants, local financial–legal expertise was consulted, resulting in a mutually acceptable formula that was offered to the board of directors in Britain. The Rigdens, however, rejected it outright, arguing that they had no wish to dilute their ownership in the American enterprise. Given that they held sixty per cent of the share capital, their position also proved decisive. At the same time, the onerous journey and detailed negotiations had so undermined Sir Henry's health that he was obliged to spend a few weeks in a nursing home, creating the impression that the Rigdens' obstinacy, as well as their recent criminal actions, had exacerbated his health problems. Indeed, shortly after the Urwicks had returned from America, the Rigden family instructed their solicitors to file a suit against Sir Henry Urwick, alleging negligence in his fiduciary responsibilities to the company, by reason of continuing absence, including a period of absence abroad (namely, the visit to the United States). The Urwicks regarded this action as incomprehensible, not to mention grossly unkind to a man who had kept the business going for most of the war, creating a conflict that would lead to the dissolution of their partnership.

Of course, the case was merely a ploy, albeit with sinister implications, because as the 1910 partnership agreement was due for renewal, the Rigdens were manoeuvring for position. Having recovered from their understandable shock, the Urwick family sought their own legal advice and discovered that the suit had little chance of success. At the same time, as a precautionary response, and especially taking into consideration Lyndall's age and undeniable shortage of experience in business activities, the Urwick solicitors recommended them to retain a consultant to review the allegations made by the Rigdens, with a view to seeking accommodation with their probable underlying objectives. Having acquired an appropriate consultant, Lyndall also personally approached the Rigden sons and secured their agreement to a review of the company's affairs. The consultant's review occupied some months of 1920, culminating in a final review session with Sir Henry, Lyndall, and the Urwick solicitors in attendance. Stark alternatives were presented: on the one hand, Lyndall could remain within the company and retain his managerial role in consort with the Rigden members, maintaining whatever ownership he could secure through negotiation, but always with the inherent rivalry in the background; on the other hand, he ought to sell the family shareholding at an equitable valuation. There could be no third way.

When the Urwick family reviewed the situation, Lyndall realized that working alongside the Rigdens would become more intolerable, rather than less, especially as they could be blamed for his father's deteriorating health. Consequently, he chose the second option, a decision which was totally endorsed by both of his parents. Furthermore, the Rigdens also greeted the deal magnanimously, because while the standing partnership agreements were due to expire at the end of December 1920, they were no longer willing to work with the Urwicks. Their only problem lay in raising funds to buy out the Urwicks. Ironically, they achieved this through the sale of the American Fownes Corporation, exactly as Sir Henry had planned during his 1919 visit, although the financial outcome was far less favourable than it would have been a year earlier. Thus, at the beginning of 1921, Lyndall Urwick found himself unemployed and with aged parents, albeit with some capital to support himself. The Urwicks had pulled out of the partnership at just the right time, because demand for gloves declined significantly thereafter, resulting in the company's eventual demise (Coopey 2003). Nevertheless, the whole episode indicates something about the weakness of governance structures in many sizeable British companies at the time, because the system had allowed the Rigdens to manipulate the situation and undermine their partners.

MANAGERIAL EXPERIENCE

In spite of the difficult issues associated with the Urwick–Rigden relationship, Lyndall Urwick had secured a substantial amount of managerial experience in his time at Fownes Brothers between the beginning of 1919 and the end of 1920. Of course, returning to civilian life understandably posed a challenge to Urwick in many ways. Whatever his personal views about the Rigdens, though, the well-being of the company necessitated working with them, albeit from the dispersed sites at Worcester and London. His greater immediate problem lay with his own father, who was visibly ailing. Indeed, a further medical consultation confirmed that his father's physique had been so seriously undermined that he needed immediate relief and relaxation. While he could be consulted for opinions or explanations, Sir Henry had to be released from the burden of active responsibility, preferably starting with an extended holiday. To this end, Sir Henry and Lady Urwick responded promptly, as Lyndall had already taken over as Worcester general manager on returning to the factory in January 1919. He did so in uniform, with the red 'Staff tabs' in his rank of Major, because although he had been granted early release from active service, he was not yet technically demobilized. That small feature may have added force to the welcome with which he was greeted within the factory, while added cachet was offered in the New Year's Honours List, when he was given an OBE (Military Division).

It took him relatively little time to take up the reins of responsibility, having been briefed on the current positions and gained the respect and support of the factory assistant managers and foremen in what was an efficient enterprise. As Sir Henry's attitude towards those he employed was solidly Liberal – they were his colleagues and friends, rather than his employees – the spirit of the workforce within the factory was also highly conducive to improved performance. During the war years, trade union membership and local consultation had become established, and internally a Works Committee had been established, in accordance with the recommendations of the Whitley Committee. When the Glove Making Employers' Federation was re-formed in 1918–19, Sir Henry was elected as Chairman of the Council, while some months later Lyndall was appointed as the Employer Secretary to the Joint Industrial Council, incidentally forming a lasting friendship with the Trade Union Secretary.

In accordance with his own wartime practices, his first main concern was to develop an effective working relationship with those who were his responsibility, not only in managerial and supervisory roles, but also the work people and ancillary staff. With regard to the operational and administrative personnel, he initiated from the outset a daily programme of visits to the factory sections and office, engaging in personal conversation during the walkabout. He attended the meeting of the in-house Works Committee, and was readily available for consultation with the local trade union representatives whenever they asked to see him. He emphasized his accessibility by a physical change: quite early after his arrival, he had the door of the general manager's office altered by replacement of the wooden panels with clear glass, and a printed notice added saying: 'If you see that I am not engaged, please knock and walk in.'

Another small incident made an important contribution to his acceptance. Walking through an operations section early one day, he chanced upon a workman sitting reading a newspaper, which was hastily folded and stuffed away. Beyond giving the man 'good morning', Urwick said nothing else, knowing the man to be regarded as a very competent operative of long employment with the company. At the end of the day, he had the man brought to his office, receiving him affably and saying that he was not intending to reprimand him for reading a newspaper in working time: instead, he wanted to ask him why he had found it necessary to thrust the paper away in such a hurried manner, virtually implying the boss to be an unreasonable so-and-so. The ensuing conversation did that boss a power of good within the factory.

In addition, a buoyant economic situation aided Lyndall's entry into the ranks of senior management at the Worcester factory. Across the nation, the popular mood in the early months of 1919 was one of euphoria, a mood that was spreading rapidly into the trading community. Restrictions on consumption, whether from imposed rationing or merely non-availability of products, were being replaced by vigorous consumer demand readily reflected in increased output, a process that strongly assisted the demobilization and re-employment of military personnel.

This period also witnessed the start of Urwick's interest in the world outside Fownes Brothers, when he accepted his first public speaking invitations. In April 1919, he was asked to contribute an address to the Fabian Society's Summer School. Choosing as his title 'The Soldier, the Worker and the Citizen', he gave his address from a self-written text that ran to eighteen pages of typescript, expounding the extent and mode to which industry and commerce could learn from military organization. Doubtless experience of public speaking at the Oxford Union came in useful here. In April 1920, one of the local citizen associations also invited him to deliver a lecture on 'The Glove Industry' in the City Hall, reflecting the high regard in which the Urwicks were held in the city of Worcester. With specific regard to his future, however, the most important event of this type was a communication from B. Seebohm Rowntree, informing the firm about the three recent weekend lecture conferences for foremen and supervisors from manufacturing companies. As there was to be another in April 1920, to be held in Oxford and involving a wider audience, supervisors from Fownes were encouraged to attend. Indeed, recognizing the potentially important educational benefits arising from this experience, Urwick at once booked two of his factory foremen and his (male) personal secretary into the conference. They participated positively in the proceedings, particularly reflecting the cooperative management style of their two main bosses, the Urwick father and son. The personal secretary took that praise further by suggesting to Mr Rowntree that Major Lyndall Urwick might be invited to address a later session of the conference. Understandably, upon the secretary's return Lyndall expressed pleasure and gratitude for that suggestion, confirming his acceptance if and when invited. Another dimension of his interest in the external world was that he became a member of the National Institute of Industrial Psychology soon after it was formed in 1919.

By the autumn of 1920, however, the economic situation was changing. In September–October 1920, the hitherto prevailing post-war economic and customer euphoria began to evaporate rapidly, gaining momentum to such extent that by the following spring the nation's industrial and commercial activity was sliding into depression, paralleled by rapidly mounting unemployment that was heading towards the one-million mark by the end of 1921. Fownes Brothers were badly affected by this trend, with sales falling and orders cancelled. These trends deeply disturbed Sir Henry and Lyndall Urwick, not least because of a growing inability to re-employ former operatives who were still being demobilized, as well as having to cut back on orders placed with their army of outworkers. Inevitably, too, fears were being generated about unavoidable redundancies within the Worcester factory. As the weeks passed in late 1920, there was nothing that Lyndall Urwick could do internally to soften the blow, because with the Rigden deal having been settled, it was known that he would himself be leaving at the Christmas break. That news had been received with universal expressions of dismay. This genuine grief was reflected in a pleasant swansong some time after his leaving, when representatives of the Works Committee invited him to an informal meeting in the city to express their thanks for his contributions. A gold watch was presented to Lyndall, as well as an album signed by over 250 employees who had contributed to the purchase. This brought to an end Urwick's connection with the Fownes enterprise, precipitating him into another career that would be of much greater significance to the business world.

2

Rowntree's

Having already experienced a full and exciting life by the beginning of 1921, and after a period of unemployment in that year, Lyndall Urwick began what turned out to be a major personal development programme that ended when in November 1928 he took up the reins as Director of the International Management Institute (IMI). While his wartime experiences undoubtedly influenced his approach towards organization, it was in the years between 1921 and 1928 as an employee at Rowntree's that Urwick dedicated himself to understanding this crucial aspect of business. It was also during these years that he linked up with the Management Research Groups (MRGs) and attended the International Economic Conference, developing an extensive reputation as a public speaker and writer on management, and contributing significantly to the nascent management movement. For these opportunities he owed much to the company's chairman, Seebohm Rowntree, who was to be his mentor and father figure. This chapter will attempt to weave all of these dimensions into an explanation of how by the late 1920s Lyndall Urwick was regarded as a key figure in that management movement, illustrating how the link with Rowntree's especially helped to crystallize his ideas on management and organization.

RECRUITMENT BY ROWNTREE'S

The new year of 1921 found Lyndall Urwick out of work, faced with the unenviable task of finding employment within a deteriorating national economic environment. While Urwick had some managerial experience, neither an Oxford MA nor a distinguished war record counted for much in the industrial and commercial context of the time. Furthermore, the prevailing conventional pattern lay in internal promotion, of rising 'up from the ranks'. Press advertising for managerial positions occurred only occasionally, while

there were always numerous candidates better qualified in terms of experience. One practical step he did take was to obtain a moderately rented
bachelor apartment in London, to be better placed to pursue his own search,
but this failed to provide anything more than access to good libraries.

Urwick spent a considerable amount of time reading, especially in the
management field, whilst also providing voluntary assistance to a community
organization which advised schools when purchasing educational supplies.
More important for his future, however, was an invitation from Seebohm
Rowntree to give a lecture to the forthcoming session of the Rowntree Lecture
Conference, to be held at Balliol College in April 1921. He chose as his subject
the title 'Management as a Science'. While not a presentation of Taylorite
themes, Urwick wanted to link his own thinking on the 'management' context
with the 'scientific method' that underlay the approach of scientists to their
analysis, emphasizing how the key feature lay in its systematic nature. In
concluding, he mentioned F. W. Taylor, emphasizing that the 'scientific' label
attached to this style of management was intended to imply 'systematic' in the
scientific mode.

While Rowntree appeared particularly pleased with the lecture, within a
few weeks a fortuitous occurrence added to his appreciation of Urwick. Major
General H. C. Davies, Commanding Officer of the local Territorial Army
Division, who was acquainted with Seebohm Rowntree as one of York's largest
employers, provided an impressive reference for Urwick, having commanded
him during the last years of the War. That informal testimonial prompted
Rowntree to take a closer interest in Urwick during the summer of 1921,
resulting in an invitation to meet at a London restaurant. On discovering
Urwick's interest in psychology, Rowntree offered him a two-year scholarship
to study at Cambridge, with the promise of a job in that area in the company
thereafter.

This was an extremely generous and attractive offer. Urwick, however, had
a major problem with Rowntree's preferred route, because in his personal
view psychology required medical competence. In addition, his own preference for employment lay in executive management, just as he had preferred
the front-line battle stations over background staff roles. Urwick consequently
responded politely and pleasantly to the invitation, offering his own reasons
for declining the offer, yet showing genuine appreciation of Rowntree's
kindness and support. Rowntree, nevertheless, remained keen to recruit
Urwick into the company, in particular to help with the progressive review
that he was pursuing with the support of a small Organization Committee.
To assist in that review, he had already recruited Oliver Sheldon, a young
Humanities graduate who had joined the Army immediately upon graduating
from Oxford. He was proving especially helpful, and to strengthen his

acceptance among the older, more traditional managers Rowntree had appointed him as secretary to the Organization Committee in 1920. Furthermore, to give him wider experience, he seconded Sheldon part time to provide assistance in developing the new Institute of Industrial Administration (IIA) in London during 1920–1.

As the review at Rowntree's progressed, the need for initiating an 'informational and education' process was strengthened. Sheldon had proposed the initiation of a staff journal for in-house circulation, providing information about management as a process of responsibility, with some indication of what were coming to be regarded as 'modern methods', alongside news of internal developments. The proposal was approved by the board of directors, with Sheldon appointed as editor, supported by a small editorial committee chaired by Seebohm Rowntree. Entitled *The Cocoa Works Staff Journal*, the first issue appeared in September 1920.

Like many other firms, 1921 was an extremely difficult year for Rowntree's. Seebohm Rowntree, having made a visit to the United States to search for ways of improving management, regarded this as a reason why the internal review should progress more rapidly. As this placed an even greater burden on Sheldon, it created an opportunity to bring Lyndall Urwick into the company, by offering him an initial role of understudy in the *Staff Journal* editorial team, with a view eventually to taking over full responsibility.

Towards the year end, Rowntree again invited Urwick to dine with him in London, in order to make his proposal in person. He could appreciate an unavoidable complexity in the early stage, because as the older Major, Urwick would have to work as assistant to a younger Lieutenant (Sheldon). On the other hand, Rowntree was willing to gamble that both men would dedicate themselves to producing a successful outcome. For Urwick, the facts were stark: after nearly a year unemployed and with little in the way of realistic prospects, the lure of regular remuneration was highly attractive, not least because he had already found the lady that he would like to marry. So he accepted the invitation to start at Rowntree's early in 1922, taking up residence in a local small hotel in York so that he could cycle to the Haxby Road site. This was not just to be a job, but a management experience second to none in Britain.

THE *STAFF JOURNAL*

Prior to starting at Rowntree's, Seebohm had already invited Urwick to write an article for the company's *Staff Journal*. Entitled 'Industry for Service', it was a short paper built around two recent contributions from Rowntree family members: Seebohm's book *The Human Factor in Business* (1921) and his cousin Arnold's address (November 1921) to an industrial conference conducted by the Society of Friends. Both had laid emphasis on what they regarded as the fundamental objective of any nation's economic system, namely, contributing to the livelihood and standard of living of its citizens. Urwick added a gloss by citing the currently accepted concepts of 'economic man' and 'psychological man', adding a third which for want of a better term he posited as 'social man'. This was for Urwick a first overt statement of his own philosophy on management, outlining how companies ought to formulate a policy that reflected acceptance of these fundamental objectives.

The editorial policy of Rowntree's *Staff Journal* was aimed at demonstrating how external managerial thinking and practice were being reflected inside the firm through the implementation of Seebohm's modernization review. While most articles carried no named byline, there was one regular exception, because each issue carried two feature sections compiled and contributed by senior managers: one named and one anonymous. The named series had the heading 'Cocoa Works Developments', presenting broad descriptions of revised activities and methods within departments, fulfilling the informational objective. The anonymous sequence, written by a succession of senior managers, carried the title 'Ideas in Management', consisting of descriptions of various managerial practices, methods, and techniques, with illustrations drawn from in-company applications, thereby fulfilling the educational objective. Each issue carried the names of the four-man editorial committee: Seebohm Rowntree as chairman, Oliver Sheldon as editor, and two senior managers. The editorial input consisted customarily of a 'leader' on managerial developments, frequently taking an external situation or event as the guideline. There followed a spread of topics drawn from a wide range of sources: extracts from contemporary periodicals with named attribution, brief reviews of significant books, and specific external events or developments. The latter pages of each issue provided a section called 'The Administrative Staff's Bookshelf', containing further book reviews and sometimes additional extracts from periodicals. Such was the editorial setting, probably unique in British industry, in which Lyndall Urwick started his new career.

Urwick's direct input to the *Staff Journal* started in the June 1922 issue, with two items that did not carry his name. One was a review of that April's Oxford Rowntree Lecture Conference, to which he was invited to attend specifically in order to compile the review. The second item was the first of a short series headed 'Output in the Office', starting with 'Approaching the Problem' and carrying on to demonstrate the systematic approach to managerial methods and practice.

While the Organization Committee speeded up the review process from the middle of 1922, Sheldon was also heavily involved in completing his book *The Philosophy of Management*. This reduced his active editorial role (though he continued as nominal editor), providing Urwick with the opportunity to make his mark. The September 1922 issue was designated as 'Volume II', with an editorial written by Urwick on the deliberately selected Shakespearean title 'Puck's Girdle'. It was to be the first of a series intended to portray Urwick's belief that management education and training could be garnered through a wide range of sources, because the fundamentals of management practice and competence remained the same, irrespective of the setting. 'Puck's Girdle' ranged widely over a series of managerial developments external to the company, based on the premise that internal changes could be more readily accepted when viewed against a wider background. This approach was further developed in the following three editorial articles (even though he was never named as the author), each of which was up to five pages in length. In succeeding issues, while content and scope remained similar, the format was converted into a succession of separated paragraphs, each covering a selected item of information from external sources, frequently reproduced from other periodicals or from addresses given by diverse named individuals.

As well as the editorial matter, Urwick provided a book review section, which reviews were substantial in length, looking at, for example, John Lee's books on management or a selected book by an American author. Another innovation was a section named 'Our Contemporaries', reproducing extracts from British and American periodicals. The *Staff Journal* consequently provided not only its recipients with a plethora of management education material, but also Urwick with the opportunity to write, think, and read about managerial issues, setting the pattern for his forthcoming career (Figure 2.1).

In addition to this work on the *Staff Journal*, apart from a major internal task to be described in the next section, there were also significant external activities. For example, at the Rowntree Lecture Conference, held in Balliol College in September 1923, Urwick was invited to conduct a session on 'The Old and the New in Business'. He adopted a broad-brush approach, reviewing change during the previous fifty years, picking up especially the recent drive to create large-scale enterprises through mergers and acquisitions. Surprisingly, though, he did not refer to changes in managerial practice, either generally or within Rowntree's. He also contributed two articles entitled 'Industrial Self-Government' and 'Scientific Management' to a new encyclopedia entitled *The John Bull Treasure Book of Knowledge*, indicating how others were beginning to recognize his contributions to management thinking. Urwick considered the practical

Figure 2.1 The Rowntree conference at Balliol College, Oxford 1923.

consideration of 'industrial democracy' as a consultative and cooperative process for the pursuit of effective manufacturing performance that served the interests of both partners as well as the community at large, including in this the joint consultative system that had been emerging in Britain since the Whitley Committee of 1917. On the second topic, which was rather closer to his own interests, he reviewed it within the American context, given its limited recognition in Britain. Mentioning key American practitioners, including F. W. Taylor, he noted their emphasis on what he described as 'a new philosophy of work . . . [and] a new attitude towards the task of organising men for the cooperative processes of modern machine production', giving this the title 'human sciences'.

By the end of 1923, as Seebohm Rowntree considered the educational objective of the *Journal* to have been accomplished, he decided to halt production. In the final issue (December 1923), Urwick's name was recorded for the first time as a member of the editorial committee, albeit only as 'Joint Editor with Oliver Sheldon'. Urwick used that issue to publish a feature article on 'The Scientific Method for Executives', which was clearly aimed at explaining the application of systematic management. While it was not entirely his own composition, his introductory paragraph indicated that the article fully reflected the company's approach to the modernization of organization and management, offering to every director and manager a checklist to monitor their own performance. Urwick's approach to these topics was clearly evolving directly out of both his wide reading and their direct application to Rowntree's, indicating how by 1923 considerable progress had been made in both respects. There was also the prospect that he would be given the opportunity to implement some of these ideas, because in December 1923 he was appointed as personnel secretary at Rowntree's.

THE OFFICE COORDINATING COMMITTEE

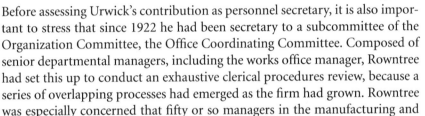

Before assessing Urwick's contribution as personnel secretary, it is also important to stress that since 1922 he had been secretary to a subcommittee of the Organization Committee, the Office Coordinating Committee. Composed of senior departmental managers, including the works office manager, Rowntree had set this up to conduct an exhaustive clerical procedures review, because a series of overlapping processes had emerged as the firm had grown. Rowntree was especially concerned that fifty or so managers in the manufacturing and product-handling departments had developed an extremely casual attitude to clerical procedures. Thus, a few months into his employment, in addition to his work on the *Staff Journal*, Urwick was asked to steer a committee that would effectively provide an in-house consultancy role, radically reforming processes in a highly systematic manner. It was a considerable compliment to Urwick, reflecting the esteem in which Rowntree held the young man.

Inevitably, though, when dealing with such a large organization, problems arose in dealing with some senior managers. One example was Urwick's desire to change the way that office circulars were distributed, making the old system devised by the works office manager look bad. As this person was a long-serving employee within a couple of years of retirement, Rowntree was obliged to step in and suggest that the embarrassment factor could be avoided if the situation was reviewed with remedial proposals, consulting the works office manager as though the issue was part of the ongoing modernization process. Having made these changes, Urwick was also able to suggest another development, the creation of a specific marketing unit within the sales and distribution department, providing the works office manager with a fresh task prior to retirement.

Continuing until August 1925, this review was a crucial part of Lyndall Urwick's education and development as a management thinker and practitioner.

Although concessions on specific items had to be made, because of internal sectional features that he had not adequately evaluated, working closely with both Seebohm Rowntree and all of the senior managers and supervisors, Urwick managed to press through most of his recommendations. Ultimately, once all the changes had been agreed, a new manual was compiled, structured in four parts: company policy relating to each department; charts illustrating that department's managerial and supervisory organization; the company's standing instructions, general and specific; and additional specific instructions, if appropriate. It proved to be a monumental task, and although one must remember that as head of the Organizing Committee Oliver Sheldon was the principal architect of the reorganization, it is important to stress that Urwick repaid the trust that Seebohm Rowntree had placed in him.

A final phase of the clerical review was a reassessment of the sales and distribution departments. As the main administrative structures had three different sections – customers' incoming orders; dispatch of products and invoicing; and customers' invoices, payments, and accounts – that could mean both customers and outdoor salesmen dealing with three separate internal units if a query arose in relation to any particular orders. It also weakened the relationship between the company and its customers. The remedy brought the male clerks in the order and dispatch units into a combined section within which groups of clerks were aligned with geographical groups of salesmen, based on regional territories, thus consolidating the threefold link between customer, salesman, and sales clerk. Although the accounting procedures did not require closer liaison, to foster cooperation Urwick proposed the mechanization of all accounting operations, with female clerks employed to perform these tasks. Within a new sales office, he placed the combined male sales clerks and their supervisors across the room, while the machines and their female operatives with female supervision were ranged longitudinally along the two outer sides. Some years later, the company gave Urwick permission to write up the full story as *Reorganising a Sales Office*.

To his great satisfaction, Urwick's colleagues recognized the value of these changes and cooperated extensively. Again, one must note that Oliver Sheldon was responsible for masterminding the reorganization, but Urwick played a leading role in assembling the manuals that became the definitive source for all procedures. Urwick entitled the whole process 'Standing Orders and Instructions', a somewhat military-sounding wording over which he was widely teased. Not surprisingly, though, in spite of raising a few eyebrows, it was not long before the everyday internal label for the manual became 'Urwick's Bible'. A Rowntree senior manager later noted that the customary reference to Urwick behind his back was the three initials GAU, designating 'God Almighty Urwick'. Urwick's response to this kind of criticism was typically robust: when an older manager remarked sourly: 'There are too many mosquitoes around', meaning bright young graduates, Urwick responded: 'Do you know what they did to get rid of the mosquitoes in the Suez Canal? They got rid of the stagnant water.' The older manager accepted the logic, admitting: 'You win, lad'.

While all this was happening, early in 1923 an important event in Lyndall Urwick's private life was his marriage to Joan Wilhelmina Bedford, a young lady he had met during his stay in London in 1921 (Figure 2.2). They agreed to marry, even though she still had eighteen months to complete of her training as a doctor at a London hospital. Although Urwick's father, Sir Henry, stated his dislike of their enforced separation, he provided his blessing and the gift of a car. Lyndall chose an Alvis, adapting the front seat so that it could be converted into a bed. Urwick described how: 'Many a Friday night I would set out from York to drive the two-hundred miles to London, around ten o'clock stopping at a roadside inn to park the car and enjoy a late supper, then fix up the car-bed and enjoy a comfortable night's sleep, rounding off the journey early morning.' There must have been occasions, of course, when he could not leave York until midday on Saturday, the morning then still being usual working time. Nevertheless, at least they had the joy of the car for weekend excursions and for holidays abroad. Mrs Urwick qualified in the summer of 1924.

Figure 2.2 Urwick's first wife, Joan Bedford.

DEPUTY MANAGER OF SALES AND DISTRIBUTION

In June 1924, Seebohm Rowntree invited Urwick to become deputy manager of the sales and distribution department, whilst keeping until August 1925 his other roles on the Organization Committee and as personnel secretary. As Seebohm's cousin Arnold Rowntree was the head of this department, it was necessary to build up his confidence, initially as distribution manager. Again, this was an attractive invitation which Urwick accepted, especially as in addition to the everyday managerial duties Arnold Rowntree sought his help in two developments focusing more on marketing orientation than sales management. One objective, linked back to the review initiated by the former works office manager, was to consider whether merging similar products would also feed into greater production efficiencies. This review brought in its train a number of difficulties in which the psychology of the consumer, the trade customer, and the salesman became dominant features. Later in life, Urwick recalled having inadequately appreciated the underlying motivations influencing those three strata of individuals, feeling that he had been too blunt and failed to recognize the strength of personal attachment developed by the individual, in whatever capacity, for something to which they had been long accustomed. It was, nevertheless, an important part of the ongoing rationalization on which Rowntree's had embarked.

The other objective lay in masterminding the launch of a new product, responding to a trend in consumer preference. Whereas milk chocolate bars had been a long-established popular product, market research was displaying a shift towards the plain chocolate that featured in boxes of chocolates. There was no problem for the production side once the range of bar sizes had been agreed; rather, the challenge was to promote the launch, a matter in which the product name would be significant. There is no evidence to say that Urwick was the source of the name chosen in the wording – *Plain Mr. York of York, Yorks* – but he worked with Arnold Rowntree to launch this product, with its slogan of a small male figure dressed in eighteenth-century style. It proved to be an outstanding success, sales rising by a factor of ten to sixty tons a week within six months of the launch.

Urwick's main activities in the sales and distribution department – a reorganization of the sales office, slimming down the product range, new product launches, and the contribution to an enhanced export framework – were not only extremely important to Rowntree's, but were also influential in giving Urwick a strong sense of the importance of marketing, a message he emphasized in much of his later work. Moreover, the book which emerged from the sales office reorganization (Urwick 1928) was influential in its own right. Yet, in spite of this work, Lyndall was not entirely happy in his new role, no doubt in part because there were some disagreements over organizational matters with Sheldon, Appleton (the director in charge of marketing), and indeed Arnold Rowntree himself. He did not have the same easy and enjoyable interactions with Arnold as he had with Seebohm, since Arnold maintained a purely businesslike relationship with him, while Seebohm had taken a personal interest in his development.

In addition to these career problems, Urwick was also unhappy about his personal life. Since his wife had qualified as a doctor, the couple had been living in a rented cottage in the village of Acomb, to the west of York. Joan had secured a voluntary role in a local hospital and occasional locum practitioner work, but could not secure an established medical appointment, largely due to local prejudice against female doctors. Nor was she at ease in that traditionally conservative rural community. By late 1925, she was also pregnant, which added another dimension to their shared dissatisfaction with life, forcing him to seek an informal meeting with Seebohm Rowntree.

Of course, Rowntree understood Urwick's personal and career predicaments. As he was also keen to retain Urwick's services, he persuaded him to persist with his current role, with the promise that alternative opportunities would arise. While the modernization programme was largely completed and the review committee had been disbanded, there were still issues requiring resolution. Rowntree was also keen to move Sheldon into a mainstream managerial role, as the head of commercial relations with the numerous subsidiary and associate companies, creating an opportunity for Urwick to become Seebohm's personal assistant. To ensure his standing within the company, he gave him the role of secretary to the Organization Committee and delegated to him functional responsibility for personnel management with respect to the commercial, administrative, and technical staff, namely, all manpower employed outside the manufacturing departments (which continued to be the responsibility of the labour manager, C. H. Northcott). Urwick accepted the transfer with effect from early 1926, as well as taking responsibility for maintaining the clerical procedures manual. From June, Joan was also preoccupied with their daughter, who was named after the month in which she was born.

In his new role as secretary to the Organization Committee, Urwick was invited in February 1926 to undertake a review of the company's management of its foreign sales. Although there was a small-scale export section, it was not large enough to expedite significant expansion. The directors had already decided to investigate how other British consumer-product companies handled their European and overseas sales, leading them to ask Urwick to pursue a much more extensive review. As his years in an army staff role had given him considerable experience of consulting with higher- ranked officers, Urwick readily accepted the project, spending several months on a programme of interviews with the likes of Brunner Mond, Carr's Biscuits, J. and P. Coats, Courtaulds, Lever Brothers, and Reckitt & Sons. He obtained a good reception in all cases and was able to provide interesting and valuable findings to his own directors, as well as having learnt a great deal about people and organizations which would later be useful to him.

THE MRGs

In establishing the new internal arrangements with Sheldon and Urwick, Seebohm Rowntree may have had in mind another pioneering innovation upon which he was particularly keen and for which he would have seen Urwick as a good person to assist in its implementation. It had stemmed from one of his visits to the United States, when he had visited the highly respected Dennison Paper Products Corporation in Massachusetts. The head of the family company, Henry Dennison, had been successful in 1923 in persuading the heads of several local manufacturing companies to join him in a cooperative framework for the exchange of experience, managerial problems, and ideas, but with a strict guarantee of confidentiality, under the name 'Manufacturers Research Association'. The experience had been highly praised by the local companies involved, as Dennison had been able to demonstrate to Rowntree during his visit to Boston. Rowntree decided to try and replicate this model in Britain, using Urwick as the principal organizer.

After ascertaining a wide spectrum of views, Urwick was sufficiently encouraged to support Seebohm Rowntree's decision to make at least a trial start. Cooperation came from the chairman of Dunlop Rubber and C. F. Merriam of British Xylonite, both of whom shared Rowntree's enthusiasm for management improvement. They formed a triumvirate, with Lyndall Urwick as their secretary and operational assistant. The major challenge facing Urwick was a notorious reluctance amongst British businessmen to talk about their own business matters. Nevertheless, the combination of Rowntree's reputation and Urwick's enthusiasm must have won through, because by year end he had secured nine firm acceptances for the first group, whose name was soon amended to 'MRG'. In parallel with those consultative activities, Urwick worked with Rowntree in drafting a constitution and proposed operating systems, while the latter undertook to select a small band of directors to add to the triumvirate as a basis for a Governing Council, of which he would be the first chairman.

During those latter months of 1926, Urwick had been continuing his York-based roles. Nevertheless, he and Rowntree agreed that a London base would be more effective for the development of the group concept. Rowntree obtained support funding from the Joseph Rowntree Social Trust (set up by his father and continued as a memorial to him) to meet Urwick's salary for half the week, while he continued drawing the other half from the company. Additionally, the grant met the cost of a small central London office at 23 Bloomsbury Square, which became the groups' administrative centre. Once the Governing Council had been formed, Urwick was appointed as its secretary, while in November 1926 he and his wife moved into a home of their own in London, satisfying their need for a place in the capital.

MRG No. 1 started its programme early in February 1927. To support its promotional activities, Urwick drafted a pamphlet explaining the concept and the modes of group operation. This laid out that the programme and conduct of proceedings were matters for each individual group to determine and agree, possibly through a small local executive committee. The broad principle recommended that rather than becoming involved in technical manufacturing matters, they should concentrate on policy, major commercial matters, marketing, human relations, and man-management, together with the principles and practices of planning and control. Each group of ten to fifteen must impose a strict code of confidentiality on its members, allowing no communication to external parties. The pamphlet also set out guidance notes for preliminary steps, for funding the group activities, and for aspects of the proceedings, with Urwick as secretary always available for additional assistance.

An early public mention of the groups occurred in August 1927, when a widely circulated magazine (*System: The Magazine of Business*) carried an article by Urwick describing the origins of the International Congress movement, in which the byline described him as 'Honorary Secretary of the Manufacturers Research Groups'. In October 1928, Urwick was also invited to address the Netherlands Institute for Efficiency, in Amsterdam, on the progress of the MRGs in Britain. This text was printed for subsequent circulation, providing information about the activities of the groups already in operation, yet without any breach of the confidentiality principle. In 1928, he wrote a booklet entitled *A Note on the Literature of Scientific Management*, published by the MRGs. This was presumably intended to indicate the main theme that the MRGs were expected to pursue (reinforced by the developments in the IMI). Another initiative Urwick pursued was to ask J. A. Coubrough, a senior manager in one of the MRG companies,

British Xylonite, to translate Henri Fayol's seminal management book into English, an exercise that is taken up again in Chapter 4.

Although it is not entirely clear how many groups Urwick was responsible for setting up in Britain, by 1930 there were eight in existence, most of which would have had some input from Urwick as the secretary. Indeed, a good deal of Urwick's time would have been spent in setting up groups, which was by no means an easy task given the secretive nature of most British companies. There was always a distinction between Group 1, comprised of the biggest London-based companies, and other groups made up of smaller provincial companies. Crucially, though, the groups not only continued in existence after the Second World War, but also expanded considerably to number up to twenty. In 1975, they were absorbed into the British Institute of Management (BIM), operating as a Special Interest Group until the mid-1990s when the Institute withdrew its support and the national framework of the MRGs was disbanded. Even so, there are still at the time of writing one or two operating as independent local associations, for example in Sheffield, illustrating the longevity of the concept.

INTERNATIONAL ORIENTATIONS

While Urwick was working industriously to build up the MRGs, he was offered yet another opportunity to expand his horizons, when Seebohm Rowntree, having been invited at the end of 1926 to represent the Federation of British Industries (FBI) at the forthcoming International Economic Conference being organized by the League of Nations in Geneva in May 1927, decided that his business commitments would prevent him from attending. Instead, Rowntree nominated Lyndall Urwick to take his place, providing an outstandingly attractive invitation that was willingly accepted. As the primary objective of the Conference was to promote the economic consolidation of Europe, with notable concern for Germany and the Balkan nations after the serious disruptions suffered during the immediate post-war years, it brought together many of Europe's leading economic thinkers. Urwick could hardly refuse such an opportunity to network with people of that ilk.

Urwick's excellent command of the French language, as well as a reasonable knowledge of German, would prove to be a great advantage in contributing to this international event. He was also well aware of all the major developments relating to management, not least the inauguration in 1925 of the Conseil International de l'Organisation Scientifique (CIOS) and its first Congress held in Brussels that year. Another movement to which he paid particular attention was the German government's 'Rationalisierung' [Rationalization], namely, its post-war recovery strategies based on scientific approaches to management and organization. The 1927 conference would consequently mean for Urwick both personal interest and intellectual enjoyment, as well as the prestige of serving as an official national representative. However, at this point he did not know that there would be even more significant consequences arising from his attendance, not least in coming into direct contact with the concept of 'Rationalization' and those advocating the wider adoption of 'scientific management'.

As far as Urwick was concerned, however, by far the most significant result of the 1927 conference was the approval given by the League of Nations Council to the formation and immediate inauguration of an International Management Institute (IMI), based in Geneva, with the specific objective of explaining and promoting the application of Rationalization internationally. The Institute would be founded, funded, owned, and governed jointly by the International Labour Organization (ILO, a subsidiary unit of the League of Nations) and the America-based Twentieth Century Fund, an educational trust formed by a group of progressive-minded wealthy heads of commercial enterprises in the Boston area, led by E. A. Filene, a retail trading millionaire. Membership (on a subscription formula) would be open to national governments, relevant institutions, industrial and commercial corporations and companies, and individuals. With a starting date of August 1927, and with one individual nominated by each of the two founding parties to serve jointly as the full-time directing heads, it was designed as a genuinely international and progressive institution that would impact widely on management practices.

It was characteristic of Seebohm Rowntree that he took up company membership of the IMI at the outset, giving Urwick direct contact with an organization that was to dominate the next six years of his life. During the Geneva Conference sessions, Urwick had also been absorbing the implications of 'Rationalization', realizing early on that the word had equivalent versions in several European languages that carried the same managerial meaning and implication as the German version. The Conference had concluded those sessions by endorsing resolutions calling upon all national governments to accept the concept and to formulate ways of applying it extensively. This was the message that Urwick and his co-delegate brought back to London for the Federation Council. However, as they realized that the customary English meaning of Rationalization was associated with closures and redundancy, the Council requested an informal meeting with a cross-section of Federation members. This meeting mostly revolved around the unfamiliar meaning and implication of the word in the Continental sense, resulting in a decision to provide a detailed explanation of Rationalization when passing the Conference resolutions to the

Board of Trade. As Urwick had clearly demonstrated that he not only fully understood them, not to mention sympathized with their intended objective, he was invited to provide that explanation. In addition, he also wrote a book on the concept (to be reviewed in Chapter 4), providing a source that has been extremely useful to both his contemporaries and historians.

The inauguration of the IMI in August 1927 was an event of considerable interest to Urwick. Much to the frustration of many people, however, the IMI soon ran into difficulties. Amid the complexities was the choice of who would serve as Director and Deputy Director. Initially, their selection had lain with the heads of the two main founding partners, Albert Thomas from the ILO and E. A Filene from the Twentieth Century Fund Trust. As Director, they decided on Paul Devinat, the incumbent Deputy Director in the ILO, while Percy Brown, an American colleague of Filene within the Fund, was appointed as the Institute's Deputy Director. Devinat had served in the ILO after an earlier background in French socialist political service, while Brown had enjoyed a successful career in management within the United States. As was to become evident within a relatively short time, though, the two men were quite different in personality, attitudes, and modes of approach to management, with further complications emerging from Brown's poor competence in the French language. Furthermore, Brown, the Deputy, was paid twice as much as Devinat, the Director, because of the differences in American and European managerial salaries. As a result, misunderstandings arose from the start, while the situation was further exacerbated by differences in personality and attitude between the two primary trustees, Thomas and Filene, because although both wanted the Institute to succeed, they were each influenced by radically different career backgrounds.

Within the Twentieth Century Fund a co-Trustee with Filene was Professor Joseph H. Willits, the Dean of the highly reputed Wharton School of Finance and Commerce at the University of Pennsylvania. Having arranged a personal sabbatical visit to Europe for the early months of 1928, Filene asked him to spend some time at the IMI office to form an objective assessment of the strains that appeared to be bedevilling the new organization. While the IMI had some success in increasing membership and expanding activities and services, it was evident to most that internal politics were clearly inhibiting greater progress. A local colleague of Filene's in Boston, H. S. Dennison, the originator of the Manufacturers' Research Association, had recommended Willits to include a visit to Seebohm Rowntree in York while in Britain. This he did, alongside visits to some of the companies active within the MRGs, bringing him in contact with Lyndall Urwick as Honorary Secretary to the Groups' Council, by now based in London. Willits found Urwick very well read in the field and endowed with a powerful commitment to contributing personally to the improvement of management. Judging Urwick to be highly trustworthy, he revealed to him the unfortunate internal situation within the IMI and how he had been asked to review the situation. Indeed, he saw Urwick as a solution to the situation, because he had already decided to secure the early resignation of both the incumbent top-level men and replace them with the MRG's secretary.

When Willits tried this thought out on Urwick, the latter was extremely surprised, because it was beyond anything that Urwick had ever had in mind for himself. It was an enormous opportunity to create a channel through which he could fulfil his post-war career choice in 'management advancement' that had first materialized in the trenches in 1915 after reading Taylor's *Shop Management*. He willingly indicated his positive interest and readiness to accept, although much depended on Filene's support for Willits's nomination on behalf of the Twentieth Century Fund. Fortuitously, as Filene was going to be in Vienna during the early summer, a meeting between Filene and Urwick was arranged. As Urwick and his wife had already prepared for a motoring holiday in Europe, Vienna was swiftly added to the schedule. After this meeting, Filene warmly endorsed Willits's recommendation (the ILO seems to have been given no consideration), and within days terms of appointment and service were settled. There was no problem about pay, because the salary offered was double Urwick's current level, providing him with an outstanding opportunity to press forward with his management work on terms that were highly remunerative.

These were not his only international activities in this period because, looking across the Atlantic, he was making friends and reading American management literature extensively. Indeed, many of the writings quoted or the books reviewed in the Rowntree *Staff Journal* were actually American, illustrating how well he knew that scene. As well as Taylor, who consistently dominated Urwick's thoughts, he was aware of and used the leading American writers such as Henry Gantt and Harrington Emerson, whose *Twelve Principles of Efficiency* he was to cite in his own *Principles*. He also struck up a personal friendship with two outstanding American women, Mary Parker Follett, whom he met at the 1926 Oxford Conference, and Lillian Gilbreth, whom he met at the 1929 CIOS Conference. Follett was to become one of his three lodestars, along with Taylor and Fayol, while the Gilbreth husband and wife team were also key figures in scientific management until Frank died relatively young in 1926, having come to be recognized as pioneers of the 'one best way' with which Urwick was also to be associated. In his talks and lectures, he became a strong advocate of the American way and American systems, as part of his criticisms of the British rule-of-thumb approach to decision-making, the employers' prevailing 'master–servant' perspective, and general anti-American attitudes. He was already on his way to becoming both the main link between American and British management and the knowledgeable historian of management that was to be a feature of his career. Much of the library that he was to create in 1929 was inevitably made up of American books.

His international links, however, were not just with America. Given his command of the French language, he was well aware of Henri Fayol by the mid-1920s, as well as other contemporaries such as Henry Le Chatelier and Charles De Freminville, each of whom featured in his own book entitled *Thirteen Pioneers*. In Germany, too, he knew enough about the work of Walter Rathenau to include him in the same book, given that industrialist's contribution to creating the Rationalization Movement. In addition, he undoubtedly learnt a lot about what was happening in other European countries at the Geneva Conference of 1927. When he moved to Geneva to join the IMI, he also became an international figure in his own right, further extending his range of international activities and interests at a time when darker forces were limiting the opportunities to engage in cross-national communication.

THE BREAK WITH ROWNTREE'S

While these international developments and the work with the MRGs were going on, Urwick also indulged in other activities, most notably writing and lecturing. In the Rowntree Lecture Conference at Balliol College in April 1926, he had again been invited to contribute, taking as his theme 'The Task Before Industrial Administrators'. This lecture laid out key tenets of the emerging Urwick approach: eradicate the prevailing anti-American attitude in British business and educate more practitioners in American industrial management techniques. He argued forcefully that the American attitude recognized the value of knowing as much about one's enterprise as possible, as a first step in understanding the cause of anything that was going wrong. This contrasted sharply with a prevailing British view, that the external environment was frequently to blame for corporate ills. Urwick then briefly explained the fundamentals of F. W. Taylor's systematic approach to effective industrial management, deploring the negative attitudes towards these principles that were so rampant in Britain.

A second important lecturing opportunity came yet again through Seebohm Rowntree, who had invited him to participate in the 1927 Summer School of the Liberal Party and to serve as a member of a working party already engaged in drafting a significant report about the nation's economy.

As many of his collaborators were eminent people in various walks of life, being among them must have been an experience of considerable satisfaction to Urwick. It is also interesting to hypothesize that one of the proposals emanating from this working party for a 'national institute of management' might well have been prompted by Urwick. The report was eventually published early in 1928 (by Ernest Benn Limited), entitled *Britain's Industrial Future*. It carried a statement of objectives that would have strongly appealed to Urwick:

The grievances of today are mainly economic: no impartial man would contend that our industrial system has yet attained an adequate standard either of justice or efficiency – so, there is a discontent widespread among the people, that discontent itself is a further cause of inefficiency.

While Urwick did not address the National Summer School of the Liberal Party in 1927, just before that event he had been invited to address the separate Summer School convened by the Liberal Party of Wales, taking as his theme 'Sharing the Product of Industry'. In that talk he claimed to be 'going to the heart of contemporary society, but bristling with difficulties'. He sketched the contemporary industrial setting, marked particularly by labour unrest (including the 1926 General Strike), bringing in train political complications focused on the Labour Party. Another significant lecture was given in the spring of 1928, to a Conference of the International Association for Industrial Relations, a body not connected with the wider-ranging Geneva-based organizations, the overall theme of which was concerned with occupational preparation for positions of supervisory and managerial responsibility in industry and commerce. Urwick's address was entitled 'The Nature of the Educational Training to Equip Foremen and Supervisors', reflecting his long-standing interest in this aspect of business.

It is also worth remembering that during the latter part of his employment at Rowntree's, Urwick wrote all or part of four books, which we shall review in Chapter 4. There were also important talks and external meetings, such as those mentioned in the preceding paragraphs. This was a substantial range of activities for someone who was also engaged in developing the MRGs, to say nothing of other responsibilities within Rowntree's, yet it reflected his desire to communicate as extensively as possible the benefits of both his own research and the ideas emanating especially from the United States.

Returning to the offer of the Directorship of the IMI, however, it is important to stress that before he could take up that role he had to settle matters back in the United Kingdom. One of these was the MRGs, because although he would have to give up his role as secretary, Rowntree was keen that he retained some active contact. Accordingly, he proposed and secured

Urwick's election as a member of the governing council, obliging him to come to London as and when practicable. Personal contacts enabled Urwick to find an appropriate person, A. J. Parker, to take over the role of secretary. At the same time, he established a lending library (under G. E. Milward) from his own very sizeable accumulation of books and journals, for use by members of the groups. This was such a great success that in 1931 it was restructured into a publicly available subscription service, operating as 'The Management Library', providing a unique source of valuable information for those interested in the subject.

The most serious problem, however, was breaking away from the Rowntree Company, and from Seebohm Rowntree in particular. Urwick readily recognized that at a critical stage in his life he had received from Seebohm enduring kindly interest, caring concern, and a great deal of personal support. He also knew that in Rowntree's mind he was seen as a serious candidate for promotion into the upper managerial levels, even if the first upward move might still be some years away, while others in the firm would have resisted the promotion. In later life, Urwick recorded the uncomfortable interview with Seebohm Rowntree when tendering his resignation. While Rowntree could recognize only too easily the attraction of the opportunity, he voiced his strong disappointment and reluctance to accept the resignation, especially as it would become active at the end of October 1928. These feelings were soon overcome, however; the board of directors even gave him a silver coffee set inscribed with their good wishes and thanks, a present customarily reserved for long-serving employees upon retirement. This indicates the high regard in which Urwick was held, given his significant contribution to a range of internal and external activities initiated by Seebohm Rowntree and the board.

In summing up this period of Urwick's career, it was, as Quail (2009) has noted, 'the making of him'. Indeed, Rowntree's had proved to be an ideal place for Urwick in which to spend almost seven years. It gave him an excellent set of opportunities from which to project his later career, not overwhelming him with purely administrative responsibilities, but providing challenging projects in internal consultancy. Moreover, there were many chances for external exposure and networking, as well as time to develop his writing and lecturing skills. In addition, his colleagues were intellectually stimulating, given that the company as a whole was arguably the most advanced in managerial techniques and attitudes to be found in Britain at that time, not least in its willingness to share and to be open about what it was doing. In particular, he owed a very considerable personal debt, as he recognized, to Seebohm Rowntree, whom he saw as the 'father of British management', and who was largely responsible for the intellectual atmosphere at the company.

In addition to the Rowntree context, he read widely well beyond the parameters of the company, building a substantial library which, as we have just noted, must have been one of the best in Britain. He was also well known to other members of the 'management movement', such as John Lee and E. T. Elbourne, as a result of the Rowntree Conferences. He expanded his knowledge of Taylor, making reference to him in most of his lectures and articles. He also read Henri Fayol in French from the early 1920s, developing such an admiration for his work that one of his first actions as Director of the IMI was to have *L'Administration Industrielle et Generale* translated into English and published by the Institute. A third major figure with whom he became acquainted in this period was Mary Parker Follett, the author of *Creative Experience* (1924), whose philosophy was based on consultation, coordination, and cooperation. One should also stress that it was mainly through Urwick's influence that she was invited to Britain in 1926 and 1928, to address the Rowntree Lecture Conferences in Balliol College, Oxford. These three figures, Taylor, Fayol, and Follett were to become central to his own philosophy, having helped to fashion its main elements by the time he left Rowntree's.

It was interesting, though, that however reluctant Urwick had been to disappoint Seebohm Rowntree, his own 'disappointment' was minimal. In later life, he recorded 'not liking continuing prospects within the Rowntree Company at all'. This was probably partly because of the likely promotion of Rowntree family members, but also probably because he had not endeared himself to some key figures in the company, Seebohm's support notwithstanding. Indeed, shortly after leaving Rowntree's, he published an article on 'How We Reorganized an Old Company' in the journal *Business* in November 1928, describing recent developments in Rowntree's, but doing so in a way which Quail (2009) has described as 'abrasive' and 'washing his previous employer's dirty linen in public'. His wife was also a positive force for the international appointment, because she realized how strongly held was her husband's keen interest in the post, even though the appointment would certainly entail abandoning hope for her own professional medical career. Once he had been able to establish a suitable residence in Geneva in November, however, the family situation was resolved.

3

The International Management Institute

While in Chapter 2 we noted the latent tensions within the International Management Institute (IMI), which led to Lyndall Urwick being appointed to its directorship, it will become clear that these by no means disappeared during his period of office. At the same time, on his arrival in Geneva in November 1928, he had the good fortune that his French predecessor had returned home and was therefore seeking to dispose of his Geneva house. This was a high-quality and well-situated chalet that appealed to Urwick, enabling his wife and baby daughter to join him immediately and resolving any personal fears he might have had. Crucially, Urwick's role as Director of the IMI gave him an international status; it is also this period in his career which has attracted the most attention from historians (Wrege et al. 1987; Nyland 2001; Walter-Busch 2006; Boyns 2007), because running through it were political and ideological undercurrents and disagreements at the IMI which have aroused much discussion, as we shall see towards the end of the chapter. Before that, however, we will examine various aspects of the structure and activities of the Institute, as well as the way that Urwick used this opportunity to strengthen his international networks.

IMI OBJECTIVES AND ORGANIZATION

The object of the Institute, as defined at its inception, was

to further the development of scientific methods of management as an essential factor in economic stability and social progress, and to this end to collect and distribute information concerning Management in its various aspects and to facilitate contact between persons and institutions interested in the subject by providing them with an international meeting ground and focus of activity.

Membership was based on financial contributions, with a full member (normally, a government or significant organization) paying at least 5,000 Swiss francs per year, and an associate member making a minimum annual contribution of 100 Swiss francs. By far the major financial burden was borne by the founding partners: the ILO provided office premises and all overhead services to the value of 80,000 Swiss francs per year; the Twentieth Century Fund paid 125,000 Swiss francs per year to provide for operational expenditures, including all staff salaries; and the Rockefeller Foundation provided an input for the first three years of, respectively, 125,000, 100,000, and 75,000 Swiss francs. Inevitably with such an organization, finance was to be an ongoing issue, since income through membership fees and sales of publications was never likely to make the Institute self-sufficient.

The Governing Board when Urwick became Director was a heterogeneous group of twenty-five members, chaired by Professor Francesco Mauro (also chairman of the Italian National Committee for Scientific Management), with two vice-chairmen representing the ILO and the Twentieth Century Fund. The other members represented a wide range of bodies, countries, and, it might be added, perspectives. The members from Britain were Seebohm Rowntree, representing the Joseph Rowntree Trust, which had made a sizeable one-off donation, and Charles Renold, representing the Management Research Groups (MRGs). During the formative months of 1927–8, the Board had translated the Institute's objective into three channels of action:

(a) Encouragement to governments and relevant national institutions and organizations to take up membership of the Institute, supporting it by the annual subscription as an associate member.

(b) Encouragement, advice, and assistance for the formation and inauguration of an internal specific national institution dedicated to the advancement and promotion of rationalization (although that nomenclature very soon changed to 'scientific management' with the French equivalent of 'L'Organisation Scientifique').

(c) The collation and provision of information on offer to assist national governments and institutions in the pursuit and accomplishment of those objectives.

Whatever the internal wranglings, the Institute's initial director and staff had been active in pursuing all three objectives, with some encouraging success. With specific regard to the third objective, a commendable library of literature, journals, and other documentation had been established within the Geneva office, the availability of which for loan was publicized in the *Bulletin*, which was issued monthly in English, French, and German from August 1927. Nevertheless, associate members enrolled by the end of 1928 totalled only about seventy, indicating slow progress on that front.

Lyndall Urwick was answerable to the Board, which met only rarely and expected him, as Director, to make the running in fulfilling the Institute's objectives and providing the publicized services. He had valuable internal support from Baron Hugo von Haan, an Austrian aristocrat whose father served in the Austrian Government. Upon graduation, Hugo had sought employment with the International Labour Organization in Geneva, securing a transfer to the IMI upon its foundation by reason of his interest in and knowledge of industrial and commercial management. During his first two months in office, Urwick found von Haan competent, reliable, and dedicated to the Institute and its members. In all respects, Urwick regarded him as a 'godsend' in overcoming both the backwash from the previous complexities and preparing for a more progressive future. In recognition of his qualities, Urwick formally established von Haan as Deputy Director, in charge of internal administrative management, including staff management aspects. Additionally, early in 1929, Urwick decided he needed, in addition to his lady secretary, a male personal assistant, with an adequate understanding of the staff role in the army sense, to whom he delegated numerous other administrative chores. This provided him with the time to devote to strategic issues, as well as the promotion of management improvement among the member nations.

THE INFORMATIONAL ROLE

As the primary objectives of the Institute were informational and educational, Urwick appreciated the significance of the *Bulletin* as a medium of communication with members, as well as with other organizations or individuals choosing to subscribe. Indeed, Urwick may well have become familiar with the *Bulletin* from its early issues, as Rowntree's had been among the first to join. As associate members were a key target category for expansion, each of these was given three copies of the *Bulletin* for distribution to their staff. This indicated how the membership fee of 100 Swiss francs (or about £4) was remarkably good value, because in addition to the *Bulletin*, members also received all of the IMI's publications. There were, of course, also a number of copies customarily circulated free of charge for promotional purposes. Well over 2,000 copies were being printed by 1933 and circulated in forty-seven countries, using three languages (English, French, and German). Just over half the issues were in French, with the rest split roughly evenly between the other two. By the time Urwick arrived, fulfilling a primary objective for the *Bulletin*, a pattern had been established, with all issues carrying reports of meetings about Rationalization, scientific management, and a range of managerial practices, forming a valuable component in the flow of innovations and ideas. While editorial policy, of course, lay with the Governing Board, as that met only three times a year, the realistic responsibility rested with the Director. Although von Haan had been involved in compiling and editing the early issues, Urwick immediately took over this role, writing either the editorial or indeed any other articles that came to mind.

Urwick had hardly become established in his Geneva office before the need arose to explain the international management situation to the Governing Board. Given that this was inadequately understood even by many of the people actively involved in the IMI, and indeed had bedevilled the early months of the Institute, Urwick wrote an explanatory article during his first weeks in office for publication in the December 1928 *Bulletin*, entitled 'The International Committee for Scientific Management (i.e. CIOS) and the International Management Institute'. The content was a factual presentation of their respective objectives, composition, activities, and progress to date, so that there could be no more cause for misunderstanding. Urwick also chose to write the editorial for the next issue (January 1929), posing the objective: 'to make available as widely as possible the most interesting and important contemporary contributions to the advancement of scientific management from all over the world'. As no Annual Report had yet been issued by the Institute, this article went on to set down the Institute's early history.

Under Urwick's editorship, the *Bulletin* developed several distinctive features. He immediately initiated a new section, 'Management Notes', to record and describe interesting innovations and developments in managerial and organizational practice occurring across the Institute's membership. While he prepared himself to enter items anonymously at times, he was far more concerned to invite contributions from external sources. Sadly, he had to start the new section with the news that John Lee, the significant British pioneer of systematic public sector management, had died on Christmas Eve 1928, just after retiring at the early age of sixty. Urwick laid particular emphasis on issuing an invitation to contribute items to the 'Notes', as well as for longer texts for reproduction in the *Bulletin*. Later in 1929, another special section was introduced, entitled 'Technical Notes'. Though not appearing in every issue, this section described corporate technological innovations that had been successfully accomplished to achieve efficiency improvements in manufacturing, machine tools, and materials handling.

While copy for each issue was partly generated internally by the Director and staff, the greater proportion was gathered through continuing contacts with the several National Committees and relevant local institutions, as well as with the Institute's membership. Two other important and interrelated subsections were 'Bibliographies' and 'Periodicals', both of which were concerned with the Institute's library. Similarly, the writing of 'case studies' for publication appealed strongly to Urwick, because in his first editorial in January 1929, he placed considerable emphasis on encouraging National Committees and associate members of the Institute to promote this kind of activity. This resulted in two case studies featuring in virtually every subsequent issue, while overall the Institute office received numerous expressions of appreciation for the practical value of the information provided by the *Bulletin*.

Another channel open to the IMI was its 'information response' service, which provided replies to personal enquiries. This avenue significantly enhanced the Institute's role and reputation, with the number of enquiries steadily increasing to 545 by 1932. Similarly, personal visitors were welcomed at the Institute office either to discuss whatever topic might be of interest to them or use the excellent library. Books were often donated by members, or purchased by the staff, while quite a number were received for review purposes, a task performed by Institute staff for the *Bulletin*. As by 1930 160 book reviews had been published, this was clearly regarded as a major activity. An incidental service from the library was the compilation of selective bibliographies for a range of aspects of managerial practice, frequently resulting in an editorial review in the *Bulletin*.

MEMBERSHIP, MEETINGS, AND VISITS

Another key role for Urwick was to make himself available, either in response to invitations from national committees and a range of other organizations, or seeking invitations from appropriate sources in countries where there was as yet neither an Institute nor a National Committee. In all, he visited twenty-one countries during his time as Director, many of them several times. In 1929, he also made ten visits to Britain. All this was not only to promote management, but also recruit more members for the Institute.

Achieving growth through visits or media was a considerable success, with the membership rising to 240 by the end of 1929, spread across sixteen countries. This expansion also continued, because by the end of 1930 it had reached 354 in twenty-two countries, while by mid-1933 it was 650, spread across more than forty countries. In viewing that trend in retrospect, one must remember the prevailing worldwide economic depression, rising industrial and commercial unemployment, and in several countries recurrent financial crises – not easy times for an international body. Crucially, this expansion of membership was critical in offsetting the withdrawal of funding from the Rockefeller Foundation. Urwick made only one public promotional appeal, with an anonymous *Bulletin* editorial headed 'Join the Institute', in October 1929. This focused on the Institute's value to industrialists, while denying any competition with the CIOS or similar bodies, an exercise that clearly had significant results.

In the interests of promoting the Institute's objectives among its membership, the Director's visiting programme was customarily spread over several days within any one country, always through consultation with officials of the host institution. The programme would include attendance at a meeting of the National Committee or institutional council, addressing a conference attended by local members and invited guests, and informational visits to companies and other selected establishments. On occasion, official governmental sessions were also included at local instigation. From the latter part of 1929 through the next three years, the Director's programme included nine or ten visits each year, selling the Institute's message, with each one reported in an issue of the *Bulletin*. The overall programme of visits gradually developed into an annual 'keeping in touch' approach, with senior members of staff frequently participating to back up Urwick's work.

For Urwick himself as Director, two important occasions were official visits to the United States. Although due to terminological differences 'Rationalization' did not resonate well with American managers, Urwick was nevertheless keen to secure at least some membership involvement, in addition to the personal participation from E. A. Filene and his colleagues in the Twentieth Century Fund. Filene readily agreed with Urwick's proposal for a visit and assisted in selecting contacts, establishing a programme for April–May 1931, and arranging introductions. As so little was known in the United States about either the IMI or the European management scene generally, it was necessary for Urwick to give an explanatory address to each host, the list of which included twenty-four professional and managerial institutions, six university business schools, twelve selected industrial and commercial corporations, and three major publishing houses specializing in managerial literature. In addition, Urwick also visited Filene's central department store in Boston. It was undoubtedly a highly enjoyable programme for the IMI Director, although when reviewing the situation for that year's Annual Report he regretted having to recognize that the outcome had been extremely poor in terms of boosting membership. He made arrangements for a subsequent follow-up visit by his Deputy, Hugo von Haan, in the following year, but that brought little better response in acquiring new members. Urwick's second visit to the United States, in 1932, was much more informal, with a select programme of visits to institutions with which contact had already become established.

Contact with America was, however, continuing through other channels; for example, in May 1931 the International Chamber of Commerce held its Congress in Washington, when Urwick's joint Report on 'Trends in the Organisation of Distribution' was presented. Urwick also established a long-term relationship with the American Society of Mechanical Engineers (one of the institutions visited during the first programme), because after it had been invited by the American government to conduct a national review of how more extensive application of scientific management could contribute to combating rising unemployment, this highly influential body took up associate membership of the IMI, with the knock-on effect that the American Management Association did so as well. Urwick also made sure that later issues of the *Bulletin* included presentations by American management institutions, including the Taylor Society, recalling its origin in 1912 as 'the Society to promote the science of management'.

Honouring a commitment made prior to his departure for Geneva, Urwick made ten visits to Britain during 1929. Some of these were to attend council meetings of the MRGs, as part of his campaign to establish a national management institute. His programme also included visits to a few major companies to solicit associate membership in the IMI, with some success, as well as nostalgic visits to Rowntree's in York. In 1930, he was invited to address the summer meeting of the British Association for the Advancement of Science, contributing to sessions on 'The Pure Theory of Organisation, with Special Reference to Business Enterprises' and 'Rationalisation does *not* lead to Unemployment'.

Attending and organizing conferences was a crucial part of his role. Almost as soon as Urwick took up office, he found himself at the 1929 CIOS Conference in Paris. Indeed, he assisted with the organization of this event, mainly to gain a closer feel for the Congress. A notable decision taken at that event was for the Congress to be held every three years, with the Director of the IMI committed to helping the local host, which was selected at the end of each meeting. It was decided that the 1932 Congress was to be held in Amsterdam, where apart from providing organizational input Urwick addressed the Congress on the progress made by the Rationalization Movement. Three years later, the CIOS conference moved to London, an event to which we will return later. By that time, Urwick had been elected to serve as Honorary Secretary to the International Committee, concentrating responsibility for inaugurating initial arrangements in London into his hands. This again reinforced his widening reputation as one of the leading lights in this world.

NATIONAL AND INTERNATIONAL
INSTITUTES AND MRGs

One of the key objectives of the IMI was to encourage the development of management institutions within individual countries, at both national and local levels, coordinating where possible international interactions. At the national level, it was hoped that countries would create either a National Committee for Scientific Management (or sometimes, 'Rationalization') or an Institute of Management, while at local levels it was intended that a range of MRGs would be formed. In the interests of promoting and maintaining what he regarded as the highly important feature of maintaining contact across the international management network, Urwick in 1929 convened a meeting in Geneva of the secretaries of the various National Committees and interested parties. The occasion was well attended by representatives, resulting in a five-page review in the *Bulletin* of the proceedings. The most positive discussions had been a survey of the progress of Rationalization in the countries attending, as well as an examination of the concept and practice of the MRGs, leading Urwick to convene this meeting annually as a means of sustaining member loyalty.

By 1931 and 1932, this meeting was being conducted on a much broader scale, with over 200 delegates from nineteen countries (including the United States, Germany, France, Italy, Belgium, Austria, the Netherlands, Czechoslovakia, Romania, Poland, and Russia). By 1933, Japan, Yugoslavia, Brazil, Hungary, and Australia had joined. Taking Hungary as an example, the National Committee had been formed as a result of the work of a number of industrial associations, led by the National Association of Iron and Steel Trades, although workers' representatives were excluded from the executive. Relations with the government went through the Ministry of Commerce, which had a right of veto on important decisions.

As Britain had no such body, not unnaturally Urwick was extremely keen to involve his home country in the network. He was obviously well aware of the specialist institutions, such as the Incorporated Sales Managers Association, the Industrial Welfare Society, the moribund Institute of Industrial Administration, and one or two others, but not one among them could realistically be seen as a focal point for the British organization. He consequently decided to use his membership of the MRG council, drafting a memorandum entitled 'The Need for a British Institute of Management' that the council might sponsor and promote as a national focus. After noting the extent of developments in a range of other countries, he advocated the need for comparable innovations in Britain, with the remainder of the document (totalling eleven pages) setting out a constitution, with indications of proposed membership, modes of working, sources of funding, and other relevant proposals. In spite of this work, however, no action ensued. Although the MRG council discussed Urwick's document, it was decided that the task of implementing the proposal would be beyond its capacity, as well as arguably being contrary to their specific purposes. With the economy plummeting into deep depression, the environment also proved hostile to the kind of innovation being proposed. For Urwick, this was a deep disappointment, not least because he felt strongly that an effective 'Institute of Management' could play an extremely valuable role in bringing the economy out of depression. The memorandum thus became nothing more than a historical artefact.

In spite of this rejection at the national level, however, much greater success was achieved in developing MRGs, something that gave Urwick particular pleasure. At his first opportunity, in the *Bulletin* of December 1928, he explained the new arrangements within the British MRGs following his own withdrawal. From that point on, promotion across Europe, and elsewhere as and where appropriate, became a major feature of his mission for the advancement of management, to be fostered through discussions with members of National Committees, and paraded whenever relevant in the *Bulletin*. The May 1929 edition carried a report of the AGM held by the British groups Council, with seven groups representing over 100 companies. The subject also formed the substance of Urwick's editorial in July of that year, when he was able to report the progress of groups in the United States, including the novel slant that some university business schools were promoting them in their local catchment areas. Indeed, the biggest difference between the MRGs in Britain and most of the non-British MRGs was the latter's focus on a single industry. The single Belgian MRG, for instance, was in the finance industry and composed of stockbrokers, while that in Czechoslovakia was made up of revenue officials in the public sector. Even in the United States, one of the groups was composed of companies in the shoe industry, while another was based in Harvard University.

The campaign to create more MRGs was further boosted by the Second International Discussion Conference, convened by the IMI in Geneva from 1–4 July 1931, which was devoted to this aspect of its mission. Urwick was pleased to see that there were sixty acceptances for this event, and even though only forty actually attended, they covered all ten countries which at that time had forty-nine MRGs involving 600 organizations. There were eighteen reports and three general discussions about the structure, scope, and experiences of MRGs, assisted by the Filene-Finlay telephonic scheme for simultaneous translation into the other two official languages. At the conclusion, a resolution was passed revealing 'the existence of a vigorous research group movement', its success in achieving 'practical results in the improvement of management technique', and drawing the attention of all concerned 'to the importance of developing as rapidly as possible . . . the number and variety of management groups'. The *Bulletin* also regularly reported the formation of new MRGs, for example, in June 1929 after four groups had been formed in Switzerland and a specialist group for retail department stores had emerged in France. By the end of 1929, five groups were operating successfully in the Netherlands, and the first was established in Germany early in 1930. In that year, four countries (Austria, Germany, the Netherlands, and Switzerland) held an informal conference in Zurich, reported in the September *Bulletin*, resulting in similar activities late in 1930 that featured in the November and December issues.

Perhaps the most international MRG was created in 1928 when E. A. Filene succeeded in persuading a number of retail trading companies in several major countries to found the International Research Group of Department Stores. Urwick assisted with this during his first weeks in Geneva by securing cooperation from the International Chamber of Commerce, based in Paris. This was a considerable coup for Urwick at the start of his tenure as Director, given the prestige and influence of this body, not to mention the support it provided for Filene's initiative. When in April 1929 the Group held its first AGM in Paris, Urwick was invited along, leading to a report in the June *Bulletin*. Within a year, the Group had adopted the 'MRG' wording in its title, when seven countries sent representatives to London in December 1930. The occasion was graced by the adoption of a specifically designed statistical scheme for inter-company comparisons of operating efficiencies. The submission of the report and the proceedings of the Congress were cited in the *Bulletin* (No. 4 for 1931), in the 'Research and publications' section.

This 'Research and publications' section was another vital component of the IMI's activities. One of Urwick's personal goals was to use his position to pursue research and offer surveys, in particular to map the management situation as it existed. Of course, such activities were not merely personal, but often the result of requests from members. Some of these he inherited, such as a coordinating role for four research projects that the League of Nations Economic Committee had commissioned in May 1928. In 1929, Urwick was also invited by a vice-president of the American Telegraph and Telephone Corporation to join him in compiling a report on 'Trends in the Organisation and Methods of Distribution within Europe and the USA', for the International Chamber's 1931 Congress. This work went on for over eighteen months, resulting in a report of 164 pages in length, with over a 100 tables.

Providing research expertise for the League of Nations Secretariat (specifically, the Economic Committee) and the International Labour Organization, was yet another valuable role played by the IMI. Urwick frequently took the lead role in these projects, with Institute staff used as research assistants. Another significant project was 'The Market Survey of Europe', because the League's Economic Committee took some interest in it. Some research was closer to consultancy, for example that requested early in 1932 by the League of Nations Supervisory Commission in the form of a review of the administrative systems, procedures, and operational performance employed internally in both its offices and those of the ILO. For Urwick, this was a near replica of his Rowntree's sales office review. There had also been an earlier consultancy review of the League's Economic Intelligence Services, conducted in coordination with a similar review for the International Chamber of Commerce. In both cases, the League's Assembly had placed on official record its appreciation of the IMI Director's service in leading the reviews.

Other research projects were internally generated. For example, Urwick decided to study the process of amalgamation among large companies, forming an international team headed by a senior staff member of the Institute. The team worked virtually full time for the best part of two years, compiling their findings into a two-volume report that was published in 1932 by the IMI as *The Administration and Management of Business Combinations*. The first volume carried the findings of the combination process and of its implications for organizational structures, delegation, and managerial responsibility, while the second took the form of an anonymized case study covering a British combination. Quail (2008: 139) notes that the report 'showed a realism and questioning approach not generally found in managerial material of the period', using it as the basis for a highly original analysis of interwar developments.

Apart from all this work, Urwick pursued other initiatives arising from external stimuli. One of these was a study of budgetary control, starting with a report in the *Bulletin* of March 1929 on the 'flexible' approach that had gained a prize from The Netherlands Institute for Efficiency. This was followed in October of that year with a report on a comprehensive control system developed and installed in Renold's, one of the leading British advocates of scientific management. The interest generated among members, especially company members, led Urwick to convene a three-day conference, with papers describing effective systems. This was held in Geneva in July 1930, with a comprehensive record of the proceedings made available in three sizeable volumes. An editorial in the *Bulletin* of July 1930, headed 'Some Reflections on Budgetary Control', summarized the underlying principles, accompanied by a series of 'Questions and Answers', providing a practical textbook on this increasingly popular managerial tool.

At the same time, Urwick also decided to initiate a research study of his own, into the managerial responsibilities associated with selling, marketing, and distribution, which again revived his own first-hand involvement at Rowntree's. This project covered several European countries, resulting in a memorandum rather than a formal report that was made available via the *Bulletin* on a request basis.

Although the scope of all this work was significant and increasing, it was only a small proportion of the IMI's activities. As well as these specific pieces of research, the IMI put out a substantial number of reports. In 1933, the *Bulletin* listed thirty-seven IMI publications, many of which were on detailed topics such as *Safety on the Boston Elevated Railway* (1932) or *Reorganisation at the Galeria Lafayette Garage* (1933), while others resulted from general studies of the application of scientific management to agriculture, railways, small factories, and textiles. A related project was to invite National Committees to compile for their own country a list of all those institutes connected to management matters as a means of increasing membership locally.

During this period, Urwick also wrote a good deal about management, partly in the form of commissioned articles for journals and papers for meetings, reflecting his growing stature in this field. For example, in 1930 he responded to an invitation to contribute a short series of articles to the European edition of an American monthly journal called *Factory and Industrial Management*. The subject matter provided an interesting insight into the diverse objectives and activities of the IMI, including the promotion of the MRG formula. In addition, he wrote wider pieces about management, such as the defensive 'Rationalisation Does *Not* Lead to Unemployment', or articles about the IMI ('An International Clearing House of Good Management'). Other pieces were about specific topics, such as 'The Idea of Management Groups' or 'Management Groups: The Business Man's University', as well as on a particular management topic such as costing. Some of his longer writings, and especially his book *Management for Tomorrow* (1933), will be reviewed in Chapter 4.

POLITICS

While much of what we have related so far about Urwick's tenure as Director of the IMI indicates that both were flourishing, in spite of the depressed economic environment, one must add that behind the scenes there were several difficult internal political issues. Indeed, as we saw in Chapter 2, right from the start there had been considerable tensions which had resulted in the exit of the initial Director and Deputy Director. Moreover, these tensions did not disappear on Urwick's arrival, with three interrelated issues developing a sinister tone. Firstly, there were unrealistic expectations of what the Institute could achieve. For example, 'Filene believed world-wide economic problems could be solved by the use of scientific management to restructure European industry' (Wrege et al. 1987: 249). In December 1928, a month after Urwick's arrival and less than two years after the commencement of the Institute, Evans Clark of the Fund wrote asking if the IMI had been successful in reducing European tariff barriers (Wrege et al. 1987: 252). Given the state of international politics, and especially the worst depression in modern history, to have even come anywhere near to achieving this objective was totally unrealistic; it would have been extremely difficult even in the best of circumstances.

Most important from the Fund's perspective, however, was the development of MRGs. Urwick himself was totally in favour of MRGs, given his experience in Britain, and understood more about the principles of operating them than anyone else. However, although more than fifty were created, the Fund was disappointed, even in the face of acute economic difficulties. To do nothing but create and support MRGs, as Percy Brown seemed to want when he became Filene's adviser, would have been a limited view of the IMI's objectives. Indeed, it would also have been impractical if there had been no informational or research roles to complement these. More than anything, MRGs needed ideas to give them a scientific management base. Nevertheless, the Fund wanted the creation and nurturing of MRGs to be the main role of the Institute. One must, nevertheless, ask whether even if more had been created and nurtured (whatever that might have involved), MRGs were the best mechanism for disseminating and encouraging scientific management practices. A major weakness was their propensity in Britain (and almost certainly in other European countries) to keep all discussions secret. Indeed, this independence and confidentiality was what made them attractive to most companies, even if this limited the impact they could make on wider business practices.

Moving away from this specific weakness, one should also stress how inter-organizational rivalries were built into the structure of the IMI through its board of directors. This rivalry was especially rife not only in the relationship between the Fund and the ILO as the prime movers and funders, but also in involving the Rockefeller Foundation, the CIOS, and several National Committees for Scientific Management, all of whom were represented on the board. As Wrege et al. (1987: 251) wryly put it: 'The difficulties of having such a diverse group of individuals on the governing board of the Institute were to become apparent as the years passed.' Almost inevitably, the representational roles created difficulties, philosophically between the Fund and the ILO (which was manifested in the third category of issues covered later), and in terms of jockeying for external power. The original idea of Devinat had been that the IMI and the CIOS would collaborate to bring scientific management to Europe, but the two bodies rapidly became rivals, with each seeking to outshine the other. The two key people in the CIOS were Mauro and Landauer, who Urwick felt believed that they 'practically owned the IMI, despite the fact that they had not contributed any funds to the costs of running the IMI'. Moreover, the ILO was felt to be 'incline[d] to the view that it is a deliberate attempt on the part of the hard-boiled Employers' Associations in Europe, which have their headquarters in Brussels, to capture the Institute and bring it completely under the control of reactionary elements' (Wrege et al. 1987: 257). As Mauro and Landauer were close to some Fascist organizations, especially in Italy, they may have feared that the IMI was threatening their status in the international management movement because it had been successful in securing the support of the various National Committees for Scientific Management. These difficulties between the CIOS and the IMI were not just the perception of Urwick, but were also shared by the Fund. However, in 1932 these issues were partially resolved when Landauer failed to be re-elected as a CIOS representative on the IMI Board.

Another key issue was Filene's perceived role, because as the main force behind the Twentieth Century Fund he always appeared to be keen to exert influence, which he did both directly and through Percy Brown, who was constantly complaining to the Fund about Urwick's activities. The Rockefeller Foundation was largely responsible for the removal of the original Director, Devinat, because of what it saw as his lack of executive capabilities. Later, in 1930, the International Chamber of Commerce also became involved in the affairs of the IMI, when it sought a role in the Institute without reciprocal membership or any financial contribution. Inevitably, this would cause further difficulties with some of the National Committees, especially in Germany.

In a talk to the Institute of Public Administration in January 1935, Urwick reflected ruefully on these problems:

In moments of difficulty, I also discovered that my own position appeared to combine almost uncannily the maximum disadvantages of both systems. It had none of the security, the dignity or the traditions which surround life in any well established public service. It had none of the direct measurement of financial results, freedom to experiment or elasticity in meeting situations which are characteristic of private business. The Institute had to produce some sort of results if it was to live at all. Unfortunately no two members of the heterogeneous group which governed it could agree for two meetings together what those results should be.

Ultimately, though, the most problematic disagreements were philosophical in nature, pre-dating the arrival of Urwick and mostly concerning the nature and responsibilities of management, and the meaning of Rationalization and scientific management. Quoting Nyland (2001: 12), 'Filene, Dennison and Brown thought of management as a firm- or bureau-centred activity and believed that if the IMI was to develop as an international management centre its officials had to concentrate on gaining the support of the business community'. In contrast, 'the ILO representatives on the IMI Board repeatedly insisted that the Institute must give equal priority to the interests of capital, labour, and the general community'. This difference was apparent at the World Economic Conference in 1927, where the final declaration 'called for the rapid diffusion of scientific management but insisted that ... [it] should be but one part of a wider movement that would enable humanity to win control of economic life' (Nyland 2001: 13). This is what it meant by Rationalization, further developed by Urwick in *The Meaning of Rationalisation*. In other words, the IMI had already been given the ILO version of Rationalization to pursue from its inception. Even after Urwick's appointment, the Americans made it clear that the Fund would withdraw its support for the IMI unless it was agreed that it would concentrate on technical problems of immediate interest to business and leave social questions to the ILO (Nyland 2001: 14). While Albert Thomas of the ILO reluctantly agreed, he still insisted that the IMI must not place too much stress on the management point of view when addressing labour issues.

While Filene may have talked about scientific management, his ideas on this subject increasingly moved away from those espoused by the Taylor Society, which saw itself as the embodiment of Taylor's ideas. Urwick, on the other hand, in his thinking and in his editorials, aligned himself with the Taylor Society and the ILO in looking to management to have a wider role and responsibility than the Fund would envisage. All of these tensions were exacerbated by the depression and resultant economic problems, while the rise of extreme politics in Europe, especially Nazism, with which some sectors of industry associated themselves, added to the potentially explosive situation. Even without the political problems outlined earlier, it seems highly unlikely that the IMI would have survived the late 1930s European political scene, not to mention the Second World War.

Where did Urwick stand amidst these tensions? On the first, he was certainly willing to pursue the MRGs and did so with enthusiasm and considerable success. Where he did diverge from Filene was in his conception of scientific management, in which he was closer to the ILO view. Urwick must have known that he was moving in directions with which Filene did not agree, but typically stood by his views based on both a detailed reading of Taylor and his Rowntree's experiences. His view was first voiced overtly in an article entitled 'Industry for Service', printed in December 1921 in Rowntree's *Staff Journal*, advocating the principle that the main objective of all industrial and commercial operations (and therefore of their management) lay in serving the well-being of its community. During the Depression, Urwick adopted the under-consumptionist view of the world economic situation which was being argued at this time by, amongst others, the Taylor Society, whose individual members were to make a considerable contribution to the Roosevelt Administration (Nyland 2001: 19). Essentially, they were arguing that the principles of scientific management, namely, planning, should be taken forward to macromanagement of the economy, whereas the business community generally strongly opposed this. The IMI *Bulletin* increasingly took the former perspective as the Depression deepened, a position that was not well received by Filene and Dennison. Indeed, in Urwick's final editorial in December 1933 he noted that: 'Over 50% of the leading articles in the *Bulletin* in the last two years have dealt with . . . the social consequences of rationalization'.

THE ENDING OF THE INSTITUTE

While 1932 could be regarded as the high-water mark for the Institute, any optimism was soon to be swamped by external events. Firstly, as the United States went off the Gold Standard, the Twentieth Century Fund's contribution was buying only 60,000 francs worth of work, rather than the previous 100,000 francs worth. Fortunately, the Institute's sound financial position could deal with the shortfall without any immediate reduction of activities, other than by stricter internal expense control and some limitation on visits. However, when in January 1933 the German Reichstag building was destroyed by fire and Adolf Hitler was elected as Chancellor of Germany, committed to carrying into reality the aims of the National Socialist Party programme, this sent political shock waves across Europe, as well as having a negative impact in the United States which had serious implications for the Institute. While Edward Filene was of Jewish extraction, putting that aside he became deeply dismayed with the prospects of European progress in general, compounding the deteriorating dollar–franc exchange rate.

These were important external dimensions of the decision to end the Institute. Equally, though, if not more important, was the worsening relationship between the two sides of the management dispute. The situation came to a head in March 1933, when von Haan, Urwick's deputy, published a paper which announced that the ILO had determined that the IMI should adopt a 'wider and deeper' conception of scientific management, meaning that workers must be allowed to participate in all forms of management activity (Nyland 2001: 21). The Fund responded by warning that its support for the IMI was 'subject to agreement upon the programme of work and other circumstances', to which the ILO in turn replied that as 'the work of the Institute did not pay sufficient attention to the social aspects of Rationalisa- tion', it had no choice but to insist on 'changes of policy in this respect'. Filene not surprisingly declared that as the Institute's 'programme of work and other circumstances ... had changed radically', the Fund could no longer finance the Institute. Although Urwick might not have been a prime mover in these exchanges, he certainly knew what was happening, given that the ILO position was in keeping with his *Bulletin* editorials. Urwick later said: 'Even then I believe they would have stuck to their guns had not the critics started a personal intrigue in the apparent conviction that the Institute would be moved to Paris if they could make its work at Geneva sufficiently unpopular with the Americans.'

Filene notified Lyndall Urwick privately in the middle of 1933 that, firstly, he was submitting notice formally to withdraw all financial support for the Institute by the end of the year, and, secondly, would not make good the shortfall in Swiss francs during the intervening months. It is worth noting that Filene was not unanimously supported amongst his American counterparts, while eighteen months later he publicly regretted the decision. Nevertheless, as Boyns (2007: 10) notes, Filene 'had always had his doubts that an ILO-linked organization, based in Geneva, could do the job that he saw as being necessary'. The situation was fatal for the IMI, because the ILO was unable to provide additional financing, and the membership subscription income was minuscule in comparison with its needs. The only solution lay in closing down the Institute, in December 1933, a decision which was a devastating blow to Lyndall Urwick and his plans to develop the management agenda.

While immediate activities continued, including compilation and circula- tion of the monthly *Bulletins*, for Urwick an important immediate concern lay in assisting his staff to find alternative employment before the end of the year. In respect of his own future situation, he preferred to let time take its course. Characteristically, the sense of devastation that he suffered from the news of impending closure was less concerned with the impact upon his own employ- ment situation than with the loss of the mechanism and the powerhouse for the continuing promotion of management knowledge. He was determined to investigate ways through which some part of that promotion could be continued, exploring possibilities with the CIOS, the ILO, and the League of Nations Secretariat. Given their limited financial resources, however, all of this came to nothing.

The year 1933 was an unfortunate one for Urwick in several ways, not least because three members of the IMI Board died, including his great supporter, Albert Thomas, the Director of the ILO, and also Colonel Raikes, whom he had brought in as his personal assistant at the IMI. As the year was drawing to its close, Lyndall Urwick decided on a last ruse, as no formal notice of closure had yet been issued; he would go over to Boston with a personal appeal to Edward Filene, even though that meant spending the Christmas period away from his family. The new Director of the ILO had already visited Filene in Boston, to plead for the Fund's continuing support, even if on a more restricted scale. This mission had failed, although Filene did agree to delay closure until the end of January 1934 and pay Urwick's salary until the end of June. Urwick's visit to Boston failed to secure any further assistance. He also came away with another item of sad personal news, that Mary Parker Follett had died in a Boston hospital while he was in the city without knowing of her illness until it was too late to visit.

His visit to America was not entirely without a brighter side, however, as he noted in his partial autobiography:

The other incident which made my visit . . . memorable was the kindness and sympathy of my American colleagues in the management movement. I think many of them were genuinely sorry that the IMI was to be closed down. While compared to many of the American Foundations it was indeed small beer, I think they wished to show me that they appreciated what I had tried to do, even if the late E.A. Filene did not. On December 20, 1933, fourteen of them entertained me to dinner in New York. At the end of the evening, they presented me with the first volume of the late Winston Churchill's *Marlborough, His Life and Times,* which had just been published. . . . The signatures on the flyleaf of the first volume read almost like a *Who's Who* of the American management movement at that time – Calvin W Rice, Lillian M Gilbreth, Walter Van Dyke Bingham, Charles H Hatch, R W Barnes, J T Person, W H Leffingwell, Harry and Rita Hopf and half-a-dozen others. I was most encouraged in a bad moment by this gesture of friendship and confidence. The volume is still one of my most prized possessions.

Before leaving for Boston, Urwick had felt it necessary for the first time to make some overt reference to the likely termination of the IMI, in the form of an editorial for the December issue of the *Bulletin.* True to his Oxford University background, he used the traditional classical salutation as a title: 'Ave Atque Vale' (customarily translated as 'Hail and Farewell'). The opening sentence read: 'With this issue the *Bulletin of the International Management Institute* appears, in the present form at all events, for the last time'. The rest of the opening paragraph confirmed the likely withdrawal of the Twentieth Century Trust funding and membership, as well as recalling the shift of concern to those 'social' aspects and pointing out their relevance within the managerial context. The following pages carried a broad review of the Institute's role, while the closing message was revelatory in reflecting the Director's thinking:

Though the Institute may cease temporarily at a moment of disillusion and economic difficulty, rationalisation cannot cease in the midst of those men and women who prefer truth above more transitory things and an understanding of natural law to the lawlessness of human misunderstandings. Where such men and women may meet and exchange ideas in any country, there the thought for which the Institute has stood will survive: it is the only guide to prosperity, stability and economic peace.

It was typical of Lyndall Urwick's concern for the well-being of his staff that in that issue he printed an appeal to readers to assist with finding them ongoing employment. On a personal note, he noted how he had enjoyed for five years fulfilment of his management mission, first formed in the trenches in 1915 upon first reading Taylor's *Shop Management*, masterminding the promotion of systematic managerial practice and knowledge across a large number of countries.

Urwick spent January 1934 rounding off Institute affairs. This involved cataloguing the enormous collection of books, periodicals, reports, and comments for orderly transfer into the library of the International Labour Organization, as well as bidding adieu to his colleagues and staff. Enjoying the benefit of a regular salary up to July, he remained in the Geneva house engaged in drafting two books that he had been planning for some time: one was concerned with organizational structure and delegation, while the second examined aspects of management and administration. However, neither was ever completed, because by May 1934 he and his family had returned to Britain. While this provided the Urwicks with a chance to rebuild a family life that for the previous five years had been constantly interrupted by Lyndall's travelling and working in the cause of the advancement of management, the demise of the IMI came as a major shock to a man who had dedicated an enormous proportion of his time and energies to his chosen mission. Overall, though, and in spite of its premature closure, being Director of the IMI had been a rich experience for Urwick, from which he emerged with an international reputation as one of the world's leading advocates of systematic management.

4

Writings in the Interwar Period

Having surveyed Urwick's career up to the mid-1930s, it is now important to assess both his interwar publications and his role in boosting the profile of the management movement. It is the latter with which we begin, before moving on to the writings which provided the principles and moral basis on which he based his entire career. It will become clear that the 1920s proved to be crucial in the development of Urwick's views on management and organization, reflecting the dynamic context within which he operated. Indeed, especially in view of the rise of a distinct management movement at that time, Urwick was part of a group that was attempting to persuade the business community to change direction. While this is not the place to discuss the extent to which any success was achieved (Child 1969; Wilson 1995; Wilson and Thomson 2006), Urwick was always optimistic and increasingly central to what was happening.

THE MANAGEMENT MOVEMENT
IN THE INTERWAR PERIOD

While there had been some important writing about management in Britain before the First World War, by writers such as Slater Lewis, Church, and Elbourne, it was insular, uncoordinated, predominantly focused on production issues, and most importantly, given little consideration by the vast majority of British managers. Moreover, the very idea of management in Britain was only partially accepted by both the directors and the general workforce: the former saw control as the perquisite of the dominant families, while the latter challenged the idea of management as a system of authority. There were of course exceptions, including Rowntree's and a handful of extremely large chemical and food companies, but the generality rarely read any management literature (Wilson 1995; Wilson and Thomson 2006).

When the term 'management movement' originated is debatable, but the ideas and activities underpinning it started to arise during and soon after the

First World War. In the post-war world, British management required legitimacy in what to many appeared to be the sharpening conflict between capital and labour. Early post-war writers such as John Lee and Oliver Sheldon were trying to provide this legitimacy by positioning management as a profession which involved two main strands: training and education to provide technical competence; and ethical standards which were based on the notion of service to the community, holding a balance between capital and labour by providing a scientific (or systematic) analysis of managerial problems. While some of these ideas were prompted by emerging concepts of human relations that originated in the war (Child: 1969), equally important were the principles espoused by German industrialists such as Walter Rathenau, the acknowledged leader of the Rationalization Movement. The management movement was largely concerned with philosophical, ethical, educational, and professional issues, rather than technical competence or production dimensions, which had been the primary concerns in the United States through their engineering associations.

The early management movement was essentially trying to identify a role for managers as intermediaries, or 'third parties', offering a professionalism based on technical expertise and operating in the interests of wider society, with the capital–labour conflict as the backdrop. As management did not have property rights to justify its authority, it needed professional status to provide its legitimacy and an ideological underpinning to contrast with the demands for industrial democracy pursued by the shop steward movement during and after the First World War. It also offered systematic thought, impartiality, and rationality, especially compared to the 'rule-of-thumb' mode of decision-making which had been dominant before the war and was still prevalent in the 1920s. Even Sidney Webb, a key figure in the development of the Fabian Society and the Labour Party, saw managers in a 'third-party' role.

Central to the early movement was Rowntree's, where Seebohm Rowntree and Oliver Sheldon offered personal leadership that undoubtedly had a considerable influence on Urwick's personal thinking. Urwick, in his *Golden Book of Management*, described Rowntree as 'the British management movement's greatest pioneer'. Not only was he concerned to bring new managerial practices into the firm, but he also set up the Rowntree Lecture Conferences which ran from 1920 to 1933, providing the only structured presentation of managerial principles anywhere in Britain during that period, initially for supervisors, but as time went on increasingly for higher-level managers. Rowntree also wrote an important book *The Human Factor in Business* (1919), based on his wartime experiences in the Ministry of Munitions, while at the same time offering moral leadership in both his other writings and actions (Briggs 1961), influencing other key individuals such as Sheldon, Northcott, and Urwick. In addition, of course, he also initiated the MRGs.

Sheldon was very much an original thinker, being the first writer anywhere to develop a philosophy of management, in a book of that title (1923). This philosophy was based on the idea of management as a profession, with special training and higher qualifications, together with ethical standards, human relations, and 'communal well-being'. Seebohm Rowntree's foreword to the book was evocative of this latter dimension, an idea which was central to the management movement and important in Urwick's own thinking, noting that

the author recognises that business has a soul; that it is not a mechanical thing but a living and worthy part of the social organism. It is not an end in itself but a means to an end, and that end is the well-being of the whole community.

Sheldon was, however, a sceptic about the production focus of scientific management, holding human values to be all-important.

Another who played an important part in the management movement was the Rowntree's labour director, C. H. Northcott, who was to become a significant figure in the Institute of Personnel Management and author of a powerful piece entitled 'The Moral Duty of Management' in the Lee compendium of 1928, as well as a later book entitled *Christian Principles in Industry; Their Application in Practice* (1958). As Urwick put it many years later, in his famous 'Letter to an MBA' (1969): 'The Cocoa Works at York in those days was a kind of practical university of management. There were a bunch of people there (O. Sheldon, C.H. Northcott, W. Wallace etc). Between us we wrote most of the British management literature.'

Outside Rowntree's a key figure was John Lee, who wrote the most important book of the early post-war period, *Management – A Study of Industrial Organisation* (1921). Lee was 'quite clear that industrial managers had emerged as a distinct occupational group whose "scientific" approach was superior to the arbitrary rule of ownership' (Child 1969: 59). This was followed by three other books, while in 1928 he edited a major compilation to which Urwick made two substantial contributions (reviewed later in this chapter). Another important figure was Edward Elbourne, who initiated the Institute of Industrial Administration, and of whom Urwick was to say much later in his 1956 Elbourne Memorial Lecture:

he was the first man in Britain to have a vision of modern methods of industrial administration as a whole, to realise the immense possibilities inherent in their deliberate study and teaching. He had an ideal. He pursued it consistently and unselfishly, often to his great personal disadvantage.

It is also interesting that Elbourne (1934: xxi) noted of the educational courses with which he was associated: 'Gradually, and largely owing to requests from potential students, classes and courses have been started at various technical and other colleges throughout the country'. In other words, demand was student- and not company-driven.

There were also institutions which, like the management movement itself, struggled in the interwar period to gain acceptance and even awareness in an industrial world which was inwardly focused. The first such body for managers, the Institute of Industrial Administration, soon ran into membership problems and went into abeyance for the second half of the 1920s, before reconstituting itself based on educational activities (Brech 2002–1). Other professional institutions noted in Figure 4.1 could still only boast by 1939 a membership mostly in the hundreds, rather than the thousands. The National Institute of Industrial Psychology, which was more of a market research organization than a professional institute, started with studies into scientific management. In line with the interests of an influential group of British employers such as Seebohm Rowntree, however, it shifted its attentions more towards human relations. The Oxford Conferences and the Management Research Groups could also be considered as parts of the institutional framework of the management movement, as we saw in Chapter 2.

In the late 1920s, the attention paid to trade unions, which had been an important theme earlier in the decade, diminished in favour of human relations, which was essentially a managerial tool, rather than a bilateral approach to operations in the workplace. The larger capital–labour struggle had in any case diminished after the General Strike of 1926. The other dimension of change was towards 'Rationalization', as evidenced by the

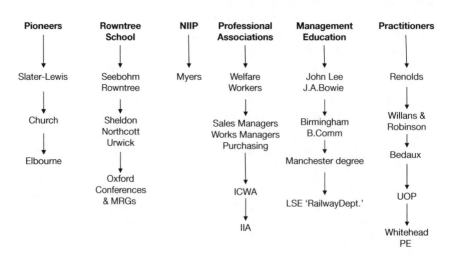

Figure 4.1 The key features of the British management movement between the wars.

Geneva Conference which, as we saw in Chapter 2, Urwick had attended. Child (1969: 86) saw this as 'an attempt to substitute organization for the rule-of-thumb anarchy of economic life'.

In general, though, it must be stressed that the management movement was always small and consisted mainly of managers, supplemented in the 1930s by an increasing number of consultants, and supported by a few prominent industrialists such as Seebohm Rowntree, Viscount Leverhulme, and Sir Alfred Mond of Imperial Chemical Industries (ICI). Almost all the writing was done by managers or consultants describing their experiences, while the publishing was done through the journals which appeared in the 1930s, such as *Industry Illustrated* (1933) and the *British Management Review* (1936), together with the house journals of the professional institutes. While the momentum undoubtedly increased in the 1930s, there was still a lack of an effective institution to provide leadership, or for that matter to represent Britain at international gatherings.

Where did Urwick fit into the movement? He was strongly influenced by the moral attitudes prevalent at Rowntree's, along with the operating principles he was learning from Taylor, Fayol, and Follett, amongst others. It should be remembered, however, that he had no direct dealings with production or the manual labour force at Rowntree's, having focused more on office and sales issues. While he certainly supported Taylor, it was the principles of systematic management that Taylor espoused, rather than the production-enhancing techniques for which scientific management was better known. Nevertheless, his attitudes to trade unions were positive. He was in favour of consultation and indeed profit-sharing, as well as being sympathetic to the plight of the less well-off, something he inherited from both his father and the man who was almost an adoptive father, Seebohm Rowntree. As we noted in Chapter 1, he also became employers' secretary of the Glove Industry Trade Association, striking up a strong friendship with the union secretary. Above all, Urwick had no strong antagonism to unions; neither did he adopt a class-conscious attitude towards them, as many of his peers with a similar background did. At the same time, he believed that management must manage, with unions consulted when necessary.

Another crucial issue to bear in mind when assessing Urwick's evolving managerial philosophy was the considerable range of experiences he enjoyed while working at Rowntree's, giving him a wider perspective than the vast majority of managers. This breadth was also enhanced through his work with the MRGs and his international reading and experience. Indeed, some of Urwick's key strengths arose out of his personal contacts in other countries, while he also read widely, building up one of the largest personal management libraries in the country. His fluency in French and reasonable knowledge of

German, again unusual for an English-speaking manager of the period (or, indeed, at any period), gave him a particular advantage. From the start, he consequently developed the capacity to be a great synthesizer. While most of the other British writers of that era based their work on either practical observation (Lee) or a priori hypothesizing (Sheldon), by the end of the 1920s Urwick was already developing the broader scope that came to characterize his work. By the time he came back from the IMI in 1934, he had also added an international dimension, resulting in a situation by the latter part of the 1930s that Urwick was unquestionably the leading articulator of the British management movement's beliefs and one of the few able to draw on international knowledge and experience.

ORGANISING A SALES OFFICE

Having made these initial observations on his status and breadth, we can now turn to look at Urwick's 1920s publications. The first was *Organising a Sales Office*, derived from his reorganization of the Rowntree's sales office, written in 1925–6 with the approval of the Rowntree directors, with a foreword by Seebohm Rowntree. Very few British companies would have been willing to make the same gesture, a point supported by Urwick in the author's preface. It was Urwick's first chance to lay out some principles in practice, although it was inevitably less about the philosophy of management than the practicalities of an internal consultancy. The book emerged as a substantial publication of 213 pages was published in 1928 by Victor Gollancz, who had been Urwick's fellow scholar at New College. It is worth noting that the book was a sufficient success to be considered worth republishing by Pitman & Sons in 1938.

Urwick started by affirming his earlier studies of Taylor's 'scientific management', making a point that he was to repeat throughout his career, namely, that scientific management had been brought into disrepute by inexpert imitation by the 'efficiency engineers', whom he called 'quacks'. In restating what he saw as Taylor's true approach, he put particular emphasis on the 'systematic' aspect of management. Moreover, he stressed that the review of methods undertaken within the firm was conducted as a faithful replication of Taylor's principles, and in particular through consultation with those employees who were going to be affected, thereby obtaining their cooperation as a prelude to successful implementation of the new methods. The project itself has already been described in Chapter 2, but it must be noted that for its time, it was a pioneering example of internal management consultancy.

FACTORY ORGANISATION

The second book, or rather parts of a book, were two chapters in *Factory Organisation*, which consisted of contributions from four Rowntree's managers. The book stemmed from the high public standing of the firm, in considerable part reflecting the esteem in which Seebohm Rowntree was held. As publishers, Pitmans invited a book on effective management as practised within Rowntree's, with C. H. Northcott (the labour manager) nominated as lead author and editor, who then selected three managerial colleagues as contributors, Sheldon, Wardropper, and Urwick. The title was something of a misnomer, since several of the topics, including Urwick's on 'Marketing and Advertising' and 'Selling and Transport' (arising from his experiences as deputy manager in the sales and distribution department), went well beyond the boundaries of a factory.

Typical of his insistence on the systematic foundation for management, Urwick's chapter on 'Marketing and Advertising' started with definitions, identifying 'marketing' as a concern for the consumer, for the product in relation to the consumer's needs, and for the modes through which the product is brought to the consumer in the market, all of which he argued was an ongoing process allowing the manufacturing company to match its market and appropriately serve the desires of consumers. This was a period when the great majority of British companies were either operating with a production focus, in which distribution issues were left to wholesalers and retailers, or a sales focus, in which the emphasis was on sales methods. As very few looked at the consumer perspective, Rowntree's was clearly well ahead of its contemporaries in advocating this approach (Fitzgerald 1995).

With regard to 'advertising', he had a different setting to review, because that was already well established, employing numerous practitioners, and well supported by ancillary services. His treatment in that part of the chapter was consequently based on reviewing the methods of contemporary practice, adding various recommendations to improve processes, and encouraging periodical systematic reviews of what had become internally acceptable, especially in the light of changes to the external environment.

The 'Selling and Transport' chapter dealt with two rather different aspects within the overall managerial supply chain of service to customers and consumers. This was actually an area in which good practice had already emerged in British business, with a professional association offering accreditation programmes, but Urwick still felt it was important to offer improvements, which included keeping customers satisfied in the longer term and enhanced management systems. While transport is ostensibly a more routine activity in supplying the customers of consumer-product firms, it is nonetheless a significant part of the supply-chain in ensuring retention of consumer loyalty. That routine character itself underlined the need for systematic formulation of practices and for systematic attitudes in the relevant managers. Although not mentioned in the title, Urwick added to this second chapter a two-page postscript entitled 'Co-ordination', in which he drew attention to the essential interrelationship of all the facets covered in his two chapters. In particular, he stressed the need to coordinate this interrelationship as a vital means of maintaining customer satisfaction.

PITMAN'S *DICTIONARY OF INDUSTRIAL ADMINISTRATION*

Pitman's *Dictionary of Industrial Administration* (as it became customarily named) was undoubtedly a landmark publication for the management movement, a point Child (1969: 87) stressed some four decades later when noting that: 'Although it is now generally long-forgotten there is nothing else to compare with this work in the history of British management thought . . . the sophistication and breadth of discussion . . . compare favourably with more recent writing'. Masterminded by John Lee, it contained over 100 articles (not all of them attributed to named authors) in a two-volume work of some 1,150 pages that covered a wide range of management-related issues, with contributions from trade unionists as well as from the managerial side. There was no intention to pursue a particular framework of thought, and contributors were briefed to pursue their own selected positions. Some of the contributions were quite short statements of current practice; others were longer, pioneering new perspectives of a more philosophical kind, for example Urwick's 'Principles', Sheldon's 'The Function of Administration and Organisation', and Northcott's 'The Moral Duty of Management', again reflecting the perceived importance of Rowntree's as the leading centre of management thought. Although Urwick's two topics had resulted from a discussion with Lee, he would have preferred to be allocated the topic given to Sheldon, but he deferred to the 'senior' author in the aftermath of his highly successful book.

Dictionary Article 1 – 'The Principles of Direction and Control'

For Urwick, the *Dictionary* provided an ideal opportunity to consolidate his own philosophies relating to the practice of systematic management, even if in piecemeal form much of that had already been expounded during the preceding few years in the Rowntree's *Staff Journal*. Child (1969: 86) describes it as a 'remarkable' essay in which Urwick 'admitted his debt to Taylor both for the functional model and for the idea that a search for principles followed naturally from the concept of scientific management. The actual framework for Urwick's principles was heavily influenced by Fayol'. In addition, Urwick acknowledged guidance from Harrington Emerson's *Twelve Principles of Efficiency*, demonstrating his grasp of the American management literature. Two fundamentals of his systematic approach were, firstly, clearly knowing what was to be done, namely, direction and, secondly, knowing how performance was progressing in the context of those intentions, namely, control. He was not looking for principles which had already been stated, but rather to pointers towards them from which he could constitute his own formulations.

True to his own standpoint of being systematic in approach, Urwick started his presentation with an introductory paragraph headed 'Definition and terms'. It is noteworthy that for the key words 'administration' and 'management', which were already causing difficulties in definition and would be an issue to which he returned many times in the years to come, he quoted Sheldon's definitions:

Administration has been defined as 'the process of determining policy, co-ordinating markets and production, setting the compass of the organization, and providing the necessary control and co-ordination of the work of management.' Management, on the other hand, is 'the process of executing the policy laid down by administration, formulating minor policies in accordance with it, and using the organization for the attainment of the particular objectives set before it.'

He then turned to 'Management and the Scientific Method', emphasizing four underlying fundamentals: factual, analytical, systematic, and subject to testing. This led naturally to a review of how Taylor had developed his principles of 'Scientific Management' (even though Taylor did not himself originate the name, but accepted it from colleagues). The ground was now clear to present the real objective of this article, Urwick's own selection of principles, which was genuinely pioneering in the management context, being a declaration of his own philosophy in determining the underlying fundamentals of systematic managerial practice. While aspects of them had been voiced in earlier lectures or articles, this was his first consolidated public presentation. He structured his presentation within six sectional headings and twenty-six sub-principles (for which only the headings are shown):

I *The Principles of Investigation*. Prior to any decision-making, the facts must be made available, leading to five sub-principles:
1. Determinism
2. Relation

    3. Analysis

    4. Definition

    5. Measurement

II *The Principle of the Objective.* It is a necessary preliminary to all activity to have a complete and clear statement of the object of such activity in the form of a policy or of instructions.

III *The Principles of Organization.* In any enterprise it is necessary to establish a structure, using five sub-principles:

    1. Functionalization

    2. Correspondence

    3. Initiative

    4. Coordination

    5. Continuity

IV *The Principles of Direction.* Once a structure is established it must be made operational based on eight sub-principles:

    1. Publicity

    2. Incentive

    3. Planning

    4. Simplification

    5. Standardization

    6. Balance

    7. Equity

    8. Mobility

V *The Principles of Experiment.* Based on improving the organization through making changes if necessary, following three sub-principles:

    1. Selection

    2. Controlled factors

    3. Decision

VI *The Principles of Control.* This involves five sub-principles:

    1. Responsibility

    2. Evidence

    3. Uniformity

    4. Comparison

    5. Utility

Urwick went on to note that while this outline of principles must of necessity be extremely tentative, and subject to constant revision as the science of management progresses in scope and definition, it would be found to include almost all of the various propositions put forward by previous writers. At the same time, while their application in practice must necessarily vary with each enterprise and problem, they represented an attempt to formulate the theoretical background which must lie behind practical action. In the complex task of conducting a business enterprise, Urwick argued, not one of them can be ignored with safety.

As Child (1969: 86) notes: 'The major step towards the construction of a priori "principles of management"' came from Urwick's remarkable essay of 1928 on 'Principles of Direction and Control'. One should also stress that these principles (Child 1969: 88–9) were derived predominantly from Fayol and Taylor. Indeed, Urwick was the first writer in English to use Fayol, even before Fayol's work was translated into English (which, as we shall shortly see, Urwick instigated). These principles were based broadly on managerial tasks, together with some general organizational precepts such as the correspondence of authority with responsibility. Furthermore, while Urwick accepted the 'insuperable difficulties' in proving the validity of these principles, he nevertheless claimed that certain principles to action are valid in all cases. This was to be an issue which would be held against him and the management movement more generally in the debate about the status of management as either a science or an art. He probably intended it as a statement to urge managers away from the 'rule-of-thumb' decision-making which dominated at that time. While he was also to refine these principles over time, they remain the first attempt at outlining universal principles of organization and his own unique and ambitious contribution to the theory of organization.

Dictionary Article 2 – 'University Education for Business'

The second contribution that Urwick made to the *Dictionary*, 'University Education for Business', was of an entirely different character. In the 1920s, the widely prevailing ethos was that 'managers are born and not made' (Wilson and Thomson 2006), paralleled by the view that the only reliable method of selection lay in the formula 'up from the ranks', with the implication that in the preceding phases of operational and supervisory employment lay the determining influence for selecting and developing managers. In contrast, as Urwick felt that an 'educated mind' was an essential *sine qua non* for the performance of effective management, he advocated that more managers ought to embark on university programmes. Interestingly, he was not at that time arguing for management subjects to be included in university curricula; rather, he was arguing for more graduates to be recruited into industrial and commercial employment. Of course, he was one of only a few voices willing to express these views publicly; most contemporaries maintained that a university education was actually detrimental to industry, other than in scientific and technical occupations (Keeble 1992). Even William Lever, who did in fact recruit some graduates, talked reverentially of 'the University of Hard Knocks'. Nevertheless, Urwick gave much greater prominence to the emerging demand for a close link between universities and business, a theme to which he would return many times over the following decades.

In defending the value of the 'educated mind', Urwick presented an argument that he had voiced on earlier occasions, namely, comparing the medical profession with the role of management. The need for intelligence and mental abilities, he argued, was no greater in the former than in the latter. For the medical practitioner, the required basic university programme of three years of physiological and anatomical studies was readily accepted as the foundation for the ensuing professional studies in medical practice, within which the newly 'educated mind' was brought into direct contact with specific medical skills. As Urwick argued, surely the importance of management service to the community required as much mental prowess as caring for physical health. While he accepted that the traditional Oxbridge emphasis on the Classics partially explained the generally adverse public attitude towards universities, he was able to name a number of recently created universities' management-related programmes, demonstrating that progress was being made (Keeble 1992).

He rounded off the article by citing international comparisons of university preparation for managerial responsibilities. Without reliable data, he estimated the overall British output of graduates with this kind of preparation to be less than 1,000 per annum, compared to 16,000 in Germany and in excess of 80,000 in the United States. Urwick conceded that traditional attitudes posed particular difficulties in Britain, principally a virtually ubiquitous 'up from the ranks' philosophy, with most potential managers being recruited at the age of 14 or 16, thereby significantly limiting the employment prospects of graduates aged 20–21. Furthermore, there was also a class dimension to be considered, as Urwick recognized. While better-off families encouraged university education for their sons, they maintained a traditional preference for 'professional' employment and an aversion to industry, except in the case of family-owned manufacturing companies. Strangely, in this article Urwick made no reference to the increasing recruitment of science and technology graduates on to apprenticeship programmes, subsequently to be trained for manufacturing supervisory and managerial roles. Overall, though, his article provided a provocative commentary on contemporary attitudes towards recruitment in British industry.

THE MEANING OF RATIONALISATION

Another notable book of the 1920s was *The Meaning of Rationalisation* (1929). This was meant to be an explanation of the proceedings and recommendations of the World Economic Conference by one of the official British representatives, rather than to reflect Urwick's own views, but there was a great deal in the book which went well beyond what was said at that event. Urwick recognized that the term Rationalization was, especially among the continental European nations, a euphemistic expression of support for 'scientific management' as promulgated by Taylor. Given the widespread British definition of this word – namely, closures, redundancies, and cutbacks – not to mention the prominent role played by Germans in advocating Rationalization, he also realized that it was unlikely that the term would be accepted in Britain. Nevertheless, in the contemporary context of the Conference and its aftermath Urwick felt that it had to be given recognition even in Britain. The first chapter accepted that the term Rationalization was little understood, followed by the explanation of its origin in Germany (die Rationalisierung) just after the First World War when post-war reconstruction was being implemented under government direction. In Germany, the phrase was especially used to describe industrial reorganization, mainly by grouping individual businesses into large combinations, thereby bringing supply and demand at the industry level into balance. This was the way in which it was understood in Britain and promoted by major industrialists such as Sir Alfred Mond (Wilson 1995). At the same time, and in stark contrast to British attitudes, Rationalization in Continental countries denoted a systematic approach to analysis and decision-making at the level of the organization, posing a major challenge to its British advocates. Urwick cited a translation of the German definition of the term, as laid down by the official Bureau for National Efficiency:

Rationalisation consists in understanding and applying every means of improving the general economic situation through technical and systematic organization.

It is consequently easy to understand why the term appealed to him, even if he would have preferred to use the more widely recognized 'Scientific Management'. The World Economic Conference itself was to adopt a second definition, namely:

Rationalisation, by which we understand the methods of technique and of organization designed to secure the minimum waste of either effort or material. They include the scientific organization of labour, standardization of both materials and products, simplification of processes, and improvements in the system of transport and marketing.

Urwick explained how the preparations for the World Economic Conference had been masterminded by two international Committees under the League of Nations, one with an industrial slant and one for commercial aspects.

These Committees had gathered information on activities that would contribute to improved economic performance, summarized in five classes:

1. The application of physiology and psychology to the working life of the individual, whether in the home, agriculture, commerce, or industry.
2. Research on such questions as wage payment systems, profit-sharing and co-partnership, industrial relations, and other methods of collaboration.
3. Attempts to provide a scientific foundation for techniques of production by a wider use of the physical sciences and mathematics.
4. Applying the same lines of thought to more general technical problems involved in the control of businesses, such as lay-out, transport, accounting, office methods, planning, routing, marketing, and the like . . . generally described by the phrase 'Scientific Management'.
5. Efforts to improve the general organization of production and distribution.

The characteristic which inspired these objectives was the belief that a more rational control of economic life was possible, and that it could be achieved by a close application of the intellectual methods and standards of science to the problems involved. It was this argument that led the Conference's Committee on Industry to decide upon 'Rationalization' as the overarching term for this range of policies, offering the definition quoted as a means of encouraging wide acceptance. This was also the central focus of Urwick's book, in addition to his restatement of Taylor's fundamental principle that 'Scientific Management' necessitated the adoption of a mental revolution that would radically replace the old rule-of-thumb traditions. To Urwick, Rationalization was not merely a new view of economic theory or a new set of methods or systems; it involved a complete change of attitude on the part of all those who worked in business, as a first step in significantly improving performance.

Although it is important to stress that in future publications Urwick rarely used the term Rationalization, because he favoured 'Scientific Management' when discussing radical changes to managerial practices, this book assisted significantly in publicizing the new ideas coming from Continental Europe. In the concluding chapters, 'The Present Position in Great Britain' and 'Some Suggestions for Action', he again highlighted the lack of progress in his home country, a situation he blamed on a combination of poor understanding of the term and the lack of agencies capable of influencing practice. This led him to argue that the immediate need was to promote better understanding of the principles of systematic management, in which an industrial or governmental lead would prove invaluable, as had happened in the United States and Germany. British governmental policies were not surprisingly criticized for being too fragmented, while the recently convened Balfour Committee on Industry and Trade was attacked for failing to consider radical alternative industrial policies. While this potentially influential Committee had collected a mine of information about a wide range of industrial issues, in omitting management as a subject of study Urwick felt that they had missed 'the cement which should bind the whole structure together and the initiative which should drive it forward'. Employers were also not spared his wrath, because they were responsible for sustaining the old traditions and failing to support such initiatives as the MRGs. On the other hand, he did not go as far as proposing within Britain the formation of an institute for management.

His short 'Conclusion' returned to the central issue of a mental revolution, commenting that

the leaders of labour have undoubtedly shown a broadmindedness and statesmanship in relation to rationalization, which is a very happy augury for the future. They have, indeed, been far more willing to view the new conception objectively and carefully, if not with favour, than the majority of employers.

Similar opinions were also expressed when he gave an address to the British Association for the Advancement of Science in September 1928, as well as in five journal articles on that theme, including one for the *Harvard Business Review*. The book itself was published in London in October 1929 without great fanfare, but it clearly made some impact because it had to be reprinted only two months later.

LEAD-UP TO *MANAGEMENT OF TOMORROW*

Although not a book written by Urwick, another publication with which he was associated was Henri Fayol's *General and Industrial Management*, first published in France in 1916. During the 1920s, thanks to his command of the French language, Urwick became aware of Fayol's work, coming to the conclusion that he was both equivalent to Taylor in importance and complementary, in that while Taylor was mainly concerned with production processes, Fayol looked at the organization as a whole. Fayol was a well-recognized writer in France, having by 1925 sold 15,000 copies of his book, while an organization to popularize 'Fayolisme' had been formed, not least to support his views that the theory and practice of administration should be taught in schools and universities.

Surprisingly, though, Fayol was almost unknown in the English-speaking world, apart from a few such as Urwick who could read it in French. While Urwick's article for the *Dictionary* surveyed earlier in this chapter was certainly strongly influenced by Fayol, few recognized the value of the French-man's work. It says something for Urwick's vision of the field that he attempted to change this situation by recommending an English translation. However, it was only when he had moved to the IMI that he had the opportunity to organize this exercise. The bulk of the translation was done by J. A. Coubrough, a member of the MRG Council, with Urwick offering advice on the more technical vocabulary, as well as writing a foreword. The English version was published in 1930 by the IMI, but only in mimeograph-typescript format in semi-stiff covers. A few hundred copies were made available by the publisher, Sir Isaac Pitman, for distribution in Britain, but none was sent to the United States. This severely curtailed the broader recognition of Fayol, until a further translation, this time by Constance Storrs, was published for worldwide distribution in 1949. For this further edition Urwick again wrote the foreword, and indeed over his career promoted the Fayol principles as vigorously as he did those of Taylor. Indeed, it is very much to Urwick's credit that Fayol became known to the English-speaking world.

At the IMI, while he did a great deal of writing in reports and for the *Bulletin*, Urwick was also interested in taking his own writing to another level. Towards the end of 1932, when the IMI's financial situation required a reduction in external visits, this provided him with the time to consider a book of his own. Three separate outlines date from this period. One draft, running to almost 200 pages, was entitled *Rationalisation and Administration*, concerned with the work of the Institute. This, however, was probably aban-doned when it became clear that the IMI would not survive. He was also interested in writing about his own interests, namely, the fields of organization structure and the delegation of managerial responsibility, expanding the themes in his addresses in 1930 and 1933 to the British Association's Summer Meetings. On these topics there are two separate sets of chapter headings, undated, but probably originating in mid-1932. One was entitled 'Organisa-tion: A Handbook of the Technique of Organisation in Theory and in Practice', which was clearly intended to be a substantial work running to more than 25,000 words. The other chapter heading is 'Staff: A Study in the Technique of Organisation', including issues which were to be of interest to him throughout his career such as the analysis of functions, the span of control, the committee form in organizations, and the staff-and-line method of organiza-tion. Whether these were intended to be two separate books, or whether the two would have become one, is uncertain. In any case, circumstances in the IMI meant that neither set of topics could be pursued. Nevertheless, they provided a background to what is considered by many to be Urwick's most important book, *Management of Tomorrow*. Indeed, Child (1969: 87) called this book 'probably the outstanding British work of the 1930s', while

Davenport-Hines in the *Dictionary of National Biography* said: '*Management of Tomorrow* was more philosophical in presentation than his specialized textbooks, but it had a long-term influence on British managerial thinking'.

MANAGEMENT OF TOMORROW

It was Esmond Milward, a personal friend of Urwick's whom he had brought into the MRG Council secretaryship and made librarian of the Management Library, who suggested that it would be a public service to make at least some of Urwick's addresses and articles connected with the IMI available to a wider audience in Britain. Milward even went so far as to secure interest from a publisher, Nisbet and Company, who had earlier produced Urwick's *The Meaning of Rationalisation*. Urwick readily went along with the proposal, but typically decided to make it more than just a reproduction of existing material, by giving it much greater original thought. In spite of its title, though, one must agree with Child (1969: 87), who notes that *Management of Tomorrow* mostly summarized his 1920s' work, rather than adding any new ideas. The book was written remarkably quickly and published in the autumn of 1933 when he was still Director of the IMI.

In the 'Introduction', he noted that all the book's subjects were linked by a common approach, 'described, for want of a better term, as scientific'. He then proceeded to forestall misunderstanding and possible criticism by explaining that in the management context 'scientific' meant methodical, systematic, and analytical in approach and application. Without becoming specifically em-broiled in the question – it was hardly a debate at that time – of whether managing was an art or a science, he argued for it being 'an art or craft', though management as a function had a scientific framework in the sense of being methodical and systematic. He also briefly mentioned Taylor's con-cepts, although relatively little was made of 'scientific management' in the book, no doubt because of the adverse reaction it had generated in Britain and to a lesser extent in Europe.

Above all, Urwick's ability to generalize and synthesize was perfectly illu-strated in the range of topics covered in *Management of Tomorrow*. The four parts make a somewhat curious group, with quite different focuses: 'The Scientific Approach to Business Management' is about process, 'Organisation' discusses structure, 'Distribution' relates to a particular function, and 'Train-ing for Management' talks about the development of a particular group of workers, the managers. Typically, though, Urwick did not mention produc-tion, even though this was still by far the most important issue as far as most employers were concerned.

The first chapter, 'The Old and New in Business', described the changing world of business, especially the increasing size of manufacturing units, increased purchasing power, and changes in the channels of distribution, all of which forced management as a process to become more professional. The second chapter, 'Management as a Science', sought to gain for management the acknowledgement and respect that intelligent people customarily accorded to science, which he took to refer to as 'a body of codified knowledge satisfying criteria of truth and capable of recurrent proof of application'. In recognizing the human dimension, he argued that the science of psychology was steadily gaining acceptance and credibility in the industrial world, while the ideas that it provided would be learned within the codified body of management knowledge. The third chapter, entitled 'Research into Management', had its origins in the MRG movement, since his concept of research was based primarily on the exchange of experience and the use of surveys, rather than the traditional scientific method of experimentation, largely because there was little of this latter type going on at that time. He did nevertheless see the need for research on a vast scale, because, as he put it, 'the roots of wealth are planted in exact knowledge' which could only come from research.

Overall, Part One sets the prerequisites of knowledge and scientific method for the application of management practice, starting with the issues of 'Organisation', the title of Part Two. The first chapter of Part Two was headed 'The Pure Theory of Organisation', bringing out the distinct advantages in modern, large-scale business of delegation, with its implicit interrelationships of responsibility and authority. This issue was a particular interest of his, taking him back to his own military experiences where he had been impressed by the simplicity of the military command structure. A second key requirement, and an area where industry could learn from its military counterparts, was in the relationship between operational command ('line') and the essential support services ('staff'). The second chapter of Part Two, 'The Organisation of Complex Business Enterprises', was largely derived from the research project on corporate amalgamation he had initiated while at the IMI. He argued that while the economics of amalgamation was well understood, little attention had been given to the administrative difficulties accompanying combination. The majority of the undertakings examined in the IMI research project had arrived at no clear view of principles on such issues as the composition of the Board, the extent of centralization of authority, and the degree to which initiative was delegated to subordinate managers. As he put it, combination is not rationalization, although it provides an opportunity for the latter.

Part Three was concerned with distribution, which Davenport-Hines (*DNB*) noted that Urwick believed to be the greatest failure of contemporary management in the interwar period. Indeed, Urwick argued in the concluding chapter of this Part that 'the present breakdown in the world's business affairs is largely due to a failure to adjust consumption and distribution to the potentialities of production'. He had, of course, had some experience in this area, both in direct management at Rowntree's and in his IMI research projects. The first chapter in Part Three was consequently 'The Marketing Point of View', which was for most British readers a pioneering text, even though the concept was simple, namely, ascertaining what the customer really wants and needs, as opposed to the traditional approach of persuading the customer to purchase what the factory happened to be producing. Urwick saw marketing as a parallel department to production and sales, with its head being 'the best subordinate manager with the most initiative, imagination, foresight and commercial judgment whom the Managing Director has available'. The following chapter was concerned with the underlying causes of inefficiency in distribution, and mainly with the lack of adequate statistics that could aid the marketing approach. He was especially critical of the lack of a Census of Distribution, although the United States had only initiated this service in 1930. In addition, he argued that general statistics ought to be produced for the needs of individual industries, perhaps arising from the activities of trade associations. As he argued, 'a well-run trade association should be a goldmine of vital information. But many Secretaries of Trade Associations are not primarily interested in statistics. They are admirable lawyers or accountants', reflecting their primary functions associated with price-fixing and other covert activities.

Part Four, 'Training for Management', was another of Urwick's favourite topics. One chapter dealt with supervisors, stressing the importance of their selection and training, providing a broad review of the contemporary industrial situation and attitudes, but without quoting either the research report published in 1922 that had surveyed a number of manufacturing managers (including Rowntree's) or the relevant books by Elbourne (1919) and Sheldon (1923), with which he would certainly have been familiar. In the two other chapters in Part Four, Urwick dealt with 'administrators' in large companies, rather than managers in general, namely, the board of directors and other senior managers. One aspect he raised was the need to broaden managers' perspectives away from the current preoccupation with functional specialization to a much more generalist management style, something which at that time was barely recognized. In addition, two further pioneering suggestions were made: firstly, that all managerial roles ought to be clearly delineated; and secondly, imitation of the performance assessment (or, 'rating', as Urwick put it) he had implemented at Rowntree's. As he recognized that to achieve these ends it was necessary to train senior managers in the diagnostic assessment of competence, he advocated intense research and experimentation at the corporate level. Indeed, in the concluding chapter he explicitly states that he had attempted to raise some of the aspects of business in which research was needed, before mentioning two other issues not covered in the preceding chapters, namely, applying scientific management to financial facilities and the potential for economic planning.

The book was Urwick's first and only full presentation of a personal philosophy of management, fulfilling an objective he had been developing since his days in the trenches in 1915. It received some substantial reviews in Britain, one of which appeared in the *Spectator*, which gave four reasons for recommending the book, the last of which was that the reader would 'have in his mind a frame of reference to which every subsequent mention or problem of management must willy-nilly be submitted'. The other significant review was in *Industry Illustrated* by A. P. Young, well known as the progressive general manager of British Thomson-Houston at Rugby. He gave the highest accolade to Part Four, first for the importance attached to supervisory training, and second for the identified need to improve the quality of 'administrators' as a prerequisite for economic progress.

PAPERS ON THE SCIENCE OF ADMINISTRATION

If *Management of Tomorrow* was Urwick's own most important book, *Papers on the Science of Administration* was one of the most important management books of the 1930s, even if it was unlikely to have attracted much attention in Britain at the time. Whilst at the IMI, Urwick had met and formed a high regard for Luther Gulick, Director of the American Institute of Public Administration. They had similar interests in organizational structure, delegation of responsibility, and functional managerial interaction. As Gulick was preparing a selection of papers on these subjects, he invited Urwick both to share the editorial responsibilities and contribute two chapters. The reason for the compilation was stated in the Foreword:

Few of these papers have been published or publicly circulated in such a way as to make them accessible to practical administrators, scholars or students. The immediate occasion for this publication is the fact that no copies of the essential papers in this collection could be found in any library in Washington at the time when the President's Committee on Administrative Management required these documents for the use of members of its research staff.

Because it was prepared for this committee, and Gulick was the Director of the Institute of Public Administration, the orientation was towards public sector administration. Nevertheless, the book represents the state of play in organizational thinking at that time, going to several imprints and becoming one of the classics in the field of management, featuring distinguished authors such as Mooney, Fayol, Follett, Lee, Dennison, Henderson, Whitehead, Mayo, and Graicunas. It was also in this book that Gulick produced his famous POSDCORB, to illustrate the functions of the manager, giving the book a status that has been widely acknowledged.

Another important dimension to this book was Fayol's inclusion, given that American audiences had barely heard of him. We have already noted that Urwick had been pivotal in having Fayol's main work published in English, while after attending the 1929 CIOS Congress in Paris he did exactly the same for A. V. Graicunas, a Lithuanian engineer with American training and experience. Graicunas had developed a special interest in the 'senior versus subordinate' relationship, within the framework of a delegated hierarchy, having intensively studied the patterns of internal relationships in large organizations. He had coined the phrase 'span of control' to designate the pattern, arguing that it became ineffectively more complex as each subordinate was added. This topic had been of great personal interest to Urwick since the early 1920s, after reading *The Soul and Body of an Army*, by General Sir Ian Hamilton. From their mutual discussions, Graicunas offered to put his findings and views into an article for the *Bulletin*, if Urwick could arrange for linguistic amendments where Graicunas's own limited command of English had failed. The article was published in the March 1933 issue entitled 'Relationship in Organisation', but was given more prominence when Urwick arranged for it to be included in the *Papers*. Urwick would also have been responsible for having the paper by Lee included, and probably that by Follett as well, because although the latter was American by background, she had spent her later years in Britain. Indeed, her paper was taken from a lecture at the LSE. For that matter, the paper by Henderson, Whitehead, and Mayo was also derived from a British source, a lecture by Whitehead to the British Association in 1935, indicating that Urwick probably had a good deal of influence on the selection of papers.

Urwick's two contributions were also taken from lectures: 'Organisation as a Technical Problem' was based on a 1933 talk to the British Association, while the paper on Fayol was a 1934 lecture to the Institution of Industrial Administration. 'Organisation as a Technical Problem' was a substantial paper of some forty-two pages, with twenty-four sections and eleven extremely detailed diagrams (which may explain why the book was published in coffee-table size). It started with an important statement:

It is the general thesis of this paper that there are principles which can be arrived at inductively from the study of human experience of organization, which should govern arrangements for human association of any kind. These principles can be studied as a technical question, irrespective of the purpose of the enterprise, the personnel composing it, or any constitutional, political or social theory underlying its creation. They are concerned with the method of subdividing and allocating to individuals all the various activities, duties and responsibilities essential to the purpose contemplated, the correlation of those activities and the continuous control of the work of individuals so as to secure the most economical and the most effective realization of the purpose.

In describing organization as a technical problem, Urwick was referring to formal issues abstracted from any human dimension, which of course he did recognize as part of reality. Much of his paper was predicated on military analogies and the need for armies to be organized, but more generally he quoted Herbert Spencer to the effect that 'socially as well as individually, organization is indispensable to growth: beyond a certain point there cannot be further growth without further organization'. He also went on to note that 'rapid growth in scientific knowledge has placed an unprecedented strain on man's powers of organization'. Many of the sections take up issues in which dimensions of this strain showed – coordination, specialization, the scalar process, line and staff, the span of control, supply, and functionalization – many of which were illustrated by diagrams derived from military manuals. Indeed, only one of the diagrams came from manufacturing industry, and that from the General Motors Export Company, the organization of which James Mooney was President and which Urwick describes as 'a very advanced form of business organization which has been developed with exceptional insight'.

The article on Fayol introduced the Frenchman as a mining engineer who became for thirty years a highly successful general manager, explaining how it was only shortly before his retirement that Fayol expounded his theory of administration in his famous book *Industrial and General Administration*. The key to this book was his benchmark definition of administration, arguing that it could be broken into five key stages: 'to plan, organize, command, co-ordinate and control'. It is also important to add that the first of these, in French *prevoyance*, had two distinct dimensions: forecasting and planning. In addition, he had fourteen principles of administration, which formed the basis of Urwick's own principles listed earlier in this chapter. Urwick emphasized Fayol's argument that

technical ability is the most important quality at the bottom of the industrial ladder and administrative ability at the top [yet] so long as technical ability and experience are treated as superior qualifications for higher posts, it is inevitable that administrative ability should be regarded as an empirical and secondary consideration, something the technical man 'picks up' in the course of his career.

Urwick also emphasizes Fayol's recognition that the structural factor cannot be isolated and the human factor eliminated. He also compared the close correspondence of Fayol's work with that of Mooney and Reilley, even though the latter were unaware of Fayol. Nevertheless, Urwick saw Fayol as unique:

Indeed the unique character of Fayol's work cannot be overemphasized. For the first time a successful business leader of long experience submitted, not the work of others, but his own duties and responsibilities to close scientific analysis. He viewed what he had to do as an administrator with a detachment as rare as it is valuable. In the first quarter century of the scientific study of business management, his is the only European figure worthy of a place beside that of F.W. Taylor.

In the *Academy of Management Journal* of December 1970, Urwick asked the question: how well have Fayol's ideas survived? His answer was that 'in the writer's view they are still largely valid and contemporary'. He very much resented how by that time his ideas, and those of Fayol, had been classified as 'classical' or 'traditional', arguing that the pejorative implication, meaning outdated and 'fuddy-duddy', was excessively dismissive.

CONCLUSIONS

Given what we have seen in this chapter, Urwick's contribution to British management thought in the interwar period was considerable. Indeed, by the end of the period he was undoubtedly recognized as a leading figure in the British management movement, with the obvious caveat that the great majority of British managers and organizations would not have been sympathetic either to his proselytizing or views; many would not have even taken the trouble to learn what these were. Moreover, as Child (1969: 70) has noted: 'With the possible exception of Urwick's work on formal organization theory, there was little produced by British management writing between 1920 and 1940 which did not rely heavily on earlier ideas.' Child also noted that the main focus was still on production and labour management issues, although moving away from legitimation and towards the technical issues with which Urwick was not greatly concerned. On the other hand, there was also a move towards models of organization structure, which certainly interested him. The assumption of and search for general principles was a natural goal in a new prospective 'science', becoming a key dimension of classical management theory which was seen as a benchmark from which organization theory progressed.

Figure 4.2 Lyndall Urwick (right) with Luther Gulick.

Urwick's writing covered a wide and eclectic range of topics; if he is now best known for his work on organizational theory and structure, his major writings at this time also covered such issues as education, marketing, office reorganization, and rationalization. Few, if any, British writers were as aware of the international management literature because, both through his linguistic abilities and experience at the IMI, Urwick had an unusually wide knowledge base that was unparalleled in its grasp of new ideas that fed directly into his own writing. While we have not said much about the topic of human relations in this chapter, this was also a frequent subject of his lectures. Indeed, he was working on the papers of Mary Parker Follett, while the Hawthorne studies led by Elton Mayo in America were a source of great fascination, leading to books which will be reviewed in Chapter 9. Above all, he was a pioneer who set himself highly ambitious goals dedicated to disseminating new ideas and expounding the virtues of the systematic approach to management, themes that run consistently through his writings at this time (Figure 4.2).

5

Urwick Orr and Partners

Having developed an extensive reputation by the 1930s, and looking for a new role after the end of his work at the IMI, Lyndall Urwick decided to use his previous in-house consultancy experience to engage directly in management consultancy. This chapter will outline how a partnership was formed, the tensions between Urwick and John Leslie Orr, and the consequences of that difficult relationship. Recently, The Lyndall Urwick Society has produced a substantial history of the Urwick Orr Partnership from 1934 to 1984 (2007), largely written by Edward Brech, which gives much more detail about the company than can be provided in this chapter. Nevertheless, one can report that Urwick Orr and Partners (hereafter UOP) was another major institutional part of Urwick's career, as well as being highly successful. Indeed, Witzel (2003: 299) states that UOP was 'enormously influential and was for many years the leading management consultancy firm in Britain', while Thomas (1986: 601) called it 'one of the world's most prominent management consultancy firms'. The chapter also reveals further material on Urwick's key role in disseminating the benefits of new thinking on management, especially at a time when firms were dealing with new challenges. Other activities during this period, such as Urwick's wartime roles and management education activities, are covered in succeeding chapters.

THE SETTING UP OF URWICK ORR AND PARTNERS

After the closure of the IMI at the end of 1933, Urwick faced a serious personal problem. He had, of course, gained an extensive international reputation, as well as having acquired a wide range of knowledge across the spread of managerial responsibility and practice. On the other hand, it would be fair to say that little of this expertise had ever been directly applied to the practice of management. As the lease of his Geneva house would not expire for some months (and he had the advantage of continuing payment from the Trustees), he decided in favour of staying on with his wife and two young children until May. Although making several visits to London in that period, he devoted himself to assessing what would be the next stage in his career.

During the Geneva years, whenever he came to Britain Urwick had included in his programme a visit to the Management Library for a personal meeting with his old friend Esmond Milward. As Milward had been in Urwick's confidence about the Institute's precarious financial situation, he suggested that if it did close his future employment could lie in the foundation of a management consultancy. Urwick had already had initial experience of that kind during some of his army phases and, more to the point, several years of internal management consultancy at Rowntree's. There was certainly an opportunity, since there was very little professional management consultant activity in Britain at that time; and that little was limited in scope (Ferguson 2002). Urwick found the idea attractive, but he felt uneasy about starting alone on a commercial basis. Early in 1934, however, Milward found himself in a position to resolve that unease, taking advantage of Urwick's next visit to London to offer a solution linked to a member of the Library with whom he had also developed a friendship, John Leslie Orr. With his permission, Milward was able to give Urwick an outline of Orr's background, to vouch for his personal integrity and to bring the two of them together in his own office, leaving them to pursue whatever path they mutually favoured.

Orr was a Scotsman, born in Airdrie in 1892. After graduating in engineering from the Royal Technical College in Glasgow, he joined the Army, in which he was commissioned in the Royal Artillery and rose to become a Major. Having suffered from gas poisoning late in the war, which led to bouts of pneumonia and a medical prescription to leave Britain for warmer climates, he married a nurse who had been caring for him. Their two-year honeymoon was spent in South Africa, Australia, and New Zealand, paid for by production engineering assignments in each country. Returning to Britain on the imminent birth of their first child in 1926, Orr joined Charles Bedaux, who was setting up his British consultancy, and soon rose through the managerial ranks of that firm to become Joint General Manager. However, he became disillusioned with the many conflicts created by the Bedaux approach, and was seeking alternative employment when Milward suggested that he should meet Urwick.

When Urwick and Orr met, they found a ready compatibility and quickly developed a mutual respect and liking, which was further developed through successive meetings. Although their individual backgrounds were radically different, in several respects they were complementary. A factor of particular appeal to Urwick in Orr's background was his spell of military service in the 1914–18 War, in which Orr had been gazetted as a Major early in 1918 at much the same age as himself. A highly significant feature was that they both held similar ethical values and principles relating to the conduct of both business generally and management specifically, both being dedicated to the improvement of managerial practice. Even the main difference between them in relation to experience was complementary; Orr operated mainly in the manufacturing and production areas, while Urwick had been mostly concerned with clerical and administrative activities. By the time Urwick returned to London permanently in May 1934, they had decided in principle to join forces and create a management consultancy to operate across the full spread of managerial responsibilities and roles. Although it would obviously take some time to develop the full range, Orr would be bringing into the partnership extremely valuable knowledge of companies where consultants had been previously used. Through his membership of the Management Library and his personal discussions with Milward, Orr was also well informed about Urwick's public educational contributions to managerial advancement and his well-established international reputation. In framing the principles and policy for their partnership, Urwick and Orr agreed that continuing that educational programme would bring advantage to their company's reputation, though Orr had indicated that he himself would not participate.

LAUNCH AND FIRST YEAR

Having agreed on the format of a private company as the framework for their service, the registration procedures were put in motion in the name Urwick Orr & Partners Limited on 6 July 1934. With a capital of £1,000 in one-pound shares, each founding partner purchased at par 450 shares, while the remaining 100 were allotted to Company Management Services Limited, which owned the Management Library and in which Esmond Milward was a shareholder with Urwick. The new partnership company would not start operating until September, but an opportunity for advance publicity had come along in June from the chance situation that the National Federation of British Launderers happened to have a progressively minded General Secretary who had reviewed Urwick's *Management of Tomorrow* in the institutional journal (December 1933) and had persuaded the Council to invite Urwick to address their annual conference. Having accepted that invitation, it proved to have an important outcome, as mention was made of the new consultancy company in ensuing publicity.

The British environment for starting such a consultancy was also favourable, since the economy was by then recovering from the major depression of

1929–33, while the management movement was steadily gaining strength. Urwick also continued to feature prominently in the literature. For example, the new monthly magazine entitled *Industry Illustrated* had published a feature article written by Urwick for its first issue which named and annotated 'the best books on business recently published'. During the first half of 1934, he had also accepted other public educational invitations, including a commission to write an obituary for Mary Parker Follett, and a review of Elbourne's classic new textbook *The Fundamentals of Industrial Administration.*

Urwick was able to provide a small office for the company, in the shape of a one-room suite in Bloomsbury Square for which he had personally held the lease since his departure for Geneva, initially forming a base for his books and documents before they were transferred to form the Management Library. For his family, he had purchased a house in Gerrards Cross in Buckinghamshire, where they had taken up residence in May. Immediately after, a family holiday in July–August was an important priority, especially for the two children, June (ten) and Alan (four). Although by contemporary conventional standards, Urwick was not wealthy, he was comfortably well off from his father's estate (shared with his mother), including the proceeds from the sale of shares in the Fownes Company several years earlier, allowing him the luxury of a long holiday that summer.

The two partners had agreed their objectives within five policy principles:

1. To develop and offer their consultant practice in consonance with contemporary British managerial attitudes, though in a progressive spirit.

2. To provide service across the full spectrum of management practice in the industrial and commercial context.

3. To establish and maintain the highest possible standards of professional practice and conduct, ensuring that all recruited consultant personnel understood and observed those.

4. To select, recruit, and train qualified and experienced men for employment in operational consultant roles on assignment to client companies, their services to be applied in accord with the defined professional standards; the recruitment specification would remain similar to that already known in Britain, though with encouragement to widening managerial knowledge and interest.

5. In the conduct of assignments always to secure and ensure appropriate consultation with the personnel employed by the client company, including consultation with representatives of trade unions as and when relevant.

Having been laid down at the outset, these principles continued to be recognized throughout the active life of the partnership. Clearly, their overall orientation was a focus on Britain, in order to differentiate the partnership from Bedaux, which was the first and dominant consultancy in Britain by the mid-1930s. Urwick also made an important point in his autobiography about the way Bedaux had distorted scientific management:

In the first place I myself thought that the so-called 'Bedaux System' was merely a sales gimmick. It was taking the ideas of Frederick Winslow Taylor and other founders of scientific management and dressing them up in an apparently 'patent' jargon as though its Directors had some secret formula to sell. To me it seemed as remote from true scientific management as I understand that term, as the quack selling cure-alls at a country fair is remote from a trained medical practitioner. The slogans and the jargon which they used appeared to me to be not only unnecessary but calculated to bring true scientific management into disrepute. . . . Their American directors had not the slightest conception of the strength, depth and fundamental good sense of the British trade union movement.

Recognizing the importance of consultation with employees and unions was something which served UOP well. A little later, Urwick made a jocular point on the Bedaux issue:

Some UOP colleagues were a little disheartened at the apparent success of British Bedaux. So I wrote a little rhyme to reassure them:

> How doth the little busy 'B'
> Improve the 'standard hour'?
> Although it smells
> The same, it sells
> Best as another flower.
> Your excess cost
> You analyse
> And multiply controls.
> What you have lost
> Escapes your eyes.
> You cannot measure souls.

This last line, of course, referred to their rival's slogan: 'Bedaux measures labour'.

Although no public announcement of UOP's formation appears to have been made, Urwick's address to the Laundry Federation's Conference in Peebles in June provided some necessary publicity. His presentation was sufficiently impressive for one member to state that he wanted to become the first client, asking when the service would be available. The new company duly opened for business in the Bloomsbury Square one-room office on 6 September, with both Urwick and Orr present, plus Urwick's personal secretary repatriated from Geneva. At mid-morning, true to his word, Mr Arthur

Blank, owner-manager of the Shaw Heath Laundry in Cheshire, walked into the office accompanied by his wife. A couple of hours were spent in discussing the firm's operations and affairs, clearly demonstrating scope for improvement. Mr Blank would have liked an immediate service, but the partners emphasized the importance of gaining a closer first-hand view before recommending an assignment. It was agreed that they would both make that inspection visit later in the month, following which a contract was placed in October.

Strangely, no issue of *Industry Illustrated* during the latter months of 1934 made any mention of the new company, even among the snippet items of ongoing events. The magazine *Business* provided indirect evidence of UOP's existence in its December issue, as it opened with a feature on Lyndall Urwick, together with a photograph describing him as 'Chairman of Urwick Orr & Partners Limited, Consulting Industrial Engineers'. The feature was a repro- duction of a long extract, carrying highly positive editorial comment, from an address that he had given in the previous July to the Industrial Co-Partnership Association. This address had also been repeated to several branches of the Institute of Cost and Works Accountants, expounding on the relevance of their professional expertise as a managerial tool for planning and control. This provided further valuable publicity, as did a talk to the newly renascent Institute of Industrial Administration on 'The Function of Administration, with special reference to the work of Henri Fayol'.

Urwick and Orr had already agreed that neither of them would personally undertake detailed consultancy services: planning and supervision certainly, but they would recruit other staff for the assignments. In addition to Orr's expertise and consultancy experience in manufacturing management, his recruiting of consultants proved to be a major contribution to the new partnership, since he knew several disenchanted Bedaux employees. The first to make this move was Malcolm W. Brown, who joined UOP early in 1935 to work on the Shaw Heath Laundry contract.

Another valuable element that Orr contributed was an ability to offer new aspects of specialist consultancy, namely, Urwick's range of skills, to companies that he had known from his Bedaux days, either as clients in assignments under his supervision or from negotiations even when no assignment had been gained. He had no qualms about such approaches because he was offering assistance in areas of managerial improvement that Bedaux could not provide, given their concentration on manufacturing and production issues. These approaches were successful in bringing in several assignments during the partnership's first year, starting with the Huntley & Palmer biscuit company. Arising from his previous links, Orr had known that the directors were planning to extend their head office premises, an area of expertise well within Urwick's competence and experience. After a preliminary review of their clerical organization and methods, Huntley & Palmer awarded them a contract, on condition that Urwick was personally involved. Fortunately, another former Bedaux colleague, H. A. MacDonald, had just left that firm in late autumn 1934, providing the operational input. The assignment started in December, when after further discussions with the directors Urwick secured their agreement to rearrange the offices, providing the basis for a widespread overhaul of the administrative system that fully matched the client's expectations. This assignment also provided another insight into UOP attitudes, because after recommending the purchase of some new office machinery, the supplier's salesman offered Urwick the customary 5 per cent commission, a deal he declined because it was contrary to the partnership's ethical code and policy.

It is clear that UOP's first year was reasonably successful, given that both partners were putting time and effort into successfully attracting clients. A one-day review conference at the Holborn Restaurant in London was convened in May 1935, at which the first set of accounts were published, revealing that consultancy income amounted to £2,512, resulting in a net loss of only £784. This was regarded as a creditable start, especially as the income was growing steadily, allowing Urwick, presiding as chairman, to predict a sound future. By that time, eight consultants had been recruited, four of whom were former Bedaux employees, while one among the other four was a marketing and sales management specialist who operated as a part-time salesman for UOP.

PARTNERSHIP PROGRESS AND MODUS OPERANDI

The success of the first conference in May 1935 led the two partners to recognize the practical value of the camaraderie generated, because by allowing the whole team to interact positively, it appeared to boost morale. Urwick consequently recommended a further conference, which was held in December at 3 St James's Square, in the premises in London's West End to which the partnership had recently moved. By that time, as there were twelve consultants supporting the two partners, the chairman was able to report assignments completed or ongoing in twenty client companies, more than half of which were household names. This meeting also set a pattern for future occasions, in that it was agreed to have two per year. These conferences had a strong orientation during the first three years towards what could best be described as 'professional' training, with current assignments used as training material to highlight the lessons they all might learn for future contracts.

Although not normally involved in detailed studies of the commissioning firms, Urwick did undertake some broader reviews. One such case was a small group of family-owned textile mills, with each unit run by a different member of the family. Although the family members had unanimously agreed to form a 'combine company', to exploit greater economies of scale, the only organizational outcome had been the creation of a central office, creating grave managerial tensions. It was also clear that as the family members were spread over two generations, this highlighted severe differences in attitude, outlook, and opinion. Urwick quickly realized that the so-called combine was entirely ineffective, leading him to recommend the appointment of a 'combine' managing director, to be recruited from external sources, with responsibility for harmonizing family relationships and coordinating all parts of the business. Understandably, in order to secure adoption of such a recommendation within the existing family structure, this called for some high-grade consultant skills from Urwick, not to mention finding a suitable candidate for the difficult chief executive post and establishing a new modus operandi for the firm. Much to his credit, years later Urwick heard that it had all worked out very successfully, with considerable financial advantage to the family.

As a result of a mounting number of successful commissions, UOP was consequently able to increase its income appreciably (see Table 5.1), the accounts for the financial year to March 1936 recording £17,846, which yielded a gross surplus of £1,202 payable to the two partners. Urwick, however, felt uncomfortable about taking all of this profit, because it had stemmed primarily from the good work carried out by his consultants. He consequently made a proposal to Orr to reconstruct the ownership structure to reflect employee contributions. Orr readily agreed to this, including Urwick's suggestion that the registered share capital ought to be increased, in order to allow employees to buy into the firm. The appropriate legal changes were duly made, including revised contracts for the two partners, with the agreed formula providing that 75 per cent of each year's net profit should be paid into a 'partnership commission account' for distribution among the personnel as a bonus, the remaining 25 per cent being shared equally between the

Table 5.1 Urwick Orr's organizational growth, 1935–8

Year	Consultants	Revenue	Revenue per consultant
1935	5	2,497	499
1936	19	18,028	949
1937	30	48,070	1,602
1938	33	63,899	1,936

two partners. For the year ending March 1936, the first bonus paid was declared at 8.76 per cent of annual salaries, while for the following year the bonus paid was raised to 30.33 per cent of annual salaries.

By the spring of 1938, the expansion in business and personnel had required a move to larger offices, at 7 Park Lane. Although the costs of this move reduced gross profits to £11,760, UOP was still able to pay a bonus of 23 per cent. Another change to their premises had occurred early in 1937, following a chance viewing by Urwick of a large house named Farnham Court in the village of Farnham Royal, Buckinghamshire. With its large rooms in the main building and stone-built outhouses, Urwick had initially seen this as a family residence. As we shall see later, though, this would become an embryonic management 'staff college', providing UOP with excellent training facilities.

Given the growth in income recorded in Table 5.1, UOP could clearly afford this extension. Indeed, this was a period of considerable growth for Britain's embryonic consultancy industry, with a series of firms appearing, each with high-profile leaders. For example, Harold Whitehead set up his own consultancy, while Maurice Lubbock started PE. Together with UOP, Bedaux (although with a changed name from the late 1930s) and PA, which was formed by Ernest Butten in 1943, these two formed part of the 'Big Five' British consultancies that dominated the industry until the mid-1960s. While UOP was never the biggest of these consultancies, it was nevertheless distinctive and innovative, and therefore arguably the most influential. Of the founders of the four other consultancies, Urwick was characterized by Tisdall (1982: 57) as 'the idealist'. In contrast, the others had very different leaders: PE was dominated by 'the aristocrats', Lubbock, d'Erlanger, and Runciman; PA by Ernest Butten, who was committed to rapid expansion; and Inbucon by the 'buccaneering' Charles Bedaux, whose aggressive attitude alienated workers. This provided UOP with a distinctive niche within the sector, an asset it exploited extensively throughout its history.

Developing this theme further, there were several aspects to UOP's innovative style. While some have already been mentioned, not least its partnership basis, it was especially notable that UOP actively sought consultation with the relevant trade unions, helping to negate some of the problematic images associated with Bedaux. It was also clear that UOP had strong ethical principles enshrined in its basic policy statement, as well as advocating the establishment of profit-sharing partnerships as a means of distributing the wealth generated from business. In 1937–8, Urwick also masterminded the introduction of a new service devoted to marketing, sales management, and distribution, having recruited two specialist practitioners in that field. The partnership then had the capacity to provide services across all aspects of managerial responsibility, which was at that time unique in the industry.

Another important dimension of UOP was consultant training, arising from the scale of professional service expansion recorded in Table 5.1 and reflected in the twice-yearly staff conferences. Two aspects predominated, the first of which was training in the practice of work study and associated techniques related to effective planning and progress control of manufacturing operations, a service that could be undertaken only by experienced consultants. The second lay in the role, practice, and attitudes of consultancy service, requiring an induction in the partnership offices by the two owners during the first couple of weeks of employment, and thereafter continued by the senior consultants through practical training during commissions. Moreover, as Ferguson (2003: 8) has stated: 'For the first time the concept of profession underpinned the approach to consultant training, a point of policy at the outset for UOP'.

In 1941, UOP was also the first consultancy firm to introduce off-the-job training. The Bedford Work Study School, founded by William Lodge in 1941 to train consultants, was the first British off-site training programme. Indeed, while Lodge resigned from UOP to set it up, his former employer was the main user of its services from the outset. In the early years at UOP, Urwick himself had provided some aspects of the training, specializing in office, clerical, and administrative practices. Another aspect of systematic manageri-al practice, where his own knowledge and experience enabled him to act as a tutor, was that related to organizational structure, the delegation of manage-rial responsibility, and the interrelationships between functional specializa-tions. From 1941, however, especially with Urwick engaged in wartime activities, these functions were increasingly performed by Lodge's outfit.

As well as this devotion to training, it is above all important to stress how UOP espoused the methods of scientific and systematic management. These methods were not being applied in the United Kingdom in their strict form until UOP, and especially Urwick, introduced them. He argued that the underlying principles of analytical review were still relevant, as reflected in the operational methods, the documentation needed, and the relevant appli-ances. This was all familiar to Urwick from his years with Rowntree's, giving him the expertise both to sell the ideas to British firms and train newly recruited personnel. The external Bedford programme in turn provided an inspiration for the management training schools that were set up by UOP and other consultants in the post-war period, an issue to which we will return later in this chapter.

This modus operandi also highlights what was arguably the most impor-tant innovation arising from UOP, namely, the 'educative' feature inherent in a consultant's role. Whatever the nature of the changes introduced by the consultant, their value lies predominantly in their permanence. This continuity depended entirely upon the way in which a client's directors, managers, and supervisors concerned with the assignment were tutored in the changes; it had to be an ongoing tutorial process, having started with the inception of the assignment and sustained as the work progressed. Particularly significant were the immediate supervisory personnel, because they were directly involved in the operational changes. This was a lesson that Urwick had first learned during his days as a junior army officer, as well as during his time at Fownes Brothers and Rowntree's. It was a feature of permanence within the continuing professional life of the partnership, substantiated as a mode of 'coaching'. Indeed, it was many years later that Urwick made his famous dictum about the role of consultancy:

The long term objective of all management consultant activities is education. The only work that is really worth doing as a management consultant is that which educates, which teaches clients and their staffs to manage better for themselves. The consultant may suggest schemes to help a client cut costs and so on, but if the consultant has not done the basic job of re-educating and altering the outlook of the client's staff, he can go back in two years' time and blush for the fees he has drawn for a job that he has not done. (*Stocktaking on Management Education*, 1961)

A final feature of UOP's style worth noting was the volume of publications emanating from the consultancy. Urwick's own writing set a standard here, of course, but he also encouraged others in the company to contribute to the literature. Latham and Sanders (1980), writing much later, acknowledged that: 'Members of the company, from its co-founder L.F. Urwick onwards, have always been fairly prolific writers of books and articles. . . . Urwick always encouraged us to read the great classics of management and those of us who have burst into print must acknowledge the grounding that these gave us.' This reflected the value of Urwick's approach to the consultancy, providing UOP with considerable publicity that was frequently recouped from additional commissions.

In September 1939, UOP could look back with understandable and justified satisfaction on five years of accomplishment across a spread of managerial responsibilities at a considerable number of clients. By that time, the initial title of 'Consulting Industrial Engineers' had been discarded in favour of 'Consulting Specialists in Organisation and Management', given the range of services offered. The two founding partners could take personal pride in what their leadership had secured, even if, as we shall shortly see, there were some difficult internal tensions. When war was declared, there was also little immediate impact on the partnership's activities, except insofar as some clients had already received war-supply contracts and were turning the assignment objectives towards the appropriate readjustment of their manufacturing activities. Fortunately, most of the current assignments continued, so that the company could maintain a sense of ongoing momentum, while also recognizing the need to avoid complacency in respect of what to many was an unforeseeable future.

EXTERNAL ACTIVITIES BY URWICK

While UOP was growing impressively, one should also remember that Urwick was also engaged in a range of external activities from the outset of the partnership. During the 1932 CIOS Congress in Amsterdam, he had been appointed general secretary to the International Committee because the following Congress in 1935 was to be held in London and he would be responsible for its organization. In the absence of any specific national management focus in Britain, the invitation had been placed with the Federation of British Industries, the council of which set up an in-house organizing committee, with Urwick as a member. This became a significant burden to Urwick in the following spring and summer of 1935 when the Congress was to be held, keeping him away from the partnership for some time.

During the week of the 1935 Congress, the council of the slowly reviving Institute of Industrial Administration (IIA) held an informal celebratory lunch, with their President, the Right Honourable Harold Macmillan, serving as host, and the CIOS officers among the invited guests. This event brought Urwick into contact with a number of well-established personalities – E. S. Byng, T. H. Burnham, T. G. Rose, Harold West, and Harold Whitehead – within the Institute who were devoting stalwart voluntary service to its continuing redevelopment and progress. Not surprisingly, in due course Urwick was invited into the IIA fellowship, to serve on the Council, and to be an assessor for the final stage of the Institute's professional examinations. He accepted all three invitations, thus beginning his period of active involvement in what many hoped would be Britain's premier management organization.

However well UOP was progressing under joint leadership, it was clear that Urwick was continuing his involvement in a national management world that was steadily expanding. While the 1935 CIOS Congress in London had produced little of positive benefit to Britain's businessmen, few of whom bothered to attend, it did offer a springboard for those voluntary pioneers to marshal additional support for the advancement of 'management' as a cause in its own right. E. S. Byng was the first to make this move, inviting the council of the Federation of British Industries to initiate discussions about the need for a major management organization. In due course, that initiative achieved some success, in the form of a British Management Council launched in January 1937. It was at least a beginning, as a somewhat informal organization constituted from two representatives from each of the professional managerial membership societies. From his previous role as chairman of the CIOS International Committee (1933–5), Viscount Leverhulme was invited to chair the new body, supported by Urwick, who was asked to serve as vice-chairman. The Council's immediate responsibility was to plan for Britain's participation in the next CIOS Congress in 1938, to be held in Washington DC. Leverhulme and Urwick agreed that the British delegation should present a report showing the existing national position with regard to scientific management, with the latter doing almost all of the writing. A preliminary draft was made available for a pre-conference event (see below) held in Oxford in April 1937, the proceedings of which were later reproduced in a special issue of the *British Management Review.*

During the second half of the 1930s, Urwick was frequently invited to make educational contributions at meetings and conferences of various organizations, in particular the steadily reviving Institute of Industrial Administration and the functional management institutes which had emerged since the First World War. He regarded this as vital to UOP, because ironically, when he had returned to Britain in May 1934, Urwick was less well known publicly at home than on the international, and especially the European, scene. Even his energetic work for the London CIOS Congress (July 1935) had barely been recognized, given the poor attendance by British directors and managers. However, his educational contributions after 1933 speedily closed the gap, so that by 1938–9 he was generally recognized as Britain's 'great man of management'. He also had the satisfaction of always being cited as 'Chairman: Urwick Orr & Partners', even if in practice his partner performed most of the routine work.

Another important aspect of Urwick's public contributions was the great enjoyment he experienced in both speaking and writing about management. Although he wrote his papers and addresses in longhand for subsequent typing, Urwick was always at ease in public, using his outstanding command of language to explain complicated ideas or make a pithy quip. Always cool under attack, he could handle his audience with ease. For example, when a scion of a Lancashire cotton family demanded at a public meeting, 'What's wrong with the Lancashire cotton industry?', Urwick's reply was blunt: 'I'll tell you in one word – Nepotism.'

Although it would be difficult to itemize every one of his external activities, several further illustrations will demonstrate Urwick's commitment to what he regarded as essential missionary work. In April 1935, he addressed the Birmingham Branch of the Institute of Industrial Administration on a favourite topic, 'The Problem of Organisation: A Study of the Work of Mary Follett'. He also wrote an article on 'The Organisation of Voluntary Associations' for the August 1935 issue of *Industry Illustrated*. In September, he was again selected to address the summer meeting of the British Association for the Advancement of Science, an invitation repeated in 1936, when his lecture on 'The Technique of Organisation' was printed in the October issue of *Industry Illustrated*. During 1935 he made eleven public speeches, thirteen in 1936, and seventeen in 1937. Excluding the professional management institutes, several of which he addressed on more than one occasion, he talked to more than twenty different audiences during the period 1935–8. In addition, he had articles or reproductions published in a dozen publications, indicating the diversity of his growing audience. This also benefited UOP, with articles such as one of those published by *Business* in October 1937 where he was described as the chairman of Urwick Orr and Partners, 'Consulting Specialists in Organisation and Management', a description which was thereafter used permanently.

During the latter part of 1936 and early 1937, Urwick was involved in three further particularly substantial educational tasks. The first was working with Luther Gulick on editing what was to be a path-breaking collection, *Papers on the Science of Administration*, which we reviewed in Chapter 4. The second major task came from his own initiative, in writing a forty-eight-page article with the simple title 'Committees in Organisation' for the recently launched quarterly journal the *British Management Review*, published in spring 1937. The item was so well received that the publishers produced an off-print version as a self-standing pamphlet. Thirdly, as we noted earlier, he was drafting a document for the seventh CIOS International Congress in Washington DC, to be held in July 1938, a preliminary version of which was presented to the April 1937 Oxford Management Conference under the title 'Britain's Scientific Management Movement'.

The year 1938 was yet another busy one for Urwick, not least due to his work at the Washington CIOS Congress, which had eventful consequences. The scientific management review first presented in 1937 had been drafted as a broad sweep from his own knowledge and recollections of the relevant literature. However, Urwick felt that the text was inappropriate for the intended international audience, especially as it provided little historical background on the period 1870–1930. At the same time, he had little time to spare to research this background, leading him to search for an appropriate assistant, initiating a relationship that for the following decades would prove most fruitful. As part of his voluntary role as examinations assessor for the IIA, he had already come into contact with Edward Brech, one of the candidates, whose work was of such quality that Urwick wasted no time in offering him voluntary research work to help with the CIOS Report. Over the following ten weeks, on three or four evenings each week, Brech spent several hours delving into records, archives, and background publications, producing reports that were typed by his wife and forwarded each weekend to Urwick's London flat. Such was Brech's effectiveness that a considerable amount of material was accumulated, leading Urwick to acknowledge in the Report's preface his 'Appreciation and gratitude to Mr E.F.L. Brech for help in the research without which this task would not have been completed'. The full text of eighty-five pages was printed in the *British Management Review*, while off-prints in booklet form were provided for the British delegation to present on behalf of the British Management Council to participants at the Seventh CIOS Conference held in Washington DC in July 1938, with the title 'The Development of Scientific Management in Great Britain'.

INTERNAL TENSIONS

It is difficult to know how far Urwick's public educational contributions helped in the generation of assignments; what is certain is that he spent a substantial amount of time on them. The two founding partners had agreed that the public programme carried a general publicity value, accumulating goodwill and increasing public recognition. At the same time, from 1936 onwards it was increasingly evident that Orr resented the amount of time Urwick spent away from the consultancy, as well as his absorption in writing addresses or other materials. Eventually, Orr raised the matter with Urwick, accusing him of 'not pulling his weight in running the Company's operations or directly selling its services' (according to the official UOP history). Of course, there was no realistic response that Urwick could offer, other than arguing that the public relations value for the Company of his external activities was considerable. He had reduced his workload by having had two of the experienced consultants on the office methods and management side promoted to senior consultant role and status, while retaining overall functional responsibility for that area. Urwick also continued to be available for specific client consultations if matters of organization, delegation, or general management arose. Furthermore, he continued to inspire the consultants and participated in the in-house training of all personnel. Indeed, he did not feel that he was failing in his own service to the company; rather, that his public programme was bringing it considerable benefits in publicizing the name. Having noted this point, it is unlikely that Urwick appreciated Orr's feeling that the balance of acclaim went primarily to Urwick, rather than to UOP.

This reveals the core issue, because at the root of Orr's accusations was envy, since while he managed the partnership almost all of the public relations acclaim seemed so consistently to favour Urwick. It was as if Orr were the junior partner, or even an also-ran, in addition to which he felt that Urwick's external activities were so general that he frequently failed to publicize the consultancy service.

Having highlighted these business differences, it is also necessary to mention a personal problem that impinged directly on Urwick's life. His wife Joan had embarked on an affair with a married Englishman while the family had lived in Geneva. Given the long spells of loneliness, with Lyndall frequently travelling abroad on IMI business, one might regard this as inevitable, although circumstantial evidence suggests that neither Lyndall nor the other wife had any knowledge or suspicion of the situation. The two couples had actually socialized together extensively, resulting in the development of a close relationship between Joan and the other husband. Joan had been able to mask her sadness at the departure from Geneva in May 1934 by claiming that she would miss 'the lovely house in Geneva', but there seems little doubt that she missed her lover more. The situation came to a head late in 1936, when the other wife died, leading the husband to travel to London to propose marriage to Joan. This resulted in a confrontation between the Urwicks, as a result of which Lyndall acceded to his wife's plea for a divorce.

At that time, the law and public opinion viewed divorce as a major issue, with a lengthy and complex legal procedure that was linked with certain conventions. One of these conventions was the wife's departure from the marital home as soon as proceedings were initiated; another was that the presiding judge would normally deny legal custody of the children to the wife, though granting maternal access. Although the Urwick divorce only became absolute early in 1938, from 1936 Lyndall consequently had legal custody of his two children, June (by now aged ten) and Alan (six). To cope with these changed circumstances, while retaining a flat in Mayfair in which he lived during the week, he decided to rent a cottage in the village of Eastleach, Gloucestershire, where he moved his mother and children. Inevitably, though, for Lyndall the disclosure had been a devastating blow, seriously damaging his sense of self-esteem even at a time when his professional reputation was expanding impressively.

While this domestic ferment was raging, Urwick's relationship with Orr was also deteriorating. At the foundation of the partnership in 1934, contemporary observers had seen the combination of Lyndall Urwick and J. Leslie Orr as a solid base for what they proposed to do. They had calibre and characteristics in common, while even their differences were largely complementary. Both had significant industrial backgrounds, providing an accumulation of relevant managerial experience. At the same time, one important difference lay in their respective experience of consultancy, in that while Urwick had one in-house experience at Rowntree's, Orr had been working for three years on freelance assignments abroad, followed by seven years in a professional company framework back in Britain. As the latter included the supervision of assignments conducted by operating consultants, as well as considerable personal experience of obtaining assignments, Orr could justifiably regard himself as 'the player', the real thing. In contrast, it was increasingly evident that Urwick felt he was 'the gentleman', or the academic contributor to the partnership. These differences in respective personal make-up came increasingly to the fore as the years passed. Urwick was a charismatic English gentleman; even Orr would have accepted that description, though probably adding 'with a strong element of arrogance'. While Urwick had a personality larger than life, sound self-assurance, and self-confidence, on his own admission he lacked patience with lesser mortals. This grated with Orr, because although they seemed to enjoy a reasonable personal relationship, it was not clear whether they shared the same aspirations for the consultancy. On the one hand, Urwick was solely interested in the advancement of the highest standards of managerial practice, while on the other hand in personality and outlook Orr was a complete contrast, being a genuine, simple man valuing integrity and honesty above all else.

While the two partners were aware that their differences were known at least among the senior consultants, both tried not to let this impact adversely on either the company's management or the conduct of its professional services. It was impossible, however, to stifle individual preferences among the senior personnel, even if they were not allowed to colour in-house activities and attitudes. By 1937–8, those preferences had begun to harden into separation, especially among those who had been longest with the firm. Indeed, individuals framed themselves into 'Urwick men' or 'Orr men', the latter including the few who had previously been employed at the Bedaux Company. It was this crystallization process that brought the situation to a head between the two partners in mid-1938, shortly before Urwick set off for the CIOS Congress. The circumstantial evidence strongly indicates that Urwick, despite an initial personal liking for Orr, had come to regard him as a 'little man'; he had even once described him as 'a Scots Covenanter'. This perhaps reflects how he was becoming increasingly disillusioned with the continuing future prospect of cooperating in the running of UOP, creating an uncomfortable work setting for the two men. Furthermore, if the situation was allowed to continue, it would only deteriorate further, with serious implications for the team. Urwick recognized this, referring to 'strained personal relations between us [as] on-going ever since the Company started' in his memoirs.

In June 1938, the two partners consequently decided to discuss possible solutions to this growing internal crisis. Urwick had already apparently canvassed a suggestion for reformulating the structure into a new format, wherein Orr would become sole managing director responsible for all general management, while he would retain the role and responsibility of chairman. The outcome of these deliberations was a decision to express their respective positions in writing as the basis for a consultative review. They also had had some discussions with three senior consultants who had been with the company from the outset. Their decision on documenting the respective views took the form of Urwick opening the discussions, at Orr's request. Urwick submitted a memorandum dated 21 June 1938 in which he noted that because of the business's success 'it would be an act of foolishness and irresponsibility' to imperil it. Nevertheless, he complained that 'during the last eighteen months, I have found my initiative cramped and my enthusiasm damped down to a degree which has very largely destroyed the value I could have for the Company. That is bad for the Company and worse, I think, for me'. As a partial solution, he suggested restructuring and enlarging the board.

Not sharing Urwick's predilection for discursive writing, Orr refused to provide a corresponding memorandum. Instead, he requested a second special meeting after he had read the Urwick document, thereafter compiling a written record dated 23 June 1938. This memo accepted Urwick's recommendations, that in order to resolve the struggle for leadership, Orr would take responsibility for the general executive management of the Company, with the title of managing director, while Urwick would focus on consultancy contacts, as well as act as personnel manager for the partnership.

As Urwick was due to go away very shortly after that exchange, to attend the CIOS Congress in the United States, involving two weeks for the return sea passage and some additional time devoted to resuming contacts with management people he had recently come to know, this resulted in a failure to make any decisions on the restructuring. In effect, both agreed to 'let sleeping dogs lie' during the autumn–winter months. It was only in the spring of 1939 that another discussion was held on this topic, and even then they decided to commission a mutually respected third party to make the key decisions. To perform this mediating role, they chose G. S. A. Wheatcroft, a well-known lawyer who had provided professional services for UOP. He was given the two memoranda and held individual personal discussions with each partner. No doubt external circumstances and his own workload slowed down Wheatcroft's consideration of the remit. It was consequently November 1939 before he submitted his own memorandum. This noted 'a serious incompatibility of temperament' between Urwick and Orr, a faulty organization structure in having two joint general managers, and 'a failure by both partners to make the difficult personal adjustments required by this situation'. Wheatcroft made three recommendations. Firstly, the functions of Urwick and Orr in the business should be altered, with Orr being appointed sole general manager with full executive power, subject only to the control and direction of the board. Urwick, on the other hand, should cease to act as a full-time executive officer and limit himself to two separate and distinct functions, as general consultant and adviser to the staff, and as chairman of the board. His activities outside the company should be a matter for him alone, provided he undertook to do nothing which in the opinion of the board would prejudice the position of the company. Secondly, Wheatcroft recommended 'that the operating board of Urwick Orr & Partners Ltd. be enlarged so as to provide an independent body of people who will share with Urwick and Orr in the direction of the Company and will not only deal with friction when it arises, but endeavour to prevent it arising'. Finally, he felt that both Urwick and Orr should make a fresh start in their personal relations.

Wheatcroft's observations confirmed that he had a sound understanding of the company's internal situation, as well as of the personal make-up and stance of the two partners. However, national circumstances rendered the Wheatcroft proposals virtually superfluous, because the declaration of war in September 1939 created a completely new set of challenges for UOP. Even issues as serious as an internal clash between its two leading figures could not be allowed to cloud considerations of operational policy and potential practice in the context of war, with a major concern being a readiness for possible assignments to aid the war effort. There was also the question of the governmental declaration of favouring evacuation from central London. During their mutual discussions at the turn of 1938–9 about potential wartime arrangements, the two partners had agreed in principle upon evacuation of the office administrative staff (ten young women), because Urwick's ownership of Farnham Court would provide the appropriate premises, affording both staff residence and office accommodation. That decision was carried into effect during the first week after the declaration of war, with Mrs Orr undertaking the housework chores for the resident staff, while she and her husband took up residence in the adjoining property, Shepherd's Hey. This brought immediate relief to the internal tension, mainly because Urwick continued to live in London, at his flat in 7 Park Lane. Moreover, as we shall see in Chapter 6, Urwick took on a new set of responsibilities during the war and discontinued all participation in the company, except for occasional meetings of the board, leaving control of UOP completely to his partner. Urwick even offered to allow Orr to buy him out of the company, in February 1940, but Orr was unable to raise the sum asked and so the offer lapsed.

While Wheatcroft's principal proposals had consequently been shelved, one of them was implemented, when five of the senior consultants (Brown, MacDonald, Coutts Donald, Boss, and Hill) were elected onto the board of directors, and Orr was appointed sole general manager. It is also worth noting that the company performed extremely well during the war under Orr's leadership, with 134 new assignments started during that period. Even so, the hostility between the two principals was still there, even to the point where Brech, who was the member of the company in constant touch with both men, resigned in July 1943 as a result of his discomfiture at the way in which they each abused the other in his presence.

URWICK ORR IN THE POST-WAR PERIOD

As Chapter 6 recounts Urwick's activities during the Second World War, it is unnecessary at this stage to go into any detail about this episode. It is merely important to note that by the end of hostilities in Europe in May 1945, and the Far East in August, Lyndall Urwick was free from his self-imposed restriction to remain clear of operational and managerial responsibilities in the company as long as the war was continuing. To assist in peaceful reabsorption, he continued for the summer months of 1945 to operate as chairman, without impinging on Orr's general management responsibility. The personal tension between the founding partners had not eased, however, implying that Wheatcroft's major recommendation remained valid and now required the two to prepare to take a new look at the situation. Both privately and in individual discussions with other directors, Urwick and Orr assessed the situation, but no indications of any likely accommodation emerged, indicating the need for a radical solution. This took the form of a ballot amongst the five directors appointed in 1940, who were asked to vote on which of the two founding partners each would select as head of the company, in the sure knowledge that the other would resign immediately, contingent upon an acceptably modest compensation formula.

Although this sounded like a rational solution, it would be predetermined personal factors that influenced each man's decision: S. H. Boss and M. W. Brown voted for Orr; H. A. MacDonald and W. Coutts Donald voted for Urwick. A. G. Hill held no attachment or predilection for either of the two founders, but his marketing expertise led him to the view that the company's progress would flourish better under Urwick's leadership than under Orr's. He came to this view on the basis of a clear recognition that Urwick's public persona was so positive for the partnership that his absence would damage

UOP's reputation. So the 3–2 vote settled the matter finally, with Orr resigning and withdrawing, along with Brown and Boss. This was a sad occasion in UOP's history, and one which should not have been necessary. On the other hand, management consultancy is a field in which rivalries are common and perhaps inevitable. As the company history (2007) notes in its preface:

Urwick himself recognized that internal problems would be a fact of consultancy management. When addressing events and conferences around the world he was frequently asked if *he* ever experienced difficulties in managing his own organization. He would reply '*You* try managing a company of people where everyone considers they are experts in management and see if *you* have problems!' [Emphasis in original]

Lyndall Urwick now had the role and responsibility of managing director formally added to that of chairman. Although he saw no need for any further change in the top managerial structure, he brought Edward Brech into the head office as his personal assistant, primarily to take over the burden of internal administrative management. Keeping the continuing external contributions in his own hands, this provided the basis for UOP's post-war expansion.

In assessing Urwick's return to the professional consultancy arena, it is important to recognize that there had been no reduction in his zeal to promote not only the practice of effective management through consultancy, but also the educational contributions necessary to pursue the mission of disseminating best practice. In other words, the mission that he had selected for himself in the trenches in July 1915 when first reading F. W. Taylor's *Shop Management* had remained undiminished. Within the company, his co-directors also accepted the enormous public relations value that his external contributions were bringing. He could consequently feel free to accept invitations at will, and as these were mounting considerably, reflecting his status as easily the most popular contributor across the British management network, UOP derived considerable benefit from this work.

During the war years, the company had also done very well in providing consultancy services, gaining an even wider reputation under Orr's general management than they had achieved in the 1930s. This was achieved in spite of minimal expansion in consultant manpower, because until a recruitment drive in 1944–5 the number of consultants had remained virtually stable at around thirty, plus the six senior consultants who were members of the board. By the autumn of 1945, there were forty-three consultants on the books, providing adequate resources to continue the established UOP modus operandi of Urwick devoting little of his time to direct supervision of assignments and focusing attention on external commitments. Indeed, the senior consultants now on the board would appear to have replaced Orr, while as Urwick's personal assistant Edward Brech ensured that the chairman was kept informed of internal developments.

The end of the war also heralded in a new era of expansion for British consultancy firms, as manufacturing businesses especially looked to take advantage of their freedom from wartime constraints to introduce fresh organizational ideas. This provided a direct challenge for the company's two development officers (or salesmen), as well as for the senior consultants, because it was part of their roles to bring in new business. Just as in the past, though, Urwick's internal role lay mainly in presiding as chairman at the periodical supervisory meetings of the senior consultants and selection committees, providing information and advice as needed, attending special 'development' meetings, and chairing the twice-yearly staff conferences. The latter occasions he particularly enjoyed, because they provided an invaluable opportunity to socialize with all of the company's staff, many of whom he rarely met during the working week. As by 1950 UOP employed 112 consultants, this was not surprising, even though Urwick sat in on all selection meetings when the senior staff chose new employees.

Clearly, over the post-war years, UOP's reputation increased appreciably. Internally, Urwick also introduced refinements that he had long sought, namely, to reduce the itinerant life of the consultant, which frequently involved week-long residences away from home. In July 1950, a North-West Area was inaugurated, because of the large number of assignments obtained there, enabling a sizeable cadre of consultants to live and work in that locality. In the following spring, a comprehensive 'Area' pattern was developed, adding the North-East (based in Leeds), Midlands (Leamington Spa), Scotland (Glasgow), the South-East, and South (based in an area office in London, separate from the head office). Each Area had a manager responsible for all services and activities, other than recruitment to the company, supported by two or three senior consultants appropriate to the scope of assignments in hand and forecast. In spring 1951, the company head office was moved to 29 Hertford Street, in London's Mayfair district, a self-contained house where the directors and chairman had their office accommodation, alongside the accounts department and administration services.

These changes had also been preceded in 1948 by the introduction of a new institutional feature to the company, with the appointment of trustees – initially Urwick, Sir Charles Renold, and Professor Wheatcroft – who held 'B' shares in the company, giving them the authority to make recommendations to the board. Over time, some extremely eminent economists (e.g. James Meade, Alec Cairncross, and Robin Matthews) served as trustees, as well as notable people from industry such as Sir Jack Scamp. Another major development was client training. As Ferguson noted (2001: 101), 'utilizing their experiences at Bedford and the personal ambitions of its founder, [UOP] formed a management training centre at Slough for the provision of training to client companies'. The Slough Centre was the first external management training school set up by a consultancy company, at a time when the Henley Management College was the only other organization providing anything similar. Although Slough and the Bedford centre operated in tandem for many years, once it became apparent that Slough was too small, Baylis House was set up in 1958. This underlines a little-noticed contribution that consultants have made to management development. While Handy et al. (1988: 169–71) describe the corporate, academic, and professional approaches to management development in Britain, Ferguson (2003) argues convincingly that the consultancy track needs to be recognized, especially in view of the work done by UOP in this field.

UOP AFTER URWICK'S RETIREMENT AS MANAGING DIRECTOR

As a matter of personal choice, the year 1951 became a watershed for Lyndall Urwick, because on his sixtieth birthday he decided to retire as managing director. Having long held the maxim that at that age men in senior positions should move aside to make room for the up-and-coming managers, he offered his resignation to the UOP board of directors. Although he wanted to remain chairman of the board and titular head of the company, contributing especially to the strategic discussions, and he accepted that the company's affairs were being effectively and competently managed by the three other board members, he felt it was time for somebody else to take over as managing director. The Board accepted his request and apart from bringing two of the senior consultants on to the board, appointed a new managing director, Coutts Donald, who was given the specific coordinating role as managing partner.

Apart from honouring his maxim, Urwick had fulfilled a personal objective in relinquishing all internal responsibilities, giving him the opportunity to embark virtually full time on what he himself has described as his 'mission at large', namely, continuing his advocacy and promotion of the advancement and spread of effective management, as well as contributing to that mission educationally through his public speaking and writing. To support his personal activities in that area, the board voted to continue paying his salary unchanged, as well as reimbursing his expenses within the activities of 'the mission', unless those were specifically covered by the host institution. The company would also provide the salary for his personal assistant and a full-time secretary, as well as office facilities. Given that he still maintained his long-established style of writing in longhand, these services were essential if he was to continue to operate effectively.

To mark the occasion of his retirement and as a sixtieth-birthday present, the board arranged for his portrait to be painted by Alan Gwynne-Jones. The finished work was presented to him, and he chose to have it hung in the head office. (See Figure 5.1) On a more personal basis, there was also a change at home. In 1941, he had married again, to Beatrice (Betty) Warrand, whom he had met socially in London, and with whom he was to adopt a son, John, and a daughter, Gillian. At the end of the war, the couple had moved into Farnham Court when it was vacated by the company's administrative staff. Bearing in mind the roving aspect likely to characterize Urwick's 'mission at large', in 1951 they decided to sell Farnham Court. While retaining a pied-à-terre in London, they replaced Farnham Court with The Manor House in the village of Poyntington in Dorset.

He did, however, still have a role to play as chairman of UOP, a responsibility that he regarded as far from nominal, spending two or three days a week when he was in Britain at the offices, as well as presiding over the twice-yearly staff conferences. As James Meade, an eminent Nobel Prize-winning trustee, put it when describing the operation of the trustees, 'so long as Urwick himself was around his decision prevailed, so whatever was formally written down didn't really apply' (*The Urwick Orr Partnership* 2007: 320). Despite his heavy programme of public educational contributions at home and abroad, after his retirement Lyndall Urwick gladly maintained active contact with UOP's affairs, especially by attending the meetings of the board of directors held some four or five times a year. He particularly enjoyed chairing the recruitment selection committee, whenever his own commitments made that possible. He also readily accepted the invitations from partnership area managers to participate in their local annual conferences, customarily held over a weekend with a social feature in the form of a Saturday dinner to which the consultants were invited to bring their wives. Crucially, he always presided at the Partnership Annual Staff Conference, held in an Oxford or Cambridge College over a summer weekend, an event he described as another occasion for 'meeting the boys'. Another event he did not miss was in November 1959, when at an in-house conference there was a celebratory dinner to commemorate the Silver Jubilee of the Urwick Orr Partnership – 'The Company's Twenty-Five Years of Professional Service and Progress'.

As well as his activities in UOP, he also played a significant role in the wider consultancy world. In 1956, he was instrumental in forming the Management

Figure 5.1 Alan Gwynne-Jones' oil painting of Urwick.

Consultancies Association, while in 1961, at the age of 70, returning to the theme of consultancy as a key strand of management development, he presented an important paper on behalf of the consultancies at the Stocktaking in Management Education Conference, run by the Federation of British Industries. Central to the paper were some important statistics, replicated in Table 5.2, which illustrate that not only were the consultancies training a large number of managers and producing a lot of publications, but also that the numbers accelerated sharply in the second half of the 1950s.

Table 5.2 Consultants' direct and indirect contributions 1940–60

	1940–55	1956–60
Student weeks of management training	11,858	43,194
Student throughput	2,276	7,042
Firms assisted in starting management training Facilities:	99	211
Number of external lectures delivered	1,813	1,973
Number of books and booklets published	64	81
Articles published	257	378

Source: Ferguson (2001)

Sadly, this was to be something of a swansong for this particular group of consultancies, since from the 1960s they were to be overtaken by both the accountancy firms that turned to consultancy and large American consultancies arriving in Britain. Nevertheless, this community had grown impressively since the 1930s, reflecting some significant changes to the general British management milieu.

Urwick gave up the chairmanship of UOP in 1961, when he emigrated to Australia, taking up the title of president. He also finally retired as a trustee of UOP in 1966, on becoming 75. The company, for its part, continued to have some successes, for example through the introduction of 'Management by Objectives', devised by John Humble, as well as the introduction of computing activities, initially in conjunction with John Diebold. It remained one of the 'Big Five', even if with the rise of major new competitors it was already apparent by the 1960s that, along with other British consultancies, UOP was in decline. Eventually, the firm was acquired by Price Waterhouse in 1984. Nevertheless, members of UOP still have at the time of writing a 'Lyndall Urwick Society', which has not only produced a history of the firm (2007), but also publishes a journal, *Keeping in Touch*, to sustain the name and honour its achievements.

6

Wartime

Although in Chapter 5 some mention was made of Urwick Orr and Partners (UOP)'s performance during the Second World War, it would be useful to say more about Lyndall Urwick's wartime roles, because he took time out from the consultancy to make a contribution to the general effort. He was especially anxious to be of service during the war, leading him, firstly, to perform an informal role in the organization of a Territorial Division, following which he had two spells of governmental service, in the Treasury and then working for the War Office's Petroleum Warfare Department. In addition, he also carried out a range of educational activities, pursuing his chosen 'mission' in spite of the difficult circumstances. As we hinted in Chapter 5, apart from contributing effectively to the drive for greater efficiency at a time of acute scarcity, this work also boosted his reputation further, confirming his position as the country's leading management thinker and activist.

TRANSITION TO WAR

The declaration of war stimulated Urwick's desire to make a direct contribution to the nation's wartime needs, even if that service had to be in 'volunteer' terms rather than commercially negotiated. Chance circumstances provided an initial opportunity, arising from Lieutenant Colonel John Smyth's role as commander of the Second London Territorial Army Division. Smyth and Urwick had first met as schoolboys in Repton and had maintained a friendship throughout their lives. Urwick had first offered his services to Smyth in 1939, and although the War Office refused to extend a formal contract, the two friends immediately started work. Having had a preliminary briefing, Urwick found himself facing an administrative situation with features resembling those he had experienced at Base Camp at Rouen during the First World War. As a consequence, he decided to commit himself full-time to resolving these challenges, albeit on a voluntary basis. As a gesture of service to the war effort, Orr also accepted Urwick's request for one of the company's office team to support him full time for some weeks.

As the personnel in this divisional headquarters, all of whom were volunteer Territorial Army soldiers, had in the main commercial and administrative employment backgrounds, for Urwick and his consultant colleague the situation was similar to an office assignment, even if all the processes and documents were specific to the military setting. Improving the organizational arrangements in the headquarters office unit proved no more difficult than in the conventional client's commercial office, calling for the customary in-depth retraining, together with the establishment of effective supervisory procedures. The Territorial Division thus had the benefit of an expert service, with Smyth declaring the outcome to be immensely satisfactory. Smyth also added a recommendation that the improved arrangements and methods should be adopted within any new Division, requesting that the War Office assess Urwick's system. It was quite some while before Urwick was invited to discuss that recommendation with the War Office, but it was speedily made clear that the military civil servants were not ready for such radical change.

THE TREASURY, JUNE 1940–MAY 1942

For Britain as a nation, the months of April–May 1940 were traumatic, with the German Army making a rapid and massive assault, overrunning the Netherlands, Belgium, and northern and eastern France, culminating in the devastating, though successfully accomplished, evacuation of almost all Allied forces at Dunkirk. The sequel was a change in government and of Prime Minister, with numerous consequential reactions in most aspects of economic and social life. The keynote of the new regime was all-out effort on war-supply production, partly to replace armaments and equipment lost in the evacuation, as well as preparing for a massive increase in the construction of military aircraft, all to be achieved with the greatest possible economy in terms of both resources and manpower.

If these objectives were going to be achieved, Urwick swiftly recognized that management consultancy services could make an important contribution. It is notable, though, as Kipping (1997: 73) has demonstrated, the British effort was not pursued as thoroughly as in Germany, where rationalization was much more intensive both before and during the Second World War. Nevertheless, considerable efforts were made in boosting the British effort, part of which was achieved through the employment of consultants. For example, three of UOP's 'manufacturing' team were invited to take over senior managerial roles in national ordnance and armament factories. As it was known that UOP also had a specialist team devoted to productivity improvement in the administrative and clerical area, the Treasury's Permanent Secretary (as Head of the Civil Service) invited Lyndall Urwick and a small team to join his Whitehall department on a full-time secondment. The two had previously shared platforms at various management conferences, convincing the mandarin that the consultant had much to offer the office research section. Urwick readily accepted, moving into the Treasury offices in May. It seems to have been a rather casual invitation, without much consideration being given on either side to what was expected as an outcome. It was in fact surprising that Urwick, given his status as arguably the leading light of the management movement, was not given a more formal invitation than the happenstance of a personal contact, but this perhaps epitomizes the way in which the British elite operated.

In spite of the informality of this invitation, it is important to stress that it implied an internal establishment appointment, rather than one as a 'seconded consultant', thus placing him on the civil service payroll. Asked what salary he was expecting, he replied that he had no figure in mind because UOP would make good any deficiency. He was consequently offered £1,000 a year, leading him to start work in June 1940. He could have raised a point of principle, because while the salary was at the top of the civil service executive grade, this did not give him the seniority accorded the administrative grade, an aspect that later caused him personal regret, as well as adversely influencing the significance of any recommendations that he would in due course be submitting. The status issue neatly reflected civil service attitudes towards administrative systems; had the internal Treasury intentions been seriously directed towards improving operational performance and manpower economy, Urwick's background would have justified his appointment as head of section with the administrative grade status. He was, of course, well aware of the situation, but was determined not to let it impair his work in the office research section in undertaking the tasks allocated to him by its head.

His first assignment was in the Ministry of Supply, a relatively new organization that had been established to coordinate the purchase of military equipment for the War Office departments. The office research section already had two members of its own staff conducting studies, to which Urwick was added as a means of extending the range of expertise available to the analysis. In this lay a first significant lesson for him, because the review was being conducted on behalf of the Treasury, not as a consultancy service for the Ministry of Supply. This was a radically different situation from Urwick's professional consultancy experience in the industrial and commercial context, when commissions were contracted directly with the client. Not surprisingly, Urwick and the team produced a considerable number of recommendations, disclosing what they identified as a seriously unsatisfactory situation in many respects, especially in terms of documentation and method. True to his own professional standards, Urwick could do nothing other than compile the findings on a 'warts-and-all' basis, producing a comprehensive report for the Head of the Treasury section under his personal responsibility. These criticisms were also supported by a programme of constructive recommendations, in order to raise the general level of efficiency of that vital Ministry. However, when in due course the report was made available to the senior Treasury and Ministry staff, the reaction of the latter was one of outrage, accompanied by a stern request for all Treasury office research section staff to be withdrawn at once. The report was rejected, simply on the grounds that it was too deeply critical, with the Ministry officials refusing to consider any of the recommendations, whatever their merit. For Urwick, the response came as a replication of the War Office reaction to the Territorial Army report several months earlier, confirming his view that powerful conservative forces were at work within the civil service.

While that review was being completed, Urwick had also been assigned to lead a similar review of administrative methods and management within another new department, the Ministry of Shipping. It proceeded for several weeks before being halted by a Cabinet decision to amalgamate the department into the existing Ministry of Transport. No consideration appears to have been given to the practical value of continuing the review. Nevertheless, other reviews were being brought to the attention of the office research section, necessitating some increase in the manpower employed. That was met in part by invitations to appropriately equipped commercial companies to second staff to the section, some of whom were known to Urwick as a result of consultancy contracts completed in the 1930s. By the early summer of 1941, the section was also discussing the possibility of creating an 'Organisation and Methods' group, given the need for some government departments to recognize that external expertise could contribute to improving operational performance and manpower economy.

Urwick continued serving in the office research section, undertaking assignments as and when they arose, sometimes as leader in a project or occasionally as a contributing member. Among the major projects in which he was active were:

1. The Prime Minister had apparently become concerned during 1941 about the excessive amount of time spent by senior officials seconded to committees on a part-time basis. It was alleged that this ran into thousands

of man-hours during a year, leading Urwick to be asked by the Treasury to investigate the situation, with a specific view to reducing this burden wherever necessary. After confirming the existence of this problem, Urwick and a small team first recommended the creation of a simple factual monthly record, to be compiled by a departmental clerk. More significantly, though, while advocating a review of committee deliberations as they occurred, this was rejected on the grounds that this could dilute the principle of constitutional departmental responsibility to the House of Commons.

2. Urwick was asked to institute a training scheme mainly for the female typists who formed the backbone of recording and communication within and between all departments. As several thousand typists were employed, with a significant turnover of staff, it was essential to ensure that adequate training was in place, in order to avoid awkward transition periods. This was enthusiastically supported by the female Assistant Secretary in the Treasury, resulting in the establishment of an office specifically responsible for the employment and welfare of female staff. In addition, Urwick devised a standard programme of intensive training that could be appropriately conducted within each major department, depending on current needs.

3. Another problem remitted to Urwick early in his service with the office research section concerned the maintenance of information about interned 'enemy aliens'. Among the crisis decisions of May–June 1940 had been the widespread imposition of internment, giving rise to a sizeable accumulation of personal information and an inevitable stream of queries that approached 1,000 items per day. For him, it was a routine 'identification, record, and filing' problem for which he devised a preliminary sorting scheme to clear the backlog and an ongoing system to cope with identifying the queries as they came into the Home Office and marrying them to the relevant personal file; when completed this was a project about which he felt particularly pleased.

4. Given the large number of civil servants that joined the Armed Forces, it was necessary to devise an appropriate system capable of ensuring that the 'salary make-up element' was paid regularly. Since September 1939, arrears had been accumulating faster than arrangements for individual payments could be maintained, while two parallel sources of payment were used, from the military and relevant civil department. Urwick recognized that clearing the backlog could only be achieved through the introduction of a single source of payment. Logic and common sense recommended that the military channel should be used for this purpose, a proposal that was

vetoed by the Civil Service Clerical Association on the grounds that civil service departmental staff would not like their remuneration coming through this channel.

5. A more satisfactory assignment was conducted within the Air Ministry, assisting the Air Members for Personnel and for Training to improve internal arrangements relating to administrative and clerical operations. This was a task similar to that performed for the Territorial Army Divisional Headquarters more than a year earlier.

6. Another major interdepartmental assignment concerned the Whitehall Messenger Service responsible for maintaining documentary interchange and distribution. After first assessing this system, Urwick felt that there was a problem with the overall standard of the men themselves. He actually described them as 'underpaid, undisciplined, untidily dressed and unhappy', criticizing poor management for this situation. Indeed, he considered everything about the Messenger Service to be poor: organization, accommodation, methods, equipment, service arrangements, supervision, and morale. A remedial programme was produced, based upon a central clearing–handling depot, equipping messengers with truck-tricycles to service programmed routes and timings, with provision built in for 'emergency special items'. Basic to his remedy was the appointment of a competent manager, to be named the 'Inspector of Messengers', preferably with military background, supported by a small team of appropriately trained supervisors. To Urwick's deep personal regret, however, the proposals were rejected, apparently without any discussion of their merits.

7. Through the latter part of the two-year period covered by these activities, Urwick was also serving as a member on the Mitcheson Committee, responsible for reviewing organization and methods in the Ministry of Pensions. In the membership listing, he was described as 'Chairman of Urwick Orr & Partners Limited, Consulting Specialists in Organisation and Management'. The Committee's deliberations resulted in the publication of twelve Interim Reports on aspects of their studies, with a substantial Final Report published in February 1942.

Whatever personal satisfaction Lyndall Urwick might have gained from these first-hand studies of organization and methods within Whitehall, it must be stressed that most of this was dissipated by increasing disappointment at the attitudes of civil servants at all levels. He was experiencing situations utterly negative to the purpose that had led him readily to accept the Treasury invitation. As well as promoting manpower economy and improved operational performance, he had harboured an expectation that his standing as a management consultant of some reputation would be accepted as a contribution to the advancement of managerial efficiency. Instead, he had to recognize that his external standing carried no weight, even in the Treasury office research section; he was just one of the team, even though most of that team would have accepted his status as a leader of Britain's management movement. Repeated rejection of apparently effective proposals could only add to the dismay and disappointment, generating over time a sense of 'derring-do' in pursuit of his primary objectives. As he later noted: 'During the whole course of this period (i.e. in the Research Section) I was determined to compel the Treasury to pay more attention to modern methods of management.' These were strong words, reflecting the bitterness that the dismay and disappointment generated. (It was not just the Treasury as an organization that had a traditional perspective. Donald Banks, whom we shall meet in the next section, had a happenstance discussion with the Chancellor of the Exchequer in mid-1941 about upgrading training and development for senior members of the Government Departmental staff, but was shocked to hear the reply that the Institute of Public Administration was not interested in taking up the matter.) The Treasury did, however, set up an Organisation and Methods Division in 1945, which was a gesture in the direction Urwick wanted them to go.

As a result of this bitterness, early in 1942 Urwick initiated a line of action that he must have known would provoke a seriously negative response in the upper levels of the Treasury. This strategy was based on external lobbying, in order to 'compel' Whitehall to adopt more effective administrative management. Selected Members of Parliament were an obvious first line of approach, with whom his external standing gained a ready response, at least for informal discussions of the deficiencies that he could describe and of the remedies that contemporary management thinking and practice could offer. Another line of lobbying lay with selected members of the official Select Committee on National Expenditure, given that in its December 1940 report it had observed that 'lessons of the 1914–18 war had not become learned'. Thirdly, Urwick made use of the chance circumstances that the managing director of one of UOP's important clients happened to be related to the Chancellor of the Exchequer, enabling him to obtain a personal interview. Inevitably, however, the lobbying came to be recognized within the Treasury as utterly unacceptable, especially as it had included the Prime Minister's official Private Secretary. Indeed, as he had seriously offended the protocols of the civil service, he had to go. Urwick was consequently requested by the Head of the Civil Service, Sir Horace Wilson, to tender his resignation from the research office section in May 1942, as an alternative to being dismissed.

Just as that unfortunate situation was moving towards its climax, an interesting coincidence occurred, the publication late in 1941 of a book entitled *The Higher Civil Service*, written by E. H. Dale, a professional civil servant who had retired in 1935. As Urwick regarded this as an extremely important publication, he reviewed it for *Industry Illustrated* in the April 1942 issue. The author had served long spells in the senior administrative grade, offering a range of mildly and politely critical comments about numerous aspects of his topic, criticisms akin to those that Urwick had generated. Keen to voice his own views, Urwick chose the pseudonym 'Narrator' as a byline, instead of his own name, and the review was presented as a feature article under the title 'The Old Lady of Parliament Street'. Early in the review, the characteristics of the typical senior civil servant were paraded for all to see, describing this person's attitude to providing information as demonstrating 'insistence on thoroughness, accuracy, clarity of reasoning and of statement, carefully adjusted to produce "safe" men holding doctrines of moderation and prudence, qualities abhorrent to enthusiasm, or at least not easily reconciled with it'. Moreover, while to the minister and within the department the obligation for truth and accuracy is absolute, it is a different affair with statements that are intended to be or may be liable to become public: nothing may then be said which is not true, but it is as unnecessary as it is sometimes undesirable, even in the public interest, to say everything relevant which is true and the facts given may be arranged in any convenient order; it is wonderful what can be done within those limits by a skilful draftsman.

Urwick also commented that it was impossible to detect where irony ceased and sincerity began in the book, even though he praised it as a first-hand presentation of how the senior civil service is recruited, developed, constituted, and motivated, conveying the 'flavour' of the service; why its members behave as they do; their mutual attitudes of understanding and internal relationships; and their tenuous feelings towards the world outside. Particularly appealing to Urwick were the criticisms that the author voiced, however mildly and politely, because they reflected what he himself had been experiencing since he had taken up his role. One other deficiency that he had frequently met, but which Dale appeared not to have noted, lay in the internal operational and human resource management, a situation stemming from the divided structure in the administrative and executive grades. While the higher (administrative) civil service was responsible for policy formulation, and for advice and service to ministers, especially when MPs' questions had to be answered, internal managerial issues and activities were delegated to the lower-level executive grade, a division Urwick felt ran counter to improved organizational efficiency.

Overall, Urwick declared in completing his three-page review that 'Mr. E.H. Dale had written a valuable book on a matter of great and immediate public interest: most valuable where it is most provocative, because at those points it is most revealing'. Although it is unlikely that the mandarins in the Treasury knew that Urwick had been the author of the review, doing this job was nevertheless a cathartic experience, providing the basis for a seven-page memorandum under the heading 'Reform of the Civil Service'. This document was presented under six headings:

1. Weaknesses of attitude
2. Weaknesses of structure
3. Weaknesses in knowledge
4. Weaknesses in recruitment
5. Weaknesses in grading and promotion
6. Weaknesses in methods and remuneration

There was also a shorter Part II headed 'Remedies'. Whether he realistically expected the civil service to adopt these remains a mystery, but he thoroughly enjoyed completing the exercise, given the acute frustrations he had experienced in the previous two years. Thomas (1988: 29), in her comparison between British and American approaches to administration, may have provided an underlying explanation of the differences between Urwick and the civil service approach: 'The British doctrines remained essentially a philosophy and not a theory of administration, embodying description, subjective attitudes and explanations rather than rigorous, systematic analysis.' Moreover, she argued (1978: 11) that '[British] administration was a means of achieving a higher form of civilization by, for example, upholding the ethic of service to the community'. While Urwick would have agreed about the service ethic, he wanted it to be achieved in a context where a scientific approach dominated, as in the United States.

While Urwick's resignation from the civil service marked the end of a significant phase of personal professional activity, he clearly did not forget this experience, given his firm belief that good management was just as important in government as in industry. In 1945, for example, he contributed two articles to the February and March issues of *Industry Illustrated*, again using his pseudonym of 'Narrator', and heading them both as 'A Tract for the Times', respectively, 'The Achievement' and 'The Lesson'. The subject matter of the articles was a review of David Lilienthal's Penguin Special book just published in Britain entitled *The Tennessee Valley Authority: Democracy on the March*. Urwick attached extraordinarily high significance to this American New Deal water-supply project, given that it demonstrated how governmental activities could be conducted through the application of systematic management while consulting the citizens whose lives were being affected by the project. It became a topic of compelling interest for him, reflected in his readiness to address meetings on 'The TVA', as well as attaching special significance to the subtitle of Lilienthal's book.

Another interesting throwback to this period occurred in 1948, when Stafford Cripps, as Chancellor of the Exchequer and therefore ministerial Head of the Civil Service, invited Urwick to visit him for some informal discussions, as part of an assessment of the need for reform. Naturally, this pleased Urwick immensely, leading to several sessions with the Chancellor, as well as a memorandum embodying his own thinking and recommendations. However, nothing seems to have happened at that time, partly because Stafford Cripps resigned with colitis two years later, both from his office and as an MP. Only in the 1980s were Urwick's ideas applied to the civil service by Sir Derek Rayner (Thomas 1986: 601), even if by then their origins had been forgotten.

Another noteworthy example of Urwick's interest in this subject came in June 1970, when he drafted an article that was submitted to the Treasury's *Organisation and Methods Bulletin*. The letter started with the wording: 'Many Happy Returns of the Day', recalling the formal inauguration of the Organization and Methods Division within the Treasury at the end of the war in summer 1945. Regrettably, his article was not accepted for publication, perhaps typifying the difficult relationship Urwick would appear to have developed with the British civil service.

THE WAR OFFICE, JUNE 1942–DECEMBER 1944

Chance again played its part in determining Lyndall Urwick's next phase of employment, when in June 1942 the War Office inaugurated a new internal unit named the Petroleum Warfare Department. Operating on a military, rather than administrative, basis, with a regular army Brigadier at its head, this department was a vital cog in the war machine. As the new department required an operational general manager, the Brigadier invited Urwick to join him in this post, given that they had been long-standing friends and fellow members of the Reform Club. Urwick was not surprisingly stimulated by the managerial challenge, but an added attraction was the obligation to become once again a serving soldier, leading to his promotion to the rank of Lieutenant Colonel. Even though located in the administrative side of the War Office, the self-contained character of the role and the military nature of the role shielded Urwick from the negative attitudes he had experienced at the Treasury. With military, naval, and air force personnel, as well as oil engineers and scientists, he also described it as 'the most mixed bag that was ever put together in Whitehall', yet highly enjoyable and rewarding.

This new department's mission was to develop and pursue into production weapons and support equipment based on petroleum. Three specific items had been identified for urgent progress: flame-throwing mobile weapons, equipment to disperse fog from airfields (code-named FIDO), and a flow line for pumping liquid fuels across the English Channel on the seabed (code-named PLUTO). Understandably, all three were highly secret, as well as requiring urgent technological development, trials, and manufacture. The first two had features in common, each needing a heavy-duty mobile chassis to be equipped with liquid fuel-burning apparatus and a mechanism for projecting flames. The third item was significantly different and far more complex in design and construction, providing the civil and military staff with a major challenge, compounded by the need to subcontract all of the engineering work to specialist firms. This created managerial tasks of planning, coordination, and supervision, offering Urwick both a challenge for his personal leadership skills, as well as the satisfaction of exercising substantial responsibility. Indeed, even though specialist subcontractors were brought in to help with PLUTO, a system which was operationally reliable over a long distance whilst allowing for the pressures of the Channel seabed, it was a formidably demanding technological project in both design and fabrication. The piping was designed to an unusual specification and fabricated in 700-yard lengths, necessitating the use of specialist jointing skills. Design and fabrication trials were conducted in a five-mile stretch across the Thames estuary, so that consequent upon the D-Day landings the pipeline could be laid immediately, to support the ongoing European conflict. By that time, eleven pipelines, each of thirty-two nautical miles in length, were successfully laid between Dungeness and Boulogne, along with a further two of seventy nautical miles between Shanklin and Cherbourg.

EDUCATIONAL ACTIVITIES

Although Urwick as general manager of the PLUTO project was extremely satisfied with the way it had been developed and implemented, in October 1944 he asked to be released from this project in order to pursue his educational interests. He had actually been participating in this area since leaving the Treasury in 1942, albeit on a part-time basis. For example, in 1942, he addressed the senior officers of the National Fire Service at their Staff College on 'Administration in Theory and Practice', the text of which would later be reproduced in the *British Management Review*. Around the same time, he gave a lecture to a conference of the Royal College of Nursing, with the title 'Bold Behind the

Battle', in which he presented his ideas on the leadership and human relations dimensions in managerial and supervisory responsibilities. This was later reproduced in *Industry Illustrated*. Early in 1944, he gave a lecture to a special advanced course conducted by the Institution of Civil Engineers, jointly with the Engineering Faculty of the University of Cambridge, with the title 'Management of a Subject of Instruction', which was also reproduced in the *British Management Review*. In September 1944, he was among the tutorial contributors to a major conference organized by the Ministry of Production in Glasgow, promoting performance improvement in war-supply manufacturing. At that conference, he also gave the keynote lecture, 'Administration and Leadership', again reproduced in the *Review*. Another governmental educational conference in 1944, under the aegis of the Ministry of Labour and National Service, included a major address from him on 'Factory Administration with Special Reference to Personnel Management', which was published in *Industry Illustrated*. It was a recognition of his status in the management field that such a high proportion of his spoken words were reproduced in journals, thus enabling him to reach a much wider audience. In addition, he secured from the editor of *Industry Illustrated* an invitation to print in three successive issues a booklet on 'Scientific Principles and Organisation' that he had written a couple of years earlier for the American Management Association. All of this was achieved while he was still working at the War Office, with the PLUTO project especially taking up a substantial amount of his time.

Having left the Petroleum Warfare Department in October 1944, Urwick was able to devote even more time to these educational activities. The invitations to lecture and write were by that time arriving in significant numbers, especially as, with the conflict in Europe apparently nearing an end, some of the professional institutions decided to resume members' meetings and conferences, while some of the technical colleges were able to restart at least parts of their pre-war courses in management-related studies. In January 1945, for example, he gave a talk to the Manchester Branch of the Institute of Cost and Works Accountants on 'Management of Tomorrow', reviewing the impact of wartime improvements to manufacturing management, especially those made by that Institute's members. In February, he also agreed to address in Liverpool a joint meeting of the local units of the Institutes of Labour Management (ILOs) and Industrial Administration (IIAs). He chose for this the intriguing title of 'Compromise and Integration', giving him the opportunity to analyse interpersonal relationships among managers in the exercise of their responsibilities, directing particular attention to achieving effective coordination, especially when functional specialization was involved. This aspect of 'line and staff' was one dear to his own interest, having featured in many of his earlier publications and lectures.

An unusual invitation that he accepted came from the London Publicity Club in March 1945. Although his topic, 'Public Relations and Industrial

Relations', was an aspect that normally did not appear to attract serious consideration in the management context, shortly afterwards he was asked by the Southern Region of the Institution of Sewage Purification to speak on a similar theme. The interesting feature of the latter event lay in its reflection of Urwick's public standing, with such an unusual institution seeking his views.

Reverting to the educational contributions in 1945, the summer months brought a further four invitations: to the Industrial Co-partnership Association in May on 'Co-partnership and Leadership'; three talks on 'Leadership and Production Management' to an Eastern Region Conference conducted by the Ministry of Production in June–July; a major contribution on 'Education for Management' to the Incorporated Sales Managers Association, the only functional institution with an established programme of professional studies and examinations at that time; and finally, an article on 'Industrial Citizenship' for the August issue of *Industry Illustrated*, which was in substance a review of a book compiled and published by Cadbury's entitled *Industry Record 1919–1939*. As this book provided a factual historical presentation of economic, social, municipal, and commercial events and developments in interwar Britain, Urwick was keen to demonstrate how this had coincided with the emergence of new ideas on management and organization that ought to be adopted more extensively.

While it is apparent that the Second World War ended on a promising note for Urwick, it is important to stress that in retrospect he was distinctly unhappy with his wartime experiences. As he put it in his autobiography: 'I was sharply disappointed with my personal performance in the World War of 1939–45.' In particular, he was unhappy with the politics:

To find that, in Whitehall, even in wartime, the fact that I was chairman of an up-and-coming management consultancy company gave me no status at all, but was in fact a handicap, a kind of certificate of freakishness, was a shock from which I never entirely recovered as long as the 1939–45 War was on . . . I have never, before or since, worked in an atmosphere so full of intrigue and personalities as I encountered in Whitehall between 1940 and 1942, and mutatis mutandis, in the Petroleum War Department between 1942 and 1944.

Tisdall (1982: 37) also quotes him as saying: 'I succeeded in forcing them to start the Treasury Organisation and Methods Division. But I had to play so much "politics" in doing it that I was poison in the eyes of the head of the Civil Service.' This may well explain why he never received any official recognition for his career in management, given that he had apparently created enemies at the head of this august British institution. At the same time, it is worth reiterating the point that by 1945 his reputation as the leading figure in Britain's management movement was untarnished.

7

British Management Developments
from the 1940s

From the 1940s up to his emigration to Australia in 1961, Urwick was heavily involved in various aspects of the development of management in Britain, in many respects the culmination of what he had been pressing for in the pre-war period. There were five main institutional developments in management in which Urwick was involved, namely, the Institute of Industrial Administration (IIA), the British Institute of Management (BIM), the Urwick Committee, the 'Staff College for Industry', and the Anglo-American Council on Productivity (AACP). A further development, the creation of the Foundation for Management Education (FME), which led to the development of university-level management education, also needs to be considered, although Urwick was relatively little involved. These are the issues that form the subjects of this chapter, providing a detailed assessment of his impact at a time when British managerial developments were increasing in range and depth (Wilson and Thomson 2006).

MANAGEMENT DEVELOPMENT 1945–65

Before moving on to these institutional activities, it will be helpful to provide a diagram and a brief discussion illustrating management development as it existed in the post-war period up to the mid-1960s. Certainly, a management movement still existed, with Urwick at its fore, but it is evident that the picture is quite different to that in the interwar period (represented in Figure 4.1), with many more and stronger strands extending beyond the core. For example, the specialized professional institutes had become much stronger, while larger companies, especially the newly nationalized operations, had become concerned with various dimensions of management development, the consultancy sector had also expanded considerably in size and scope, and new private bodies had emerged, notably Henley and the FME. Successive governments had been involved in several of these new developments, including the formation of the BIM and the Urwick scheme of management education. In addition, it sponsored the AACP and its successor, the British Productivity Council, created the National Economic Development Office, which immediately identified management as a key issue, and passed the Industrial Training Act at the end of this period.

As well as the institutional developments revealed in Figure 7.1, there were various trends which facilitated a surge in interest in management development. The increasing scale of business was an especially important factor, in that it required much more complex structures, culminating in the movement towards M-form organizations led by the arrival in Britain of the American consultants McKinsey & Company in 1959 (Wilson 1995). These more complex structures required more managers, while more generally there was a significant increase in the number of managers in the post-war period. Associated with this growth were a retreat from patronage and a need to look to university graduates for recruitment, not least because the bright young men who had formerly been brought into companies at the age of 15 or so were now staying on at school and going into further and higher education. Industry and its managers were also under attack as the weakness of the British economy became increasingly evident during the post-war period, with a spate of books criticizing Britain's economic performance. Furthermore, American management methods had percolated into Britain, in part from reports such as the AACP, but probably more through the increasing number of American multinationals operating in Britain, usually outperforming British companies and releasing managers

Figure 7.1 The management movement in the post-war period.

with experience of American methods into the managerial labour force (Wilson and Thomson 2006).

While all of these were positive forces for change, there was still a great deal of resistance by British companies and their leaders who preferred the old ways, a point powerfully illustrated by Keeble (1992). The narrow individualism of British companies, their focus on the short term, their preference for 'personality' (or innate qualities) in managers, rather than any recognition of the role of education or training, were only some of the forces which Urwick saw as his enemies. When a body as central and influential as the Federation of British Industries could say in 1947, 'a B.Comm. course is not appropriate for full-time study and . . . can hardly be regarded as a qualification of significant value for entry into industry', it must be wondered what qualification such a body might accept. To borrow from Keeble's chapter headings, for most of industry at least until the mid-1960s there was a rejection of both formal education and planned experience. Meanwhile, most of the universities were unwilling to pursue management education, especially as several of them had experimented unsuccessfully with this field in the interwar period. As late as 1963, the Robbins Committee on Higher Education was extremely ambivalent about whether management could be taught, even if it did recommend setting up two major postgraduate schools. Additionally, with a few exceptions such as Urwick and the Browns (J. A. C. and Wilfred), there was relatively little British writing about management to stimulate thinking.

THE IIA

As Urwick had been extremely knowledgeable about the IIA's activities and sympathetic to its objectives (Brech 2002–1), being a fellow and chairman of the education committee, as well as its examinations assessor, he was keen to see it develop further from its limited interwar base. Indeed, its membership did increase during the early 1940s, rising to just over 5,000 by 1948, when the BIM was formed. Inevitably, though, a complex and difficult relationship existed between the two institutions, with Urwick and many like-minded people preferring the IIA perspective on management to that of the BIM.

Urwick had worked closely with the IIA since the 1930s, a relationship that continued to flourish in the 1940s. Coincidental with taking up the appointment in the Petroleum Warfare Department in June 1942, he was invited to give a series of five lectures at weekly evening meetings of members of the IIA's London Centre on 'The Elements of Administration'. In a seminal contribution, he set out to present a logical scheme, in part culled from a range of pioneering contributors of different nationalities, based upon the premise that 'the art and science of administering social groups, large or small, and increasingly characteristic of our civilisation, have emerged during the past quarter of a century as a *technical* skill'. (His customary use of language at that time accepted 'administration and administering' to mean the same as 'management and managing'.) The lectures were then revised into a book of the same title, published by Pitman, which is further reviewed in Chapter 9, providing Britain with a significant innovation in 'management studies'.

In December 1944, at the Annual General Meeting (AGM) of the IIA, he was elected onto the governing council and reappointed chairman of the education committee. In this latter role, he had the important and to him attractive task of masterminding revision of the Institute's syllabus and examination scheme leading to the award of the professional diploma, the only established professional educational programme for general management. He had the satisfaction of gaining committee endorsement for an innovation that he regarded as particularly significant, adding to the broad revisions of the existing subject matter two new sections of fundamental management knowledge, respectively named 'Management: principles' and 'Management: practice'. The former provided management knowledge with a foundation that Urwick had envisaged since his return to civilian life in 1919, prompted by reading Taylor's *Shop Management* in the trenches. The second aspect, 'practice', had the special purpose of emphasizing the unity of the managerial process and its responsibilities within different settings, whilst also accommodating the specialist functional features that contemporary circumstances were bringing increasingly to the fore. These were to have a significant influence on Urwick's later work on the Committee on Education.

Another important development came when accepting an invitation from the Leeds Centre in April–May 1945, to provide a substantial educational input through a series of five lectures (one each week), entitled 'Business Administration'. Urwick used this series for several years thereafter, in over a dozen different places connected with the IIA, resulting in the conversion of the lectures into a fifty-eight-page booklet for presentation to participants. Although never commercially available, it was also used abroad: in Oslo (1948), Montreal (1950), Geneva (1951), and at five Canadian locations. At this point, these programmes were probably the main focus of management education in Britain, with Urwick as probably the main teacher of management.

Urwick also performed for the IIA in other ways, having been invited in 1947 to give the opening lecture to the London Centre on the revival of the Institute's Higher Management Programme. He also continued to serve as chairman of its education committee, providing talks to various provincial centres throughout this period. In the second half of 1956, these occasional lectures suddenly increased for no apparent reason to seven in six months, one of which was the first annual memorial lecture, 'Management Studies and Training for Management', jointly sponsored by the IIA and the BIM in honour of E. T. Elbourne, the pioneer of professional institutional management studies in Britain.

It was in 1957 that the IIA amalgamated with the BIM, bringing with it some 6,000 members and many local centres. Urwick was actually against this move, fearing that such was the deference to big business within the BIM that this would harm the efforts of the IIA's individual members to professionalize themselves. Many years later, Urwick noted in his foreword to Light's *The Nature of Management* (1968):

When the original Report of the Committee on Education for Management appeared in 1947, no British university was prepared to regard management as a serious educational subject. Consequently the former IIA, which had done the spadework in introducing education for management into this country, was compelled to cut its coat according to its cloth. That is to say it was concerned . . . with the teaching of management in technical colleges and the needs of the type of student who used the technical college at that time, predominantly a student who was coming up the hard way and who was determined to equip himself for higher responsibilities by night work. . . . In the intervening years the idea that managing could to some extent be taught has made considerable headway.

This reflected his deep disappointment with higher education, a feature of the British scene that was especially slow to evolve.

THE URWICK COMMITTEE ON EDUCATION
FOR MANAGEMENT

During the winter months of 1945–6, it was as well that Lyndall Urwick was not burdened by Urwick Orr and Partners (UOP) responsibilities, because he was invited to undertake a national task of considerable importance in the field of 'education for and in management', a cause very dear to his heart.

During the years 1936–9, a quartet of functional management associations (Works, Office, Labour, and Purchasing) had pursued a programme to develop a syllabus of 'management studies', with both generic and dedicated features. The work had been completed by the summer of 1939, with a view to commencing operations in polytechnics and technical colleges in the September. Although this was postponed because of the declaration of war, during the 1940s both the Ministry of Aircraft Production and the Ministry of Labour and National Service also designed selective programmes of managerial and supervisory studies, with tutorial facilities provided within the further education system.

It was only once hostilities in Europe ended that the colleges and the educational authorities started to display interest in reviving the suspended programme. Urwick came into the consultations by virtue of his role as chairman of the IIA's education committee, whose programme of part-time studies for its professional diploma had been continuing during the war years. The Ministry of Education took the lead by holding a consultation conference in September 1945, an event attended by representatives from eleven institutes that had management subjects in their professional curriculum. There was unanimous agreement that the field should be comprehensively and thoroughly reviewed, especially giving specific consideration to the topics that could be regarded as common across the institutes. There was also unanimous agreement that Lyndall Urwick should be invited to preside over the review.

The Ministry's Further Education Division responded positively to this by appointing a departmental committee composed of six members selected for their knowledge and involvement in the domain of 'management studies'. Urwick accepted the invitation to preside as an additional member, supplemented by a ministry assessor and a departmental secretary. From the first meeting, held in the Ministry offices in November 1945, the committee understood and accepted their chairman's emphasis on the historic character of their mission; it provided the opportunity to establish the first ever British national syllabus for the study of professional management in principle and practice, oriented to functional responsibilities and roles across the industrial and commercial spectrum. The committee set itself sizeable tasks, both in terms of consultation across the various Institutes that had a managerial element within their professional qualifying curriculum, as well as studying the many submissions received. Oddly, though, quite early in the committee's deliberations severe delays were experienced as a result of workload congestion within the Ministry's typing service. This was only overcome once the chairman had secured departmental agreement to have that task taken over by UOP, under Edward Brech's direct supervision.

Supported by prompt input from the institutes, the committee's deliberations proceeded rapidly, enabling a draft report to be compiled by August 1946 for consultative circulation. It is also worth noting that the broad response to this draft was positive, because the preceding consultation process had been so constructive. Within a few weeks, the committee had been able to accommodate the few queries and modifications, establishing a definitive report in time to allow adequate consideration prior to attendance at the Ministry's conference in early December 1946. The purpose of the conference was to resolve any lingering difficulties, so that the Minister of Education could have the report printed and formally presented to the House of Commons for acceptance as a national policy programme in April 1947. For Urwick, that was an occasion of considerable personal satisfaction, not least because the committee and report were from then on customarily associated with his surname.

After accepting that theoretical study alone cannot make a manager, the report's recommendations started from the argument that the professional institutions should accept an obligation to include in their syllabuses as much about general management as possible, confining specialized demands to a bare minimum. It was also agreed that all professional managerial institutions should adopt a common curriculum for an intermediate course consisting of three parts: an introduction to management, the 'background' subjects, and the 'tool' subjects. There should be two types of final course, one for those who wished to qualify for specialized management, the other for those who wished to qualify in general management. Both intermediate and final courses should lead to qualifying examinations for the professional institutes concerned, although students could not take a final examination in specialized management before the age of 25, or in general management before the age of 28. Students should not be expected to give more than 100 hours a year to formal part-time instruction at any stage of the courses, with the possibility of day release to be considered by employers. Immediate steps should also be taken to secure an increase in the supply of trained management teachers, both part-time and full-time. At the same time, the Ministry commissioned a team to investigate and report on the facilities in the United States for management education, while an Advisory Council on Education for Management was set up, to be associated with the proposed Central Institute of Management (namely, what became the BIM). Urwick had hoped, perhaps even expected, to be the first chairman of this advisory council, but that recommendation was never implemented in the way intended, a fact that undoubtedly adversely affected the effective introduction and progression of the scheme. Instead, for administrative purposes, the Ministry established in February 1949 a Joint (Examinations) Executive Committee of ten members, two from the Further Education Division and eight representatives of the institutions involved in management studies, excluding Urwick from future involvement with the scheme.

Urwick's direct link with this scheme was consequently as chairman of the IIA's education committee, in which capacity he organized and presided over a week-long summer school held in an Oxford college in July 1947, with informal support from the Ministry. The declared purpose of this event was 'to provide for selected persons responsible for teaching management subjects (whether full-time or part-time) in education, industry or professional institutions an opportunity to explore the syllabuses proposed by the Ministry Departmental Committee and to discuss the practical teaching problems arising therefrom'. This was repeated the following year by the Ministry's Further Education Division, with Urwick again presiding, focusing more on practical considerations of the first stages of the national syllabus which were due to be inaugurated at the polytechnics and colleges in the following September.

While these developments represented a major step forward, for a number of reasons they were never destined to be as epoch-making as Urwick would have hoped. One of the most significant obstacles to success was the failure to involve the universities, because the high-quality staff or students could not be attracted to polytechnics or technical colleges. A second factor was that the specialized institutions wanted more control of their own qualifications, while a third was that the BIM in its early days showed little interest in management education. Perhaps most importantly of all, though, the system did not attract the interest of employers. As a result of these factors, only 810 certificates and 640 diplomas had been awarded by 1961. As Brech has sadly noted (2002–5: 256): 'After hardly more than ten years, the interrelated professional management studies scheme aimed at by the Urwick Committee had been abandoned. It had been replaced by a defined higher level qualification in general management leaving the functional and sectional management societies to continue pursuit of their own professional specializations.' How this came about is recounted in Urwick's relationship with the BIM, a story that must now be recounted.

THE BIM

We noted earlier that the lack of a central institute had been a considerable weakness and embarrassment to British management in the 1930s (Brech 2002–1). Although Urwick had written a draft constitution for such a body while he was at the IMI, and then became involved in the formation of what was effectively an interim body, the British Management Council (BMC), little of substance had happened on this front. In November 1945, and after a lot of manoeuvring during the latter part of the war, Sir Stafford Cripps, as President of the Board of Trade, announced that he was setting up the Baillieu Committee (after its chairman, the chairman of Dunlop Rubber) to consider the steps to form a central management institution.

While the story of these developments, and of the BIM thereafter up to 1977, is comprehensively told in Brech (2002–1), it is worth noting that in January 1947 the Board of Trade accepted the creation of 'The British Institute of Management'. Crucially, as Tisdall (1982: 37) noted: 'There is no doubt but that . . . [Urwick] played a large part, behind the scenes, in its formation', reflecting his significant national reputation. Urwick not only had the ear of industrialists – Renold, the first chair of the BIM was one of his first clients at UOP – he was also regularly consulted by government officials on such matters. Together with McKinstry, the chairman of Management Research Group No. 1, he was also influential in selecting the first council of the BIM. Urwick was selected as one of the appointed members of the council and nominated as one of the two vice-chairmen, alongside McKinstry. A steering committee composed of Renold, McKinstry, and Urwick was also responsible for drafting the constitution, policies, and some aspects of a working programme. However, arguably the most important task entrusted to him by the council and chairman was the selection of a full-time chief executive to serve as Director. While this post had to be publicly advertised as a matter of principle, this was done only in a cursory fashion in April 1947 because Urwick had already found a man, Leo Russell. It was the combination of an exceptional wartime military record with a forceful character that attracted Urwick to Russell, resulting in a strong recommendation to the council that Russell was the best person available. As we shall go on to see, however, this was not Urwick's best decision.

In its early years, the BIM struggled to make much of a difference, given that it reflected the philosophical differences between the progressive and traditional sides of British industry. Several interrelated issues were ever-present: the 'managers are born not made' mentality, the criteria for membership, the education of managers, the nature of management as an art or a science, and whether management could be considered to be a profession. In essence, the majority of the council, including Renold as chairman and Russell as Director, supported the traditional views of British industry on most of those issues, rather than those of the 'management movement'. This is hardly surprising, given the numerical disparity between the traditionalists and the progressives in British industry as a whole. On the other hand, one might have thought that Urwick could have used his influence to greater effect in such key appointments. Of course, he had much to say on these matters in council debates. At the same time, because the BIM also had wider problems, his comments were often lost. For example, the BIM's influence on national developments related to management was marginal, an example of which was its failure to be represented on the AACP and the British Productivity Council. Crucially, it had only limited success in obtaining the sort of members it sought to recruit. Russell did not want a membership incorporating all managers; rather, he preferred the 'great and the good'. To fulfil this aim, he obtained a list of some 1,500 notables, but only managed to secure around 500 of them. He was more successful in recruiting 'blue-chip' companies as corporate subscribers, producing a balance that resembled the Federation of British Industries (FBI) and which further frustrated progressives such as Urwick. There were also continuing financial problems, given the slow growth in membership. Nor, after an abortive start, was there any representation at local level. Russell also had little time for relationships with the other management institutions, including the IIA, which he regarded as second-class operations. This view was shared by Renold, the first chairman, who resigned all contact with the BIM when the IIA and BIM amalgamated in 1957. All in all, in its first decade the BIM was a divided, even retarded, organization.

For his own part, Urwick attended council meetings several times a year, and made several other contributions. However, no doubt because he was less influential than he would have wished on the key issues noted in the previous paragraph, he was never as enthusiastic about the BIM as he had been for the IIA. Nevertheless, he was chairman of the BIM's education committee (as well as that of the IIA), in which role he was able to set up a scholarship fund in 1950 to select two participants for the one-year programme at Harvard Business School. Even for this prestigious programme, there was difficulty in obtaining suitable candidates due to the unwillingness of companies to release staff. Urwick was also invited to participate in BIM programmes, contributing as early as 1948 Occasional Paper No. 1, *A Short Survey of Industrial Management*, followed in the Winter Proceedings of 1948/9 by an address on *Problems of Growth in Industrial Undertakings.* He also used his role as vice-chairman to argue for a management education delegation to America, as we shall see below.

Although in 1950 Urwick was re-elected to a second term of three years as a member of council, as well as reappointed to his role as vice-chairman, by February 1952 he had resigned from this body. This action was partly prompted by impending trips to the United States, but more importantly it reflected the dismay that he had for some time been expressing about the Institute's inadequate progress; as he reported, 'I can't persuade Russell to listen to those of us who have been in the British management movement since the beginning' (Roper 2001b: 326). There were clearly fundamental philosophical differences between Urwick and the other key members of the BIM hierarchy, leading to a schism that was never fully bridged.

Having noted this point, after his United States trips Urwick was involved in three activities related to the BIM. The first was work on a four-week full-time advanced management study course called 'The Executive Development Programme', on which Urwick provided tutorial input. This programme was conducted four times a year at the BIM's London offices, with an intake limited to twenty-four participants, headed by senior BIM staff, but with tutorial input from selected visiting specialists. Another activity was an obituary tribute at the BIM's annual conference to Benjamin Seebohm Rowntree, whom he cited as 'the father of British management'. A third related to an internal tangle that had been ongoing almost since the Institute's foundation, over whether or not the practice of management amounted to a 'profession', with a strong section of the Council membership inclined towards a negative view. As Urwick was very much inclined to argue in favour of a positive view, he wrote a pamphlet entitled *Is Management a Profession?*, which was published in June 1954 by UOP. This pamphlet was widely reviewed in journals, undoubtedly contributing towards the more positive trend of opinion in institutional and commercial circles that emerged towards the end of that decade. It is also an issue that is taken up in more detail in Chapter 9.

Although in 1956 he was entreated to rejoin the BIM Council by Imrie Swainston (of whom more is discussed later), the continuing battles over the management studies scheme discussed in the previous section resulted in only a short tenure of office. By that time, a joint working party of the BIM and the IIA had evaluated the programme and produced severe criticisms, to which Urwick took exception. This review also led to acrimonious debates within the BIM, where by this time Urwick had numerous enemies such as Russell intriguing against him. The reality by this time was that Urwick had an ongoing personal commitment to a system that was never going to work within the British system, even though it had fulfilled the terms of reference given to the Urwick Committee, and indeed reflected what was a general consensus when proposed a decade earlier. Not surprisingly, very upset by this episode, in 1957 Urwick again resigned. He also wrote a sixty-page analysis of a BIM working party's report on the diploma scheme, arguing that this represented 'a charter for reaction'. Thereafter, even though for five years from 1965 the BIM held a series of lectures in his honour, Urwick rarely had much to do with this body, having decided that it was never going to support his ideas.

A STAFF COLLEGE FOR INDUSTRY

Urwick's ideas for an industry staff college had been germinating for a long time, stretching back to his admiration for the Army Staff College (ASC) in the First World War, whose courses had such a significant impact on personal command and leadership qualities. He first publicly aired his thinking on this topic when invited to give an address in Amsterdam in 1929 on 'Training the Administrator', by including the concept of an industrial staff college in the full military sense. However, the times were not propitious, because within months of his presentation the world was sliding into global economic depression.

It was only after returning to Britain in 1934 that further work on the idea materialized. Urwick had become a regular participant in an informal dining group of some nine or ten Management Research Group (MRG) participants who came together on a weekday evening approximately once a month in a private room at the Reform Club to discuss aspects of administration and management. It was during these lively conversations that the concept of a 'staff college for industry' surfaced from time to time, encouraging Urwick to pursue his objective. As we have already noted in Chapter 5, it was that objective as much as the attraction of the house itself that prompted his purchase of the Farnham Court estate in 1937. Among the frequent participants in the dining group were two men who would play significant roles in pursuit of this goal: Donald Banks, his mentor at the Petroleum Warfare Department, but at that time director of the General Post Office, and H. Imrie Swainston, managing director of the Associated Independent Department Stores Limited.

Urwick seized an opportunity to test public reactions to this idea when invited to address the Oxford Management Conference in April 1939, offering a presentation of the concept in his theme 'The Making of a General Manager'. As he knew that it would in due course become available for wider readership when reproduced in the *British Management Review,* it proved useful in gauging opinion. Inevitably, though, it was swamped by the outbreak of war, as were the informal dining group sessions. Nevertheless, as we noted in Chapter 6, Donald Banks continued to talk to the Chancellor of the Exchequer about such issues, leading to a resumption of Urwick's connections with Imrie Swainston in order to resurrect serious discussion about 'a staff college for industry'. The group then expanded to take in two others, the Reverend Michael Clarke, Headmaster of Urwick's alma mater, Repton School, and John Rodgers, managing director of Britain's leading advertising agency. Early in 1942, a formal group was set up, with Banks presiding, Swainston as honorary secretary, and Rodgers and Urwick as members. The first meeting was held in the Reform Club in March 1942, at which point they decided on an extensive programme to promote the concept across a wide range of influential people.

This decision necessitated two consequential implications: a title for the project and an information document. Urwick undertook to compile a first draft of the latter, while the 'National Administrative Staff College' (NASC) became the agreed title. In the following months, the group met several times, in part to finalize the document and in part to select and agree a list of individuals and organizations to which the document would be circulated. The Urwick archive actually contains repeated typescript drafts of the proposed letter, most of them carrying a considerable amount of amendment, indicating that the group took their responsibilities very seriously.

Once the document was finalized and extensively circulated across their personal networks, it is clear that the early responses were sufficiently positive and encouraging to justify a public declaration in January 1943, the text having been agreed for publication as a printed pocket-size booklet, bearing the agreed name 'NASC'. The contents contained a number of topics, including the origins of the idea; its scope and curriculum; staffing; admission and fees; constitution and finance; canvassing public opinion; and the next step, seeking the cooperation of government departments. Perhaps the most interesting of these issues was the proposed scope, which envisaged students drawn not only from industry, but also areas such as government, the professions, voluntary associations, and trade unions. Another important dimension was the curriculum, which was based not on 'commercial' subjects but on Fayol's six main aspects of administration, namely forecasting, planning, organizing, commanding, coordinating, and controlling.

Discussions also continued about the memorandum and articles of association, again conditioned by numerous redraftings within the group. During the early part of 1943, Lyndall Urwick compiled a revised version of the text for more extensive circulation, while the group extended its membership and adopted the title of 'The Committee for the Administrative Staff College'. At their meeting on 10 February 1943, they recorded that they had discussed from time to time with Sir Donald Banks and Major Urwick 'the possibility that they might respectively be offered and accept the position of President and Principal when the time comes to fill these two positions'. It was carefully recorded that there was no commitment on either side, and indeed as the College was not then in existence nobody could be committed. Nevertheless, the committee noted that they 'would feel bound to bring this minute to the attention of the Court [of Governors] as soon as the question of the appointment of a President and a Principal arose, and to recommend that Sir Donald Banks and Major Urwick should be invited to consider these appointments'.

It was in July 1943 that Geoffrey Heyworth informally attended a meeting of the committee, an event that was to have significant consequences. Heyworth had started working for Lever Brothers Ltd straight from school, as a clerk on 15 shillings a week. By 1941, at the age of 46, he had become chairman of Unilever Ltd, one of the country's largest companies. Heyworth has since been credited with transforming Unilever during his chairmanship; indeed, he was well known for his forward-looking views on management practice, leading the group to secure his services. Before he would accept, however, Heyworth asked for assurances on several matters: that the group was not committed to any particular person as head of the College and that there would be one supreme head of the College responsible to the Court of Governors. The committee resolved to give Heyworth these assurances, and at the same time they rescinded their previous decision to recommend to the Court, when the time came, that Banks and Urwick should be 'invited to consider' appointment as President and Principal, respectively.

Another matter which was then brought into the open was the length of the course. While this had not been made explicit in the group's public statements, it was known that Urwick favoured at least one year. Having been appointed to a financial and legal subcommittee, Heyworth reported back to the following meeting of the full committee that what were described as 'certain ambiguities in the arrangements for the College' would have to be removed, so that a sensible budget could be produced. The full committee then decided on 5 August 1943:

1. to revert to the original plan for the executive direction of the College, that is, there should be one executive head;
2. to plan the first courses for three months only;
3. to plan the first courses for 100 students only, but to bear in mind that the College should be capable of housing up to 200 students; and
4. to plan the tutorial staff on the basis of one staff member to eleven students.

At the next meeting, held on 8 September, Urwick asked that his dissent from the first two of these decisions should be recorded. On the first, Urwick argued that if the Principal was to be made responsible for public relations, he would be unable to devote the necessary attention to developing the entirely new types of teaching and research called for in the College; on the second, he felt that three months were too brief to inculcate the principles of administration and leadership. Later in the meeting, Urwick said he could not see his way to sign the memorandum and articles of association of the College, the formal documents of incorporation which were then in draft form.

That was the last meeting Urwick attended. Shortly afterwards, in reply to a letter from Swainston inviting his continued presence on the committee, Urwick wrote on 11 October 1943 expressing appreciation for the invitation, but nevertheless asking Swainston to accept his disassociation from the group. It was a sad incident, not well handled by the committee, because Urwick (and Banks, who resigned at the same time) had played a major part in developing the staff college idea and in laying the foundations for the establishment of Henley.

In spite of this unfortunate end to Urwick's formal links with the Henley scheme, it is important to note that he did maintain an interest in developments, making an enthusiastic public presentation about it in September 1944 in an address to the Birmingham Centre (Branch) of the IIA. The ASC at Henley was incorporated in October 1945, with Geoffrey Heyworth as chairman of a Court of Governors and with Professor Noel Hall as Principal. The first course, of thirteen weeks full time, commenced on 31 March 1948 because fuel and heating problems had delayed the intended opening five months earlier (Rundle 2006). Urwick continued to maintain his interest and accepted an invitation from Hall to visit the College. It was as a memorial to his involvement in the pioneering group that UOP donated all his personal and public papers and documents to the College archives. Staff colleges of a similar kind were also set up in various other counties, including Australia, New Zealand, India, Pakistan, the West Indies, and East Africa, testimony to the concept that Urwick was among the first to identify.

AACP

Urwick's links with the United States proved to be extensive in the 1950s, starting with his AACP mission. This body had been set up by the Board of Trade to improve British productivity, by sending teams to the United States to examine and be instructed in American systems, to bring back American best practice, and thereafter to disseminate this throughout British industry. The British section of the AACP was composed of representatives of employers' organizations and trade unions, with forty-seven industry teams and twenty-one specialist teams visiting the United States. Although the BIM was not involved directly in these missions, Urwick used his role as a vice-chairman to persuade the Board of Trade to set up a management education team, which he led, composed of thirteen members, in addition to its leader, as well as an official secretary (Figure 7.2).

From late 1950, Urwick used his extensive network of American contacts to plan a six-week schedule of visits and discussions, with return travel by sea adding a further two weeks. The team set off in mid-April, using the voyage to turn the scheduled programme into a time-tabled action plan for each member. To prevent possible difficulties arising from terminological differences, the team agreed to use only the single umbrella title of 'Administrative Studies' and to concentrate on the use of college and institutional

Figure 7.2 Education for Management—The Anglo-American Council on Productivity group, 1951. (Urwick is third from the right).

managerial educational facilities. As a consequence, twenty-nine university colleges and educational institutions were visited, as well as sixty-six corporations and firms, each of which was interviewed by one or two team members. The team review was completed before mid-June, the return voyage being devoted to preparation of the report.

The team's report (of eighty-six pages) was published by Her Majesty's Stationery Office (HMSO) in November 1951, covering twenty-plus pages of text and some sixty pages of appendices. Its key points were:

1. The close connection between productivity, management, and education.

2. The integration of theory and practice.

3. The volume of higher education. (In 1950, over two million American students were receiving a university education, with 617 institutions offering degree courses in business and commerce. More first degrees were granted in these subjects than in any other.)

4. The 'graduate' business schools were also winning increasing support. (They usually required two years of full-time study, on top of the four years for a first degree.)

5. Professional qualifications. (A great deal of the instruction organized by professional bodies in Britain was undertaken by universities in the United States)

6. High-quality teaching in which staff were encouraged to do part-time work in business.

7. A large volume of part-time studies.

8. Close liaison between business and the universities.

9. Widespread executive development in both organizations and universities.

10. The prestige of business encouraged many of the best students to choose business as a career.

11. An emphasis on human relations.

12. The whole development of administrative studies in the United States was dynamic. (The team believed that it was essential that arrangements should be made to maintain continuous contact between those concerned with the subject in the two countries.)

The report devoted little space to the state of administrative studies in Britain, beyond stating a few facts which were common knowledge. As no comprehensive study of what was being done to teach administrative studies in universities and technical colleges in Britain had been compiled, the team requested that such a study should be undertaken as a matter of urgency. Nevertheless, in view of these findings, they wished to draw the attention of British industry and education authorities to their key conclusion:

We have not attempted to review corresponding developments in this country or to make definite recommendations as to whether the American example should be followed and if so in what respects. We believe, however, that American experience has shown that productivity and education for management are closely related. The subject is of such vital importance to Britain that industry as a whole should study means for promoting education experiments for executive development; individual firms should review their training programmes in the light of American experience, and education authorities should consider how they can best encourage and develop administrative studies.

The impact of the AACP was not as great as had been hoped by its originators (Tiratsoo 2004), largely because the traditional reluctance of British managers to consider anything outside their immediate environs. The most important follow-up publication was Graham Hutton's *We Too Can Prosper* (1953), published for the British Productivity Council, which grew out of the AACP. The book was 'about the implications for Britain today of the sixty-six AACP Teams' experiences in comparing British and American industrial efficiency' (Hutton 1953: 7), focusing on 'the promise of productivity'. It focused especially on the role of management in the United States, which had been a common thread running through almost all of the reports. Although Hutton did quote Urwick's committee report on the close relation-ship between productivity and management education (Hutton 1953: 44), the book mainly focused on the direct issues leading to higher productivity, such as a better division of labour, improved planning and decision-making, more cost-consciousness, effective use of technology, greater concentration on quality and design, and the like, rather than the longer-term focus required by management education. When longer-term issues were taken into account, they mainly related to attitudes, such as the internal and external acceptance of management, its professional status, and the willing-ness to change, with which Urwick would have been fully in agreement. When discussing ways to improve management, Hutton felt that the most important were the shortages of instructors and the obstacles that were 'largely matters of organization', in terms of 'the appropriate arrangements for time off, shifts, etc' (Hutton 1953: 121). This narrow focus was hardly what the 'Education for Management' team would have wanted. On the other hand, while the exercise seems to have given many of those who participated something of an inferiority complex, Kipping (1997) notes that when a group of German Reichsausschuss fur Arbeitszeitermittlung (REFA) engineers visited the United States at much the same time they were not impressed and pointed to the lack of uniformity of work study in America compared to Germany.

Overall, as Clark (1999) argues, the AACP was a failure, with the British section more concerned with quantity of production for relatively short-term economic ends, while the American section had its own political goals. Whatever the case, nothing emerged with specific regard to management education, while the British Productivity Council, as the British section became, focused on local associations, rather than lobbying for institutional change. Clark (1999: 65–6) also argues that 'representatives of employers and management within the British section played a significant role in sustaining embedded patterns of management practice.... The AACP was a failure because the American section could not successfully position its arguments and findings in the British section'. In effect, the British side fought 'to sustain unscientific management' (Clark 1999: 77), and that 'improvement in training and development was not forthcoming because existing production systems did not require this' (Clark 1999: 81). In such a context, Urwick's arguments were never going to succeed in persuading anybody of the need for change.

THE FME AND UNIVERSITY-BASED MANAGEMENT EDUCATION

An additional aspect of the management development scene which needs to be recognized was the move towards involving universities in management education, with the FME playing a lead role in lobbying government and orchestrating university interest. Ultimately, this led to a reluctant acquiescence in the need for management education by the Robbins Committee (1963) and the establishment of the Franks Committee (1963) that fashioned the London and Manchester business schools formed in 1965. The FME's founding father was John Bolton, a Harvard MBA who had made a considerable amount of money by selling his electronics firm, Solartron. He used some of his wealth to pursue his interest in management education, specifically by pump-priming the FME. He and Urwick, of course, knew each other, having exchanged correspondence on mutually held views concerning the need to change British attitudes towards management education.

A question emerges, of course, as to why Urwick was not more directly involved in creating the FME, especially as he had been one of the principal advocates of change in this respect. It might be that he felt too old to involve himself in yet another institutional development; it may also be that he was too close to moving to Australia (in 1961), since the FME only held its first formal meeting in that year. Another factor could have been that in the late 1950s, he was fighting to preserve the BIM model. Nevertheless, it was something of a paradox that this path turned out to be the most influential agent of change in the longer run. Indeed, it was largely pressure from the FME which led to the momentous Franks Report, while the FME created an offshoot, the Council of Industry for Management Education (CIME), to raise money for the first generation of business schools.

While Urwick would have been delighted at the creation of these business schools, his argument had always been that Oxbridge set the tone of Britain's intellectual life. Indeed, he felt that 'as long as they refuse to provide a course of studies leading to a degree, squarely based on the vocational requirements of those contemplating a business career, so long will management studies be regarded as academically dubious, a little "below the salt"'. A second dimension of his views about university-based management education was that 'schools of management and particularly graduate schools of management for students already engaged in business should be administered by business-men *not* by academics'. In addition, he would not have been enthusiastic about what he called 'the insidious temptation to glorify research' at the expense of teaching which he identified even during his life, a feature of twenty-first-century business schools of which he would have been highly critical.

CONCLUSIONS

These episodes in the development of management were all logical possibilities in the context of the contemporary British situation, encapsulating a vision of the future that could have been realized. To Urwick's considerable regret, however, none of those activities with which he was directly linked was ever converted into direct results. Perhaps his hopes were too ambitious. In the case of the management awards scheme, for instance, he should arguably have been prepared to cut his losses and move to a different model; similarly, in the case of the ASC, although he was right about the long run, in the short run Heyworth's view was the best that could be expected from industry. As to whether the BIM could have been more effective, that depended to a large extent on personalities, and Urwick must take some of the blame for putting the wrong people in key positions. On the other hand, the context within which these schemes were enacted must have contributed to the outcomes, in that the anti-intellectualism in most of British industry limited the impact of Urwick's ideas. While in the United States and European countries such as Germany and France there was an extremely active market in management ideas, this had yet to emerge in Britain. In simple terms, Britain lacked a power base on which to launch ambitious management development institutions, a factor that seems likely to have contributed to Urwick's decision to emigrate to Australia.

8

A Mission at Large

While the phrase 'a mission at large' sounds like an extrapolation based on Urwick's extensive activities, it was actually of his own making to describe the work he did outside his consultancy duties and institutional commitments to take the message of management to a wider audience of managers, students, and indeed the general public. As we shall see, this involved a large number of speaking commitments covering a wide range of topics, many of which were published as articles, consolidating his role as the leading management speaker and writer of the period. What did Urwick mean by the 'mission at large'? For more than a century preceding the outbreak of the Second World War in September 1939, the prevailing ethos in Britain amongst managers and the public regarded managerial competence to be essentially an inborn skill derived from a combination of personal qualities, characteristics, and attitudes (Wilson and Thomson 2006). If a man had those within his make-up, he would succeed in business management: if he did not have them, successful performance would not be possible. The basic tenet that 'managers are born, not made' derived in part from the preponderance of small- or medium-scale businesses, rendering the process and practice of managerial responsibility relatively simple. The prevailing notions of class and genetic inheritance were also important contributory factors in this debate. A first breach in this belief came with the exigencies of war supply in the 1914–18 conflict, and while in the interwar era there was relatively little further modification, the Second World War acted as a substantial additional catalyst for change, resulting in an increasing recognition that knowledge, know-how, education and training, and a more systematic approach could add to managerial competence. It was to the promotion of this viewpoint that Urwick's mission was directed, and for all the momentum that was developing, there was still, as we have already seen in the Chapter 7, a great deal of work to be done, and not just in Britain, but around the world.

THE MISSION IN BRITAIN UP TO EMIGRATION

During the post-war period up to his emigration to Australia in 1961, it could well be argued that Urwick's public educational contributions held pride of place in his personal agenda. Even when he was still acting as managing director of Urwick Orr and Partners (UOP), since he knew that the operational management was in competent hands, he was more than willing to make the time and effort required for numerous addresses, lectures, and for writing articles, not least because they also gave him considerable personal pleasure. In the immediate post-war years to 1951, Urwick gave something like 120 public lectures, the majority of which were to professional institutions, trade associations, or educational bodies. One particularly important event was a lecture at the Birmingham Central Technical College, not least because it marked the inauguration there of a Department of Industrial Administration. Urwick's lecture, entitled 'The Scope of Management' and subsequently reproduced as a booklet, was also used again in 1950 at the College, when he was invited to provide a series of five lectures twice daily within a single week: once during the day for some 150 industrial and commercial directors and managers, and in the evenings to the part-time students attending courses in Management Studies. Again, a booklet was produced, this time with a preface by the head of the College which noted: 'Down the years there will be many Birmingham men – and men who have sojourned here – who will be able to say, "Yes, I heard Urwick – it was in 1950".' He was also at times invited to give a lecture to the students and staff in the Management Studies departments of various senior technical colleges which were keen to know more about the new national programme of which he had been the inspiration as chairman of the Education Departmental Committee.

After his retirement as managing director of UOP in 1951, he continued in much the same vein in the following decade, although with a considerably higher proportion of his activities conducted abroad (to be dealt with later in this chapter). In fact, between April 1952 and February 1954 he gave no talks at all in Britain, while over the following decades there were other long gaps in his home-country mission. Nevertheless, there was little if any slackening of the overall workload as he approached 70, while the versatility of his coverage if anything increased, reflecting the growing interest in the various dimensions of management.

Invited lectures continued to be the main bulk of his activities, many of which were followed by publication of the text in related journals. The topics on which he talked were extremely varied, although as one might expect they reflected both his interests and activities at a particular point in time. Thus, following his surveys in America incorporated in the Anglo-American Council on Productivity (AACP) and American Management Association (AMA) reports, there was a great deal of interest in hearing more about American management education. Amongst others, he addressed: the National Institute of Industrial Psychology (March 1952), the Royal Institute of Public Administration (twice in 1954), the Sheffield Chamber of Commerce, the American Chamber of Commerce in London (twice in 1954), Manchester University College of Technology, and the Institute of Public Relations. His principal message in these talks was always that professional education can play a major role in the development of managerial competence, illustrating how he never missed an opportunity to publicize his 'mission at large'. In addition, other themes such as leadership, the managerial span of control, and management as a profession were subjects of his lectures and publications to specific companies, nationalized industries, professional institutes, and trade bodies. He also did several talks for the BBC, mostly on radio. One of these, which he must have particularly enjoyed, was about Seebohm Rowntree's life and pioneering contributions to managerial advancement. In November 1955, he also gave a televised press interview about the objectives, practices, and the profession of management.

Beyond the talks he was, of course, continuing to write. As well as the principal publications that will be reviewed in Chapter 9, there were many minor works, including articles, book reviews, forewords, and the like, many of which were also published by the sponsoring organization. Magazines such as *Business* or *The Manager* also commissioned him to provide articles. While most of these were on his main subject areas, sometimes he wrote on topics such as 'Business Organization and Public Relations' or 'Urwick v Oxford', or 'Tomorrow Begins Today'. One of the most widely read, and demonstrating Urwick's versatility, was a feature article for *The Economist* on aspects of general management practice, entitled 'Minding Other People's Business'.

A somewhat unusual piece in February 1955 was an article in a French industrial journal and written in French on aspects of Henri Fayol's ideas and attitudes. It was also in 1955 that he wrote a major article in *The Times Review of Industry* which argued the need for British industry to adopt a much more professional approach to management. He could also write rapidly, for example in February 1958 when he produced four articles in one month. June 1958 saw an article entitled 'Behind the Charts: Men and Methods', published first in the journal *International Management Digest*, which was replicated in the journals of both the Irish and the Indian management institutes. This was not uncommon; indeed, a lot of his articles were republished in foreign journals. He also wrote various articles or booklets which were published by UOP, notably 'Is Management a Profession', which is further reviewed in Chapter 9. Another unusual request came from the George Cohen 600 Group in 1961 for a light-hearted article on management, resulting in an article entitled 'Are Managers Gentlemen?' Drawing from the long-standing British cricket convention of 'Gentlemen versus Players', he used the analogy to bring to the fore the widely prevailing cult of 'the amateur' in Britain, an institutional rigidity he felt ought to be completely eliminated from the business scene.

In addition, there were other modes of expression, for example, through a number of book reviews. In 1955, he did a long review of Peter Drucker's new book *The Practice of Management* for *The Times Review of Industry*, which he praised highly. Later in the year, he reviewed it again for the Industrial Welfare Society's journal. He was much less complimentary about *The Boss: The Life and Times of British Businessmen* by Lewis and Stewart, which he felt was not a serious contribution to management studies because of its cynical tone. In 1958, he reviewed Joan Woodward's book on *Management and Technology*, commending it for the many valuable findings that could be used when teaching management studies. Early in 1959, he had a request from the *Financial Times* for reviews of two recent publications: *Management in Britain*, the report of a research survey by the University of Liverpool; and *Promotion and Pay for Executives* by G. Copeman. At the end of that year, he also reviewed G. E. Milward's book on *Organisation and Methods* for the British journal *Engineering*, with the unusual title of 'Quiet Flows the Office'. While that book was a pioneering masterpiece in its field, there was an added pleasure in reviewing it because of his long-standing personal friendship with the author.

Forewords to books were another vehicle to publicize his ideas. In 1955, he contributed one to a book entitled *Teaching Management* by H. Newman and D. M. Sidney, while in 1957 he did three: Cleghorn Thomson's *Management, Labour and Community*, Arthur Roberts's *Management Notebook*, and Seymour Melman's *Decision-Making and Productivity*. Writing for newspapers also kept him busy. For example, in 1956 he offered 'What Makes a Manager?' to *The Economist*, in 1958 he wrote to the *Financial Times* on 'The Boss', in reaction to a contributed feature article, while in the same year he contributed to the *Journal of Westminster Chamber of Commerce* on an objective appraisal of professional management consultant services derived from his experiences at UOP.

Given this workload, one might well ask how he could be so productive at an age when most people had retired. Two answers come to mind: firstly, he was often able to choose his own topic; and secondly, even if the title was different or unique, the content was often similar to previous talks. His habit was customarily to draft a new text for each presentation, whilst frequently

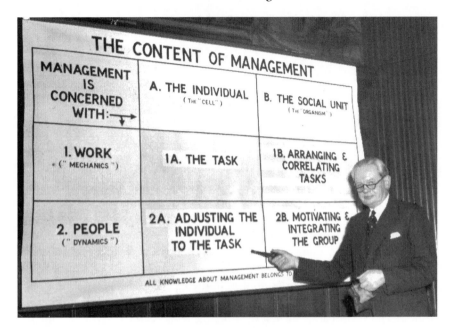

Figure 8.1 Urwick lecturing in front of one of his charts.

absorbing into the later draft passages from earlier versions, thereby economizing on effort (Figure 8.1).

In addition to these activities, there were also quite different types of commitments, such as his seventieth-birthday tribute lunch in April 1961, attended by some 200 people, most of them the great and the good of British industry. (Interestingly, however, judging from the titles on the attendance list, only one was a professor, reflecting his poor relations with academia.) This event was arguably the high-water mark of his recognition in Britain. Another occasion was to propose the Civic Toast to the Lord Mayor and the Corporation of the City of London at the formal dinner in October 1961, as a member and past master of the Worshipful Company of Glovers.

This period ended with Urwick and his wife emigrating to Australia. As Betty had family connections in Australia, this seemed like a conducive place to retire. They established a home in Longueville, Sydney, where with a touch of nostalgia, they took the house name 'Poyntington' with them from the Dorset village where they had lived for many years. The Dorset 'Poyntington' was a substantial old manor house with ten main rooms, where Raleigh had allegedly stayed the night before his last journey to the Tower. While there, apart from his management activities, Urwick had done a good deal of research into some of the local great houses such as Longleat, Clevedon, and Fairleigh, pursuing his considerable interest in genealogy. He was never idle for long.

BRITAIN AFTER EMIGRATION

After emigrating to Australia, although nominally this represented a move into retirement, until the mid-1970s Urwick still made two trips a year to Britain, in the spring and autumn. Although predominantly to see family and friends, as well as addressing UOP events, Urwick never neglected his 'mission' activities on these trips. For example, he wrote a memorial to Seebohm Rowntree for *The Manager* in February 1962, entitled 'The Father of British Management', in which he again paid homage to the progressive role his mentor had played in Britain's evolution of effective managerial practice. He also added a personal touch by offering a warm tribute of gratitude for the start and support provided to him in the 1920s. Another article that year was in the October issue of *The Times Engineering Supplement* on 'Work-Study from the Start', probably the first time that he had ever written on this subject. There were actually only two 'mission' talks that year, and only one in 1963, apart from the particular pleasure of addressing the jubilee conference celebrating the fiftieth anniversary of the Institute of Personnel Management, founded in York out of Rowntree's in 1913. Typical of Urwick's quixotic tinge, the address was given with the quizzical title 'You Can't Always Be Nice to People'.

Thereafter, formal engagements tapered off, with only one each in 1964 and 1965. In 1966, there were three public lectures, including one to an international conference of management consultants in London, an unusual event for Britain. In 1967 and 1968, no public lectures at all were given, indicating how his absence from Britain meant that he was rarely in the public eye. In 1969, his customary spring visit was concerned with UOP activities, although he did write 'A Plea for Semantic Sanity' for the Shell in-house journal. During his second visit to Britain that year, he accepted an invitation to address the staff and students of the University of Aston's management studies department, reviewing the current embryonic stage of progress in British management education. He was also awarded an honorary DSc for his contribution to management. Over the next four years, he gave further lectures at Aston on management pioneers. Interestingly, his DSc was his first and only academic award from a British university, while he was never even invited to visit the two leading business schools in London and Manchester. Other than his Aston lectures, in 1973, he gave only two external lectures and wrote just two articles, one of them for the *Journal of Imperial*

College, using an esoteric title 'Semantic Hay' and concentrating his attention exclusively on the word 'organization'; it is clear that semantics had become something of an obsession in Urwick's later years.

In the early months of 1974, he was laid low with a long-lasting bout of pneumonia that left him seriously weakened for several months, necessitating the abandonment of his customary visits to Britain. He resumed his trips in the autumn of 1975, when he was entertained as a guest of honour at a dinner for members of the British Institute of Management (BIM), gracing the occasion with an inspirational after-dinner speech. In the spring of 1976, he made his last trip to Britain, the highlight of which was a dinner arranged by a large number of 'old boys' from UOP to celebrate his eighty-fifth birthday.

NORTH AMERICA

As we have seen in previous chapters, Urwick had excellent links with North America from the 1920s, on which he built extensively for his mission activities. Indeed, by far the majority of Urwick's foreign trips were to the United States, with him spending almost two years there between 1951 and 1961 in a series of visits. Even before he retired from the managing director-ship of UOP, he was well known in America through his work at the International Management Institute (IMI), the path-breaking book with Gulick (amongst other writings), continuing contacts with International Committee for Scientific Management (CIOS), and enduring friendships with many Americans. Moreover, both when he led the British AACP team on management education and then headed the AMA survey, it is no surprise that there were plenty of places in North America that were only too happy to invite him for a visit, especially as he presented his views in a forceful and ebullient style that appealed to Americans. After his emigration to Australia, he understand-ably made far fewer trips there – indeed, only four in total. Nevertheless, he was still sufficiently well known to be asked to write an obituary of Lilian Gilbreth, receive a fellowship from the American Academy of Management, and be involved in the second edition of *The Golden Book of Management*, all when he was in his eighties.

Although we have already dealt with his major visit to America as leader of the AACP management education team (see Chapter 7), something even more substantial arose from his knowledge of the American scene. In 1951, with financial support from the Ford Foundation, the American Fund for Adult Education had proposed to the Council of the AMA 'a survey of the nature and extent of educational activities within American business'.

The Council accepted this proposal, adding that they would like Lyndall Urwick to head the project. Urwick must have realized and relished the high compliment being paid to him in being invited, though a Briton, to conduct a major survey in the United States. Preparations were started in February 1952 through correspondence with the three commissioning parties, resulting in the formulation of an agenda based on five questions:

1. What are companies doing to contribute to internal improvement of managerial practices and competence?
2. What is the nature and extent of external facilities used in connection with the foregoing item?
3. What are companies doing to encourage non-supervisory grades to participate more fully in the life and progress of their employer company as well as within the community within which it is set?
4. What results have been accruing from the activities conducted within the foregoing three items and what impacts have those activities had on the individual executives and supervisors?
5. What assessment would be made of the overall result accruing from the foregoing activities and what has been their significance?

Four ways of obtaining the requisite information were devised:

- A postal questionnaire sent to 6,710 enterprises, of which just over 2,000 replied.
- Some thirty area discussion groups covering 253 people occupied with the internal consultative review process.
- A further 120 individuals fed in individual contributions.
- For the 'management development' aspect, there were internal case studies with thirteen corporations involving active participation from forty-nine persons.

To provide administrative support, Urwick brought over his British personal assistant from UOP, R. G. Simpson, who remained at the committee's disposal for several months. The whole complex project had been initiated by the early summer of 1952, Urwick himself having masterminded the whole set-up, following which he undertook four study visits ranging between one and four months each between February 1952 and July 1953.

The findings were published by the Association in February 1954, composed of four parts, of which Urwick himself wrote the first. The text of Part I ran to 136 pages, with seven chapters:

i. Historical Background
ii. Operation Stopgap

iii. The Profile of an Executive
iv. Operation Future: The Intellectual Factor
v. Operation Future: The Problem of Recruitment
vi. Operation Future: The Practical Factor
vii. Conclusion

Urwick worked on the drafting of his own contribution back in Britain during the late summer of 1953. The historical first chapter was especially long, tracing the development of managerial practice and education in America over the previous century. In chapter ii, despite its strange title, Lyndall Urwick turned to his favoured topic of management development, in part to foreshadow the findings set out in later chapters. Chapter iii, 'The Profile of an Executive', was a remarkable contribution, much of it serving to underlie development practice. Chapters iv, v, and vi conveyed the findings and outcome from the full spread of the project, even though there were three supplementary reports from other authors. From Urwick's own personal standpoint, however, undoubtedly the most significant section was the thirteen-page 'Conclusion' that rounded off his 'General Summary'. In the course of the project, and especially in the context of management development, he had come to recognize that its outcome had a relevance reaching well beyond the United States. He saw the conclusion as the gospel embodying his 'mission at large', displaying and illustrating his ideas on the effective exercise of managerial responsibility in all countries, as well as the benefits to be gained for both companies and the wider community.

Arising from this project, another major visit to the United States took place in 1957. As the report had attracted considerable attention beyond the confines of the AMA, a punishing fourteen-week lecturing schedule was arranged for Urwick. The venues, thirty-two in all, included several smaller cities such as Amarillo, Charlottesville, Knoxville, Madison, San Bernardino, and Schenectady. The programme in effect put Britain's management expert on public parade, combining lessons in management with Urwick's highly entertaining way of lecturing. Urwick took his 30-year-old daughter along to serve as combined secretary, logistics manager, and chauffeuse, having elected to travel by car in the interests of flexibility and informality for something like half of the 22,000 miles covered. As the programme was based on informal objectives, he did not prepare set texts for the sessions, though he did actually give some fifty addresses extempore from notes. There were, however, a few more formal occasions slotted in for which he had pre-prepared texts. During the visits, he also responded to local corporate invitations to address managers in-house, including such prestigious names as General Electric, Monsanto, Hughes Aircraft, and AT&T. It was a major tour.

Other invitations can be split into several categories. First, there were university visiting professorships of several months, such as those in Toronto (1951), Minnesota (1955), and Los Angeles (1959). Each of these visits was also associated with invitations to give institutional addresses on aspects of management. For example, while based in Toronto, Urwick gave four talks in Canada and three in the United States; a somewhat similar set of activities was replicated during the other visiting professorships.

Another category of activities was those connected with professional institutions, and especially the AMA, an institution in which he became extremely well known. When visiting the United States, Urwick had usually been invited to lecture on the Association's series of general management courses for senior managers, mostly with special reference to organization structures and managerial delegation. In connection with these lectures, two booklets were published: in April 1952, *Notes on the Theory of Organisation*; and in June 1953, *Profitably Using the General Staff Position in Business.* The American engineering institutions also invited him to speak, something which was never replicated in Britain. Moreover, they were happy to hear him talk about subjects well beyond engineering. For example, in 1960 he addressed a joint meeting of the local chapters of the American Society of Mechanical Engineers and the American Institution of Electrical Engineering in Seattle, taking the unusual theme 'Leadership: The Need for Simplification'. He was also invited to contribute a chapter on 'The Philosophy of Management' for a compendium publication produced by the Mechanical Engineers Society. On a reduced scale, he also lectured on that subject to members of the Society's chapter in New York, followed by a second address on 'The Engineer's Debt to Management'. Finally, he addressed the Canadian Engineering Institution, selecting as his title the curious wording 'Management: Horse-Trading or Trusteeship?'

A further type of activity was the single event or short series, of which there were several, usually as a result of an invitation from a university. Thus, in April–May 1958, he spent six weeks in the United States and Canada fulfilling formal lectures, initially in Toronto, then in Los Angeles. He also responded positively to requests for informal educational visits with institutions where he was already well known. For example, he gave seminar–discussion sessions at the universities of Chicago, Western Ontario, and Toronto, as well as spending time with the Canadian subsidiary of UOP, Urwick Currie Limited. He then travelled to Boston for a talk to the Chamber of Commerce, followed by New York to address the Methods–Time–Motion Consortium, moving on to North-Western University in Chicago to lecture. Before leaving North America that year, he gave a final lecture on 'Evaluating the Policy-making Function' at one of General Electric's New York offices. He found time in the meanwhile to write an article for a Canadian magazine on a theme not previously found in his repertoire, 'Why Cannot Industry Learn from Experience?' All these added up to a huge commitment over six weeks.

After Urwick had moved to Australia, he made fewer visits to North America, mainly because Britain became the main focus of his travelling. In fact, he only made a further four trips to North America: in 1963, 1967, 1968, and 1973. Two of the visits were for special reasons, most notably in 1963, when he was invited to speak at the fiftieth anniversary celebrations of the foundation of the Taylor Society, by then called the Society for the Advancement of Management (Figure 8.2). As Taylor had been such a major influence on Urwick, he was extremely pleased to be involved in this event, taking as his main theme 'Management's Second Half-Century'. The 1973 visit was to be elected as a fellow of the American Academy of Management (AAM), an occasion described in more detail on pages 173–4. Of the other visits, the main focus in 1967 was the University of York (Toronto), where he gave a series of seven lectures covering many of his favourite topics, such as management semantics, line and staff, and leadership, while that in 1968 was also to lecture in Canada.

Figure 8.2 The Golden Anniversary of the Society for the Advancement of Management, 1963. (Urwick is on the far right).

Although he was rarely in North America after 1961, this did not stop him writing a plethora of articles for US journals, some of which proved to be extremely important. Typically, they covered a wide range of topics, usually on big general subjects. Some of the more important articles were for the *Journal of the American Management Association*: in 1962, he wrote on a theme unusual for Urwick, 'The Board of Directors. An Asset or an Anachronism?'; in 1963, his subject was 'Management in Perspective: the Tactics of Jungle Warfare'; and in 1965, he provided a memorial tribute to Sir Winston Churchill, entitled 'The Greatest Manager of Our Time'. A 1967 article, under the curious title 'Organisation and Theories About the Nature of Man', was published in the same *Journal*, prompted by a contemporary critique of the attitudes and behaviour of directors and managers in 'big business'. While not disputing the views expressed, Urwick chose to respond by citing the numerous management practitioners and writers who for many decades had portrayed the essential honesty and social purpose inherent in the concept and practice of management. As Urwick argued, the true objective of 'business and enterprise' had always lain in providing for the livelihood and standard of living of the community, the financial benefit to the entrepreneurs stemming from fulfilling that objective competently and effectively. It was a seminal expression of what has come to be regarded as a stakeholder, rather than shareholder, view of the firm, putting Urwick at the epicentre of a raging debate across American business and society.

Other significant articles he published in American journals included 'Management and the American Dream', for *Advanced Management* in April 1966, a topic which illustrated his status as an honorary American. In the following year, he wrote an article for the *Journal of the University of Michigan* on 'What Have the Universities Done for Business Management?'. While Urwick would have been highly critical of British institutions, he was positive about the contributions of American universities, reflecting his greater empathy with a system that proved much more conducive to the acceptance of his ideas.

The high-water mark of his writing during this period came in 1969–70, when he wrote nine articles or chapters of books for American audiences, an output which would put modern management academics to shame. Two of them worthy of particular note were 'Are the Classics Really Out of Date? A Plea for Semantic Sanity' for *Advanced Management*, and for the same journal, 'Lines to a Newly-Installed Computer', demonstrating that he was familiar with new technology. At the turn of 1969–70, he also wrote a lengthy tribute to Peter Drucker in a memorial book compiled by the University of York Press, describing him as 'the managers' professor'. Urwick especially highlighted the way in which Drucker consistently emphasized the contributions made by his predecessors in the development of management, an approach he regarded as all the more valuable because it was becoming fashionable to denigrate pioneers.

Another important article in January 1970 for *Advanced Management* carried the seemingly esoteric title of 'Theory Z'. For an American readership, however, it would have been readily understood as a commentary on the juxtaposition of 'Theory X and Theory Y' that had been actively discussed since its publication by Douglas McGregor in 1960. While Urwick recognized both facets as significant, he argued that the 'commercial objective (Theory X)' could be effectively attained only if the 'human side (Theory Y)' had been thoroughly embedded, a view that had been intrinsic to his own 'Theory Z'. In March, a further article for the *American SAM Journal* also carried an esoteric title, 'Paper Tigers'. Drawing upon illustrations from his managerial experience and as a Staff Captain in the First World War, he reviewed the handling of paperwork involved in managerial activity. The substance of the article was 'taming the tiger', or reducing red tape, while ensuring that managerial responsibility was suitably supported by appropriate information.

In July 1970, he completed a long chapter on 'The Span of Control', a particular interest of his since the IMI, for a major collection organized by the University of Miami. As was his custom, he began by providing a historical setting, identifying the first presentation of these ideas in the book *The Soul and Body of an Army* by General Sir Ian Hamilton (1921). He paralleled this book with the American industrial contribution from an April 1922 article in the *Bulletin of the Taylor Society*. He also cited the Graicunas 'limitation' feature, showing that no one had yet proven the reasoning invalid. Yet another special article in 1970 was for the *AMA Journal*, 'Papers in the Science of Administration', replicating the title of his 1937 book edited with Luther Gulick. This article indicated that 'a number of persons of some authority in the field of management within the United States have been very kind enough recently to warrant that 1937 publication as a landmark in the development of thought about management'. He went on to recall how that early volume had come to be compiled, arguing that it was not only unique for the 1930s, but also way ahead of its time, having a strong resonance even in 1970, judging from recent publications.

The scope and intellectual significance of these publications were quite remarkable for someone in his late seventies. In May 1971, by now aged 80, he also published an article reviewing the contemporary management education and training scene, written for and published in the *Journal of the American Society of Mechanical Engineers*. This was followed a year later by an obituary of an old friend, Lillian Gilbreth, as well as a broad survey of management, both for the *AMA Journal*. It is especially interesting that the leading American management journal asked Urwick to write these pieces, reflecting the status he had achieved in a country that prided itself on the many contributions it had made to management development and education.

INDIA

In 1955, Urwick was invited by the Indian Government to undertake a tour giving advice on five topics for which help was particularly needed, a commitment he eventually undertook in February–March 1956. The five issues were:

1. An overall national policy and programme for the provision of systematic management studies, similar to the one inaugurated in Britain in 1947 as the outcome from the Urwick Departmental Committee;

2. The formulation and inauguration of a national 'Institute of Management', its role and structure having to take account of the immense distances separating India's major cities and industrial centres;

3. Proposals for a central Administrative Staff College (ASC);

4. Advice on the recently established Organization and Methods Division within the Department of Home Affairs;

5. Similarly, advice on the recently inaugurated professional Institute of Public Administration.

Beyond the named tasks lay a range of invitations to lecture and attend conferences, as well as some press conferences. The subject matter for the programme of formal addresses generally lay within the range that Urwick had established during the previous decade for his own educational contributions. In all, there were twenty-three formal events scheduled between 13 February and 15 March, in addition to several informal events. These informal meetings often contributed towards the educational nature of the visit, because Urwick was frequently asked to give a short talk, either of his own choice or arising from a suggestion by the member presiding over the meeting, leading to an open discussion. In such instances, Urwick used neither text nor record, given his total grasp of his subject matter.

As extensive as Urwick's institutional programme of formal and informal events in India was, they were far from being the full story of his activities. Fulfilling the requirements of giving advice in respect of the five tasks necessitated a considerable amount of personal investigation and consultation. The fourth and fifth tasks were especially specific, each requiring a few days of preliminary investigation, supplemented by discussions with committee members, officials, and a cross section of institutional members, either for clarification or to test out ideas on possible recommendations. In the case of the fifth task, these consultations included committee members and officials in the major cities where the Institute already had established branches. Task three (the staff college proposal) required more selective identification of people and institutions for consultation, although the prior contact of certain individuals with Henley helped a great deal. On the national institute of management, there had already been some consideration of the concept by an internal planning committee, resulting in a proposal for an All-India Council of Management, with the central focus in Delhi, and regional associations based in a major city organized by a locally elected governing council and honorary officers. Urwick agreed with this proposal, arranging for the BIM to provide further advisory assistance.

Understandably, the national programme for management studies called for the heaviest input of personal and group consultative discussion. For Urwick to provide information as to the fuller scope of 'management knowledge', he was able to supply the full programme set out in his 1947 Report. However, the niceties of the mission called for extensive consultation. The obvious starting points were the Institute of Management in Delhi and the local university's business administration department, following which he talked to the All-India Manufacturers Association, creating a pattern for replication within all of the eleven cities that formed the consultative programme. There were, though, almost universally additional local requests for consultative sessions arising from Urwick's known presence in the city concerned, frequently creating the occasion for the informal events cited earlier. To all these would undoubtedly be added social events, a welcoming reception, a formal dinner, or a festive lunch, giving Urwick little time for sightseeing or relaxation.

His final report was compiled for the two ministries, which immediately circulated the document widely. A typescript of eighteen pages, plus two appendices, in some respects it was a strange document because it did not record findings and recommendations as an outcome of the mission in the conventional mode. Instead, Urwick used the final report for educational objectives. An encouraging finding was the widely prevailing interest in, and enthusiasm for, management. On the other hand, the document is curious in other respects, because there is an oddly apologetic tone to the early paragraphs, emphasizing that the recorded views in the document are no stronger than 'impressions' gained from such an extensive programme of visits and meetings. This was most un-Urwick-like, in that all of his other reports contained specific recommendations based on committed views.

In fact, although no longer available in his personal archive, it is known that Urwick did submit specific recommendations on each of the five tasks to the appropriate organizations. Many of his lectures were also reproduced in local or national journals, precipitating an avalanche of personal letters of appreciation from those who had met and talked to him. One of these letters informed him that the Indian Council of Management Associations had been inaugurated in accordance with his recommendation. Indeed, overall the programme could be considered a considerable success, further strengthening his international reputation.

AUSTRALIA

Before emigrating to Australia, he had visited that country in 1960 to address the opening session of the CIOS Congress in Melbourne, following which he travelled to New Zealand. Arising from this visit, he was also invited to return in February 1961 to give a series of addresses to the Australian Institute of Management, when he decided on Australia as a suitable base from which to continue the active pursuit of his educational and promotional 'mission at large'. Why did Urwick emigrate? He was after all 70 and could be excused if he had wanted to cut down his activities. He himself said: 'When I hit 70 I decided to come and live in Australia. That was purely personal: my wife wanted to live here' (Tisdall 1982: 40). While there is no reason to disbelieve this, however, he could have been excused for feeling some disillusionment with the state of British management and disappointment at the limited impact that his efforts had achieved.

Nevertheless, although now living at a great distance from his two main countries of interest, Britain and the United States, he certainly did not reduce his commitment to the 'mission at large'. In the first place, he rapidly became involved in the Australian management scene, taking up a range of invitations from different types of organizations to lecture and advise. In 1962, he had ten commitments with a range of different organizations, indicating considerable prior recognition of his abilities. He was in addition spending some three months in Britain every year, with more limited visits elsewhere, demonstrating that emigration did not equate to retirement.

Apart from the Australian Institute of Management, Australian universities were amongst the first to make use of his presence, again in stark contrast to their British equivalents. For almost a decade, both the Faculty of Engineering and the Department of Business Administration of the University of New South Wales regularly invited him to give lectures. These started in 1963, when he gave a series of three lectures which were a real *tour de force* that provided a wide-ranging historical review of the evolution of managerial practice. Two sets of three lectures in 1964 and six more in 1965 were with one exception on general managerial topics. By 1966, however, he returned to the historical theme, talking about Taylor, while in 1967 he gave a series of five lectures on 'Great Names in Management' (Fayol, Rowntree, Dennison, Follett, and Mayo). In June 1969, there were a further three lectures with historical connotations, on 'The Foundations of Management', 'Management since Taylor and Fayol', and 'An Example of Management'. The last one was an account of his own managerial experiences in the battle areas of Flanders in 1914–15, focusing specifically on liaison with the higher levels of military command. He also gave talks to other educational bodies, including the universities of Sydney and Melbourne, as well as the New South Wales College of Nursing.

A second main focus of his activities was naturally the Australian Institute of Management, to which he gave a series of lectures almost every year in the 1960s. While the main topics in the University of New South Wales had been historical in orientation, to the Institute audiences he kept to day-to-day management issues for the most part, although in 1969 he did provide four lectures on the origins and development of management. During the 1970s, however, his contributions waned because only in 1972 and 1976 did he feature in its *Journal.*

Especially during his early years in Australia, Urwick also did a substantial amount of work for public sector organizations. Two addresses in November 1962 to the Australian Department of Defence in Melbourne were followed early in 1963 by a programme for the senior staff members in the Department of Works. The latter was also replicated in Canberra and Melbourne, in each location as a series of three lectures, respectively, under the titles 'The Nature of Management', 'What Is Management?', and 'Line and Staff Relations'. July 1963 took him back to the theme of organizational structure, when he gave an address to the Australian Police College, while in 1964 he lectured four times to senior civil servants in Canberra, to be repeated later in the year in both Canberra and Melbourne. Clearly, Australian government departments, like Australian universities, were more interested in listening to him than their British counterparts.

Nor did the private sector ignore him. In mid-1963, Urwick had three commitments with business groups, again showing that they were aware of his contributions to management thought. One was for a company called the Construction Management Advisory Services, on systematic management in construction projects, while the second was the opening address at a three-day residential management conference for the Australian and New Zealand Pulp and Paper Industry Association on 'Management and Technology'. At the end of the year, he was also invited to give the opening address for the Retail Trade Conference held in Sydney. In addition, he talked to a range of other organizations: the Sydney Rotary Club; the Australian Institute of Chartered Accountants; the Business Men's Dining Club in Sydney; the Sydney Division of the Institution of Production Engineers; the Australian Administrative Staff College; and the Australian Institute of Professional Management Consultants, amongst others.

Apart from lecturing, Urwick was frequently asked to contribute articles and book reviews to Australian publications, mainly *Australian Manager* and *Modern Administration*. He also wrote a chapter for inclusion in an Australian book with the overall title *Monopolies and Management* (Paterson 1964), focusing on education and training. Two of the book reviews must have pleased him, one being about *The Successful Executive* by Peter Drucker, the other for John Humble's *Improving Business Results*, a practical illustration of the author's advocacy for what he called 'Management by Objectives' (MBO). The latter was particularly relevant for Urwick, because UOP had already become well known for its successful launch of MBO. In 1969, for the Australian magazine *Modern Administration*, he wrote a memorial article on Seebohm Rowntree, while a few months later the same publication asked him to write about Elton Mayo and Mary Follett.

Given his absorption into the local management scene, however, it is surprising that he played no formal role in the UOP subsidiary that by the mid-1960s had become a well-established professional consultancy service in Australia. Nevertheless, just as with the parent company, Urwick did respond positively to invitations to participate in occasional informal social gatherings of directors or senior managers from client firms. He was clearly still valued as an asset to the firm, even if the expatriate managers insisted on running the subsidiary without his direct input.

In September 1970, he had an unusual request for assistance from McGraw-Hill, which was considering a proposal to commission the production of a film and a videotape on organizational structure and the span of control. This was the only time that Urwick compiled guide notes for the content and exposition of the subject through the media of film and tape. Although those two topics had the same subject matter with similar titles, Urwick decided to establish their content in different modes, with the film coming first. He drafted a script for an in-house discussion among three or four senior executives in a fictitious American corporation where a management consultant had recommended an additional managerial appointment. The story was told through a discussion, enabling Urwick to explain historically how 'span of control' had originated and developed, including bringing in Graicunas and an 'Englishman named Urwick'. The film involved no action among the cast, other than their presence around the table and spoken input. For the videotape, Urwick took up a lower echelon of managerial responsibility based around Taylor's proposals for 'functional foremen' within a manufacturing context.

The 1970s understandably saw a sharp downturn in his activities, even in Australia. There were four lectures in 1971, another four in 1972, one in 1973, and only one more in the rest of the decade, mostly at Australian universities. In 1971, fastening on to his favoured topic of 'terminology' – though he himself preferred the word 'semantics' – he wrote an article entitled 'Clearing the Jungle of Management Obscurity' for *Rydges* magazine.

OTHER VISITS

While the great majority of his 'mission' was carried out in Britain and North America before emigration, with the addition of Australia thereafter, Urwick was so well known elsewhere in the world that organizations in other countries frequently invited him to visit. One of the principal sources of these invitations was through CIOS triennial international meetings, which he always tried to attend, or regional meetings, either because of his proximity or through invitations arising out of the meetings themselves. For example, the Stockholm Congress of 1947 prompted two invitations to Norway, while arising out of the Brazil Congress in São Paulo he was invited to Portugal. Similarly, as we saw earlier, the proximity to the Melbourne CIOS generated a visit to New Zealand. In May 1965, as the CIOS Pacific Chapter was held in Tokyo, while there he addressed two sessions at the Japanese Productivity Centre and one at the Japanese Economic Research Centre, followed by one in Hong Kong. He obviously went down well there because the Hong Kong Management Association invited him for a further three lecture series. He also gave the opening address to the European Chapter of CIOS in Vienna in 1959.

Outside the CIOS connections, there were also occasional visits to European countries such as Belgium, France, Italy, Switzerland, and Germany. In 1958 and 1962, he attended the meetings of the newly founded International Academy of Management (IAM), of which Urwick was one of the first elected fellows. Given his ability to converse in several languages, he was much appreciated in Europe, especially as so few British and American management experts bothered to communicate in anything other than English.

After emigrating in 1961, activities outside Western Europe inevitably increased, partly because he could stop off on journeys between Australia and Britain. In 1963, he had an invitation to give two addresses to the Turkish Management Association in Istanbul, following which he attended the American University in Lebanon. In April 1964, he was in Cairo to conduct three educational sessions, while in connection with his spring 1966 visit to Britain he stopped over in Athens to contribute to a course conducted by the Greek Management Association. In Asia in 1962, he visited Manila, while in 1965 he spent another spell there with the Philippines Council of Management for a programme called 'A Week with Lyndall Urwick'. As he was invited back there in 1973, to give four lectures to the Malaysian Institute of Management, he was clearly appreciated in that region.

In addition to these lectures, Urwick was also writing a good deal. For example, he wrote two substantial papers for the IAM meetings in Italy, while articles such as 'Theory Z' (1970) were published in several languages. There was also a request in 1958 from a Japanese publishing company for a 'Foreword' that would be translated into Japanese for *The Pattern of Management*. Later, the *Journal of the Indian Institute of Management* published articles on 'Morale' and 'Whether Management and Training Are the Same Thing or Are Differentiated?', indicating that his views were sought from groups in many different countries.

INTERNATIONAL AND DOMESTIC HONOURS

One of the features of the post-war period was the number of international accolades and honours which Lyndall Urwick received. While this reflected his standing on the international management scene, it contrasts sharply with the paucity of awards received from his native country. One of the earliest awards he received was from the International Chamber of Commerce, which in 1934 as a mark of gratitude and respect for his cooperation when working at the IMI gave him a silver medal. In 1932, Urwick's status had also been recognized through an invitation from the Belgian government to attend the centenary of that country's elevation to independent statehood.

It was in the post-war years, however, that awards came his way in significant numbers. In 1948, for example, the Norwegian government made him a Knight in the Order of St Olav, in recognition of his contributions to management development in that country. At the 1951 Brussels CIOS Congress, the International Committee gave their Gold Medal to Lyndall Urwick as 'an honour richly deserved'. In making the presentation, the vice-president cited 'the long and eminent service you have rendered to the cause of scientific management as thinker, writer and teacher, and as pioneer in the practical application of the principles of administration, in your own country and internationally'. In his reply, Urwick noted that 'this is the first occasion of the CIOS award given to a Briton and I would like to feel that it is given not to myself personally as to the many men and women of British stock who have laboured devotedly ever since 1918 to bring a British Management Institute into being'. The CIOS Gold Medal award (the sixth made since its inception in 1929) was marked in Britain by an editorial feature in the *British Management Review*, providing a full appreciation of the citation and a lengthy summary of Urwick's response. Among Britain's management experts, there was considerable satisfaction at the high regard implied across the international managerial network not just for the nation, as Urwick had specified, but far more deservedly for the man himself.

Perhaps the most prestigious awards, however, came from the United States. In leading the Anglo-American review, in 1954 Urwick was elected to Honorary Life Membership of the AMA (Figure 8.3), a privilege replicated in the same year by the American Society of Mechanical Engineers. In May 1955, he was selected to receive the highly prestigious Wallace Clark Award, given that it

Figure 8.3 Award of Honorary Life Membership of the American Management Association, 1954. (Urwick is in the centre).

was a joint commemoration from the AMA, the American Society of Mechanical Engineers, the Society for the Advancement of Management, and the Association of Consulting Managing Engineers. The Award was made at a ceremony held in a prestigious New York hotel attended by 130 specially invited guests, with the presentation conducted by the dean of the Massachusetts Institute of Technology. The citation highlighted significant phases and aspects of Urwick's professional and educational contributions to the advancement and promotion of management knowledge and practice, making particular mention of his valuable role on the international scene during his years at the IMI. Urwick replied suitably, appreciating particularly being a British recipient.

Even more prestigious was his selection in September 1961 to receive the major American management award honouring the memory of Henry L. Gantt, the first time that award was made to a non-American. As Gantt was one of the pioneering innovators in the advancement of manufacturing management, specializing in systematic planning and progress control, Urwick took great pride in this honour. The memorial award, inaugurated in 1929 jointly by the AMA and the American Society of Mechanical Engineers, had an Awards Committee of eminent management specialists responsible for the selection of recipients and for the conduct of the procedures. The 1961 occasion, celebrating the centenary of Gantt's birth, was held at a commemorative lunch in New York's Roosevelt Hotel. The formal citation read:

Recognised authority on management, with unusual ability in the field of organization, whose pronouncements have world-wide recognition; devout apostle of the professional stature of the manager; creative leader in adult education for managers; constructive and generous contributor to the world community through his profound works in management in both government and industry.

To make the presentation, the awards committee selected H. B. Maynard, another eminent American management pioneer, who gave a long address outlining aspects of Urwick's professional programme to date (Figure 8.4). The citation had started by saying

We are meeting today to honor one of the great pioneers in the field of scientific management who has been called the greatest speaker, writer, teacher and authority of the Management profession in the world. It is particularly appropriate that the names of Henry Gantt and Lyndall Urwick should be joined together in history through the occasion in which we now participate. Both have evidenced in their lives and work a sincere conviction of the importance of scientific management in the development of a better and more productive world. Both have had the ability to recognise and formulate the basic principles for many of the situations which the manager encounters in his daily task of managing. Above all, both have had the ability to develop from

Figure 8.4 Award of the Gantt Medal, 1961, by H. B. Maynard.

those principles practical solutions to problems which have stood the test of time. Colonel Urwick is probably best known to most of us as the world's foremost authority in the field of organization: a distinction not easily won.

Two years later, in September 1963, Urwick was awarded the other most prestigious medal in American management, the Taylor Key, by the Society for the Advancement of Management (as the Taylor Society had by then been renamed). Moreover, it was on the special occasion of the Society's Golden Anniversary, and again it was the first occasion it had been awarded to a foreigner, 'for the priceless legacy which his thinking, example and inspiration will be for the coming generations of students, teachers and managers in all lands'. In response, Urwick gave a far-sighted paper on 'Management's Next Half-Century'.

An honour of a different sort was being asked to present the CIOS Gold Medal in 1972 to Peter Drucker, with whom he had an ongoing correspondence. He used the occasion to present another of his little ditties, starting 'There is a Professor called Peter'. In that year, Urwick was also awarded an honorary doctorate at York University in Toronto. His final honour was received in 1973, at the AAM, when he was elected as a life fellow, a rare honour for a foreigner and an even rarer one for somebody who had spent none of his career in academia. He gave an address entitled 'Professors, Professionals and Practitioners' on this important occasion, and another at the formal dinner of the Academy on 'Some Americans', a review of the American pioneers in management.

Compared to these recognitions of a lifetime of service to management thought and practice, his awards in Britain were limited. We have noted his honorary doctorate from Aston University, while in 1968 the BIM awarded him the James Bowie Medal. On the other hand, the political and academic establishments failed to offer him the kind of recognition that others in North America and Europe felt were richly deserved. While this is an issue to which we shall return in Chapter 10, the absence of awards remains something of a mystery.

REFLECTIONS ON 'THE MISSION'

Having examined Lyndall Urwick's 'mission' in various different countries after he retired from the managing directorship of UOP, it is now time to reflect on various issues. Table 8.1 provides a breakdown of how his activities were divided, separating the periods before and after emigration to Australia. Inevitably, the numbers presented are not necessarily the whole story, because there were many occasions when Urwick gave informal talks, while some lectures might not have been mentioned in the archives. On the writing side, published versions of talks have not been included to avoid double counting, although this problem might not have been entirely eliminated because a talk might be turned into an article under a different name and some time later. Nevertheless, the data are sufficiently robust to give a broad indication of his activities by location.

Before commenting on the breakdown between countries, what can be said about the impact of the mission? One aspect was the sheer quantity, especially for somebody who had ostensibly retired. Another aspect was his powerful and articulate delivery; indeed, the continued quality of his speaking was exemplified by the frequency with which his talks were turned into articles or booklets. Making an impact through the spoken word at a time when oratory was rare was also unusual in a field like management. Furthermore, when to this was added an underlying passion for and a deep background knowledge of his subject, it is not surprising that people remember to this day when they listened to Lyndall Urwick. Many of these people would never have read about management in print; many others who read him in their professional journal or some other magazine would never have read him in a specialized book.

Table 8.1 Urwick's activities after 1951 by location

Location	1951–61		Post-1961	
	Talks[a]	Articles[b]	Talks[a]	Articles[b]
Britain	64	32	19	6
North America	98	12	22	31
Other countries	19	5	37	5
India			23 (47)	
Australia	9	0	99	21

[a] Talks are mainly formal ones. In India, for instance, there were forty-seven 'events' in which Urwick would be expected to perform in some way, of which twenty-three were formal talks.
[b] Articles also include chapters of books, forewords, book reviews, and major letters to publications.

Moreover, in contrast to the way that modern gurus preach, the mission was not about a single message. Rather, he covered a wide array of different topics, although all involving a systematic view of management. It is also vital to stress that as fulfilling the mission depended on being invited to speak, Urwick proved to be a highly popular speaker in a significantly large number of countries and communities.

Before 1961, although Urwick spent most of his time in Britain, he was also abroad for substantial periods. This was mainly why between April 1952 and February 1954 he gave no talks at all in Britain. In total, his time out of Britain probably amounted to more than three years over the period 1950–61, when there were more than twice as many talks in countries other than Britain. Furthermore, while the vast majority of talks in Britain were single events, many of those abroad were part of a series. In 1957, to take an extreme example, he gave thirty-two scheduled talks on his post-AMA survey tour, and another six which were not part of the AMA-organized schedule.

After 1961, of course, it is apparent from Table 8.1 that the number of talks and articles in Britain declined markedly, even though he was visiting for six-week spells twice a year until the mid-1970s. At the same time, the number of talks understandably decreased in North America, due to the very much reduced number of visits. On the other hand, the number of articles written for American journals increased sharply, reflecting his acceptance in that circle. Moreover, the number of activities in Australia rose dramatically, indicating that he was both well known and welcome in Australia and that there were institutions that could make use of him. In addition, the number of talks in other countries increased substantially, perhaps mainly due to him being able to stop off between Australia and Britain, but also indicating his recognition in countries such as Egypt, Turkey, the Philippines, and Greece.

Why was there such a difference in the levels of activity inside and outside Britain? Several reasons suggest themselves, none of which relate specifically to Urwick, yet connect with the lack of management development in Britain. One of the most obvious was the lack of contact with the university world, because prior to emigration he only visited one university (Glasgow), while during the 1960s and 1970s only Aston invited him to provide the kind of lecture series which was staple fare for American universities. Another key factor was the relative feebleness of the BIM, especially compared to the AMA or the Australian Institute of Management, both of which invited him to carry out a wide range of activities. One must also stress the continued domination of industry by an old guard which still regarded development as an experiential process, rather than one based on instruction of any kind. Even in 1964–5, the so-called Savoy Group attempted to thwart the creation of two university business schools, reflecting the conservative nature of much of British business at that time (Wilson 1995).

Above all, though, in explaining this difference it is vitally important to emphasize how Urwick concentrated his attentions on North America. While there is a paradox here, in that this was the area that had least need of his services, he felt much more at home, intellectually and psychologically, in a country in which his 'management heroes' (Taylor, Follett, Gantt, Drucker, etc.) had enjoyed their greatest successes. The professional and educational institutions were also willing to invite him to speak on management and organization, encouraging him to visit there as frequently as he could. Urwick was always much closer to the AMA than the BIM, while the American engineering institutes similarly held him in high regard. That the same was true to a lesser but still considerable extent in Australia merely serves to illustrate the situation in Britain. Finally, one should conclude by noting that his activities after 'retirement' were a monument to his commitment and passion; age did not seem to dissipate these characteristics. Indeed, two of his most active years were 1969 and 1970, when he was on the verge of 80. While no doubt his family suffered from the constant absences, he sustained his 'mission at large' for many years, to the point when most people would have settled back into a comfortable retirement. After all, this was Urwick's life, his very driving force.

9

Later Writings

In the second phase of Urwick's writing from the Second World War onwards, rather than developing theoretical work, he was more concerned with consolidating his existing material. This covered a wide range of topics – as Pugh et al. (1971: 107) note: 'Indeed, there can be few topics in administration on which Urwick has not something to say' – in a significant number of publications. While it would be impossible to cover the whole range of his writings in this chapter, we are going to attempt to illustrate his breadth of interest and ability by looking at twelve topics that represent the most significant of his very considerable range of writings in this period. As this was also a period in which new ways of thinking about management were developing, we have depicted in Figure 9.1 a context within which management thought can be placed.

DYNAMIC ADMINISTRATION: THE COLLECTED PAPERS OF MARY PARKER FOLLETT

As one of the key figures in the history of management, Mary Parker Follett was as eminent in her field as were Taylor and Fayol in theirs. While the latter two were concerned with the structural working of organizations, she was concerned with their human dynamics, and particularly the reconciliation of individuals and groups. The key for Follett was to give groups a community objective, making coordination the central process and goal. As Urwick and Brech noted of her thinking in *Thirteen Pioneers* (2002: 52–3): 'In the last analysis there is no such thing as a final authority inhering in the senior executive and delegated to him by others. Modern industrial organization, built upon specialized functional and sectional service, gives to almost every individual in the enterprise specialized responsibility for a particular field or task.' While she recognized that there must be differences within organizations, and that this conflict could be creative, the key aspects of management – authority, leadership, and control – depend on the analysis of the objective

Organisational
Analysis
(1960s onwards)

Organizational Change

Argyris, Senge, Pettigrew, Morgan

The Organizational Environment

Burns, Lawrence and Lorsch, Hofstede

Organizational Decision-making

Simon, March, Vroom, Crozier

Structural Analysis

Weber, Aston Group, Chandler, Mintzberg

Humanistic
Perspective
(1930s to 1980s)

Behavioural Sciences

Cyert

Human Resources Perspective

Maslow; McGregor; Likert

Human Relations Movement

Barnard; Mayo; Roethlisberger

Administrative Principles

Fayol; Follett; Barnard; Urwick

Classical Perspective
(1880s to 1960s)

Bureaucratic Organizations

Weber; Parsons

Scientific Management

Towne; Taylor; Gantt; Bedaux

Pre-Classical Perspective
    (upto 1870s)

Functional Approach

Smith; Babbage; Ure

---------- // --
1780   1900   1950   2000

Figure 9.1 The evolution of management thinking, 1870s to 1980s.

facts of the situation. This gave rise to Follett's famous phrase 'the law of the situation' to govern the decisions taken.

Urwick had been a personal friend of Follett from the time when Rowntree had invited her to one of his Oxford Conferences. Although American, she spent most of her last years in Britain from 1928 until shortly before her death in 1933. Indeed, in 1933, she summarized her whole doctrine in five lectures at the London School of Economics (LSE), entitled 'The Problem of Organisation and Co-ordination in Industry'. On her death, Urwick wanted to make her papers available to the management world. This was a simple enough objective, but there was a snag, in the form of H. C. Metcalf, the Director of the American Bureau of Personnel Administration, who had many years previously effected Follett's entry into the world of Boston industry, giving him some claim to the publication of her papers. While Metcalf accepted the idea of a memorial to her, he was less enamoured of it being done by a non-American. Years of desultory correspondence passed between the two men, leading Urwick to drop his plans because so many other projects took up his time, not least the early development of UOP. While a compromise was finally reached in 1939, involving both protagonists acting as editors, but with Urwick alone writing the Introduction, the onset of war put a stop to the agreed collection of essays. In 1940, Urwick handed the file to his personal assistant, Edward Brech, and asked him to publish the collection. However, as Urwick had not by then completed the introductory essay, Brech was given the task of converting his boss's notes into a cohesive chapter.

It is consequently ironic that neither of the two named editors played any part at all in the publication of *Dynamic Administration*, although Urwick donated a signed copy to Brech expressing his gratitude and appreciation. It was also Urwick who persuaded Seebohm Rowntree to write the foreword. Crucially, the initiative provided by Urwick and Metcalf had resulted in a valuable book which filled a gap in our knowledge of Follett's contribution to management thinking, given that she had only published books on political science, rather than management. A second edition of the collection was also produced as late as 1973, in which Urwick this time collaborated with Elliot Fox, who had written a Ph.D. about Follett's work.

THE MAKING OF SCIENTIFIC MANAGEMENT

This series of three books was to become perhaps the most popular and best known of Urwick's works, going through several imprints, most recently by the Thoemmes Press in 2002. It originated as three sets of articles for *Industry*

Illustrated, the first of which was written by Urwick and the other two by Brech, although all of the books carry both names. A considerable amount of the material was taken from the British report to the 1938 International Committee for Scientific Management (CIOS) Conference, entitled 'The Development of Scientific Management in Great Britain', on which Urwick had invited Brech to assist with the research. At the CIOS Conference, Urwick realized from the discussions that very little was known about the men who had contributed to the development of scientific management, so on his return to Britain he proposed to the editor of *Industry Illustrated* the idea of dozen articles, each devoted to an individual.

The first book, entitled *Thirteen Pioneers*, resulted from these articles. Six of the articles were about Americans (Taylor, Follett, Gantt, Dennison, Gilbreth, and the President's Committee on Administrative Management of 1937), three each from Britain (Babbage, Rowntree, and Elbourne) and France (Fayol, Le Chatelier, and De Freminville), and one German (Rathenau). This was the start of Urwick's considerable contribution as a historian of management, with the initial chapter, on 'Scientific Management and Society', serving as an introduction to all three books. In it, he explained that as his subjects had 'recognised that the antiquated scheme of business principles . . . bore no logical relation to the intellectual standards, the mode of thinking customary in the exact sciences', they had therefore attempted to apply the methods of science to the problems of direction and control, even though some (like Taylor) had often been misrepresented. In order to move forward he argued, just as he had in *Management of Tomorrow*, that

the work of research to be done is immense. The sheer weight and complexity of measurable and ascertainable fact which must be marshalled before we can begin to be more scientific in the sociological and political fields, is literally staggering.

But he accepted that the work of the individuals needed to be set against a background of the larger developments in industry, and this was the objective of the second book, while the third dealt with the Hawthorne experiments, which 'constitute the most complete piece of controlled sociological research at present carried out in connection with the management of industry anywhere in the world'. In the conclusion, he noted that 'no student of scientific management can comprehend his subject unless he sees behind the textbook technique, the reflection of the individual human beings who have lived and laboured to add to our store of exact knowledge'.

When the initial articles on the pioneers were nearing completion in the early summer of 1941, Brech suggested a continuation of the series in a rather different format, relating to individuals and phases in the evolution of management in Britain. Although Urwick thought this was an excellent idea, he emphasized that he was too busy to participate, offering instead to recommend the series to *Industry Illustrated* under Brech's name. Brech, however, preferred the continuity of having both names associated with the series. The second series began in November 1942, with sixteen articles under the title 'Management in British Industry', which became the subtitle of the second book in the series. Although Urwick discussed the articles with Brech, they were almost entirely the latter's work. Much the same happened with the third volume, after Brech had suggested to Urwick that they should round off the series with a volume on the Hawthorne project at Western Electric. Brech consequently wrote eighteen articles under the subtitle 'The Hawthorne Investigations'. The foreword for this last book, which was published in 1948, was written by Elton Mayo, and starts: 'Lyndall Urwick was the first person to take public notice of the successive studies of human relations in industry undertaken by the Western Electric Company. He was at that time Director of the International Institute of Management at Geneva; and somewhere in the early 1930s he published a monograph on the Hawthorne experiments.' Little did he realize, perhaps, that Brech had been more responsible for the articles and the book.

THE ELEMENTS OF ADMINISTRATION

This book was based on a series of five lectures given to the London Branch of the Institute of Industrial Administration (IIA) in May and June 1942. It proved to be extremely popular, running to a second edition and in all seven reprints, given that it was a consolidation of Urwick's views on administration, starting from Fayol's framework but also taking principles from a range of other writers. Indeed, it is generally regarded (Subramaniam 1966) as one of the standard works on classical management theory, alongside those by Fayol (1949), Mooney and Reilley (1931), and Gulick and Urwick (1954).

The intention behind the lectures had been to design an ideal model of organization through a technique of administration, on the grounds that if this could be achieved, then the rest would follow. Nevertheless, as he acknowledged in the preface: 'At the moment there is, admittedly, an insufficient basis in the physical sciences for an exact science of administration.' His principles of good organization were founded on the conviction that a logical structure is better for efficiency and morale than one allowed to develop around personalities. As he had said in his article on 'Organisation as a Technical Problem' in *Papers on the Science of Administration*, 'the removal of much of the routine of management from detailed personal control to the operation of the system eliminated an important source of friction from industrial life'.

The main chapters are based on Fayol's six main aspects of administration, which fall into two main groups related to process and effect:

> *Forecasting* leads to a *Plan*,
> *Organizing* has as its object *Coordination*, while
> *Command* issues in *Control*.

Urwick added three principles, 'investigation', 'appropriateness', and 'order' to these six aspects of process and effect, which Fayol does not provide (since his analysis deals only with actions). 'Investigation' is necessary because all scientific procedure is based on an investigation of the facts; 'appropriateness' involves seeing that the human and material organization are suitable for the objects, resources, and needs of the undertaking; while 'order' ensures material and human order.

The second main dimension of the book is Mooney and Reiley's logical scheme (adapted from a German author, Louis Anderson) that every principle has its process and effect. Thus, 'leadership' has as a process 'delegation' and an effect, which is known as the 'definition of functions'. Moreover, if these have been correctly identified, the process and effect will in their turn have a principle, a process, and an effect. The outcome of incorporating all three of these dimensions is a series of interacting triangles, as depicted in Figure 9.2.

This figure, which illustrates Urwick's predilection for complex diagrams, is a summary of the material discussed in the previous chapters, incorporating twenty-nine principles and (by coincidence) the same number of sub-principles, drawn from the descriptions of a range of writers, including Fayol, Taylor, Graicunas, Mooney and Reiley, and Follett, as well as his own article in 1928. They were

HFP: Henri Fayol's list of Administrative Principles – 15 examples
HFAD: Henri Fayol's list of Administrative Duties – 20 examples
HFAA: Henri Fayol's Aspects of Administration – 7 examples
MR: Mooney and Reiley's Principles of Organisation – 26 examples
FWT: Frederick Winslow Taylor's Principles – 8 examples
GR: Graicunas's Principle
MPF: Mary Parker Follett's Principles – 7 examples
LUDC: Principles of Direction and Control listed by L. Urwick – 17 examples

As one can appreciate, comparing the terminology and intentions of different writers in relation to the principles is a complex and difficult operation; to bring all of the twenty-nine principles from different writers together into a single diagram is consequently a considerable feat. This highlights once again

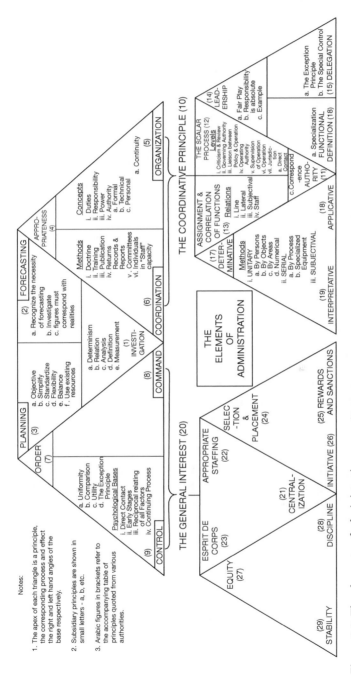

Figure 9.2 The elements of administration.

Urwick's great skill as a synthesizer of the various strands of management thought, a skill for which he had a wide reputation.

The chapters follow a somewhat similar pattern, but due to space constraints it is only possible to examine the first, on 'Forecasting'. It starts by saying that as research underlies the process of forecasting, it must be conducted within certain intellectual principles, taken from his 1928 paper, namely, determinism, relation, analysis, definition, and measurement. He notes how although it is vital for business to form a judgement about the probable course of events, the means of achieving this by using the available scientific data was badly underdeveloped. While a number of large organizations had recently been making a conscious effort to forecast, Urwick was highly critical of the methods employed, suggesting that a much more systematic method would help to dampen down the cyclical effects experienced at that time.

As the book brought together most of Urwick's views on management. George's path-breaking book *The History of Management Thought* (1972: xvii) noted that it provides a major contribution because of its 'collection, consolidation and correlation' of the principles of management. On the other hand, because Urwick's framework was regarded as extremely rigid – the 'one best way' – it has been criticized for being overstructured. Indeed, it was perhaps understandable that many managers found it daunting, although Urwick did make it clear in his conclusion that 'the raw material in which administration works is human beings', even quoting, a little surprisingly, given their disagreements over the International Management Institute (IMI), Edward Filene to the effect that labour could not and did not act like a commodity. As Child (1969: 144) has also noted, by the 1950s Urwick (and Brech) had adopted a more flexible view of administration, or management as it was increasingly being called. Rather than having essentially static principles, they recognized the dynamics of behaviour at all levels in the organization. As a result, the 'one best way' became less plausible. Moreover, interest in the application of the principles as a main guide to action diminished, even if the basic principles of Fayol continued to be recognized as central to management.

Leadership

Leadership was a subject very dear to Lyndall Urwick's heart, stemming from his keen early interest in and active involvement with the military, initially in the University Officer Training Corps, continuing as a Territorial Army Officer and onto the 1914–18 War. His own record of the severe 1914–15 fighting demonstrated deep thinking devoted to ensuring high morale and cooperation from the men under his command, whatever the tasks to be performed and difficulties encountered. Indeed, the detailed study of military command systems gave him a sound foundation on which to generate his own thinking, leading him to argue consistently that industrial management could benefit considerably from the application of these ideas.

Building on these ideas, his two main contributions to leadership studies were, firstly, five unpublished lectures given to the IIA in 1943, and, secondly, *Leadership in the Twentieth Century*, published by Pitman in 1957. His military background meant that he did not focus on prevailing views of leadership, such as the view held by the scientific management movement, which held that leadership should come from knowledge, namely, a technocratic perspective. Neither did he accept the notion that leadership can be seen in the sense of helping to resolve the labour–management problems through new ways of managerial leadership, as for instance in paying attention to 'secondary' social needs (Child 1969: 49). Nor, for that matter, did he pave the way for modern concepts of leadership, such as transformational or transactional leadership, except for his emphasis on subordinate leadership, what would now be called distributed leadership.

Urwick's views can best be understood by examining the 1943 lectures, which broke the issue down into five questions:

- Why should we be interested in leadership? Urwick noted: 'It is vain to discuss administration, its rules and procedures, unless at the same time we consider this vital human element in the equation.... While the two subjects must be separated for convenience of exposition, that separation is entirely artificial. In reality they are two halves of the same subject.'

- Why do we need leaders? We need leadership to make group coordination possible. But also, because, as he put it 'human beings, being the queer, odd, emotional, unpredictable creatures that they are, cannot by any stretch of the imagination be made into a perfect fit to any formula.... One of the consequences of this humanity is that they crave for leadership'. He also made a strong point about the importance of subordinate leadership – the leadership of the Lance-Corporal or the Charge-Hand – to create good relations within the smaller group, without which it is difficult for the individual's attitude to the larger group to be satisfactory: 'Loyalties to larger purposes which may seem somewhat abstract are built up out of experience of the smaller, more close-knit groups in which men share a personal comradeship.'

- How are leaders chosen? They can be appointed by higher authority, they can be selected from within the group, or they can push their way into a position of leadership by personality and an assertive ego.

An increasing proportion are chosen by the first method, is a fact of profound significance for our subject . . . whether in business or in government the appointed leader responsible to those who have chosen him for the ends he serves, and for winning the willing adherence of those he leads, the leader who is removable and accountable, is likely both to be a better leader while he is in office, and, what is even more important, to leave behind him a healthier social group when he quits office.

- What should be expected of our leaders? The functions of leadership are: representation of the organization and the cause for which it stands; initiation or as Urwick put it, 'intellectual midwifery'; administration; and interpretation, or modifying policies to bring them into line with changing circumstances, while key outputs are: delegation of authority without delegating responsibility, engendering the spirit of cooperation to build morale, the ability to get things done, and organized self-control.

- What are the qualities required in a leader? This is no easy task. A fundamental quality is integrity, meaning not just honesty but its derivative sense of unity; a man who would lead others must be 'at one with himself'.

It is possible to list a dozen other qualities desirable in a leader . . . manhood, presence of mind, sense of purpose and direction, intelligence, a sense of timing, quickness in seeing an integration, friendliness and affection, keeping people informed, a taste for being disagreed with, a sense of human and technical curiosity. . . . But the important point to remember is that it is not this or that isolated quality which matters, but the balance and unity of qualities in the individual.

The last few pages of *Leadership in the Twentieth Century* were a savage tirade against Urwick's enemies, accusing them of a lack of national leadership. In particular, he attacked 'these two national vices, indifference to intellectual values and advancement based not on professional skill but on the "old boy" nonsense', as manifested in the British Army of the nineteenth century up to the First World War, and in business itself up to his time of writing, supported in their position by the major universities' lack of willingness to take responsibility for educating business leaders and the British Institute of Management's (BIM) internal disputes about whether management is or is not a profession. Even these are a 'cover story', he argued, because

what is really being called into question is that there is a body of knowledge about leading a business which can be taught and which should be learned. . . . In the second half of the twentieth century, this attitude is not only half a century out of date, it is desperately dangerous. We must export or starve. We shall not continue to export in a competitive world unless the standard of leadership in all areas of our economic life is at least the equal of that found in other industrialized peoples.

These were damning words, typifying his long-held views about the need to change attitudes from the top.

THE PATTERN OF MANAGEMENT

This book is an example of Urwick's series of lectures in American universities, which were presented as the Merrill Foundation Lectures at the University of Minnesota in April 1955 to an industrial and commercial (rather than student) audience. It was based on five topics:

1. Management in an Adoptive Society
2. The Marriage of Theory and Practice
3. The Main Outline of Management Knowledge
4. The Principles of Government and Leadership
5. The Principles of Government and of Management

The University's School of Business Administration reproduced the full text as a book, which was also made available in Britain. Typifying his modus operandi, Urwick used the material in a reduced form at the Summer School of the IIA, much of which was reproduced in the autumn issue of the *British Management Review* (and translated into German for a national journal) which Urwick then used as a Christmas present for favoured recipients.

This book is perhaps of less interest for what he said, much of which was taken from what he had written over the previous quarter-century, than for how he said it. Although the material was largely culled from the various pioneers for whom Urwick had developed a particular affection, he also used his considerable knowledge of the wider literature to expand on these ideas. In the first talk, for instance, he quoted Herbert Spencer, Thorstein Veblen, Ortega y Gasset, Sir Arthur Quiller-Couch, A. E. Housman, Darrell Huff of *How to Lie with Statistics* fame, R. F. Hoxie, and Sir William Slim, as well as management writers such as Taylor, Mayo, Filene, Whitehead, and Drucker. Other non-management writers whom he was fond of quoting included Alfred Marshall, General Sir Ian Hamilton, Von Clausewitz, David Lilienthal, and Bernard Shaw. He was also capable of reaching out to little-known books far removed from management, such as Helen Waddell's *The Wandering Scholars*, to draw an analogy between the itinerant clerics of the Dark Ages who carried over into modern Europe the rhythms of the Greek and Latin poets, and the way in which management knowledge had emerged and spread. Eclecticism was indeed his great forte.

THE GOLDEN BOOK OF MANAGEMENT

This somewhat strangely named book was developed on behalf of the CIOS, a committee member having suggested such an extension of the *Thirteen Pioneers* work after he had been presented with the International Gold Medal in 1951. The fuller version was undoubtedly an attractive task for Urwick, especially as he still had the services of a personal assistant and a secretary courtesy of Urwick Orr and Partners (UOP). Published early in 1956, *The Golden Book* was a roll of honour of the great management figures of the past, described by Urwick himself as

An historical record of the life and work of seventy pioneers, edited for the International Committee of Scientific Management: notes on the work of seventy pioneers in eleven different countries who in the opinion of that Committee have made outstanding contributions to the world body of knowledge about management or administration. Concerning each person selected the book gives a portrait or photograph of the individual: the reason for his inclusion: the main facts of his career; a note on his personal characteristics; the titles of his most important written works on management. There are two bibliographies: a chronological list of the key management books and papers authored by the individual concerned and a select bibliography of publications covering the history of management.

What this description does not include is the generosity of Urwick's attitude to his subjects, many of whom had been his friends. Indeed, some would not have been widely recognized had Urwick not provided these portraits, which made him what he still remains, the leading historian of the pioneers of management. The volume was, of course, a contribution of international value and significance, so much so indeed that some twenty years after its publication the American Management Association (AMA) commissioned a second volume of thirty-eight additional pioneers who had died since *The Golden Book* had first been published. With Urwick's permission and active assistance, the second book was edited by William Wolf, although just as the book was about to go to press the publishers heard of the originator's death. It is also worth noting that although nine countries were represented in the second volume, Britain was not among them, a measure of the lack of British progress in this field since the 1950s.

In his preface to the second volume, Wolf was fulsome in his praise of Urwick, noting:

I wish to express my appreciation for the inspiration and help given by Lt. Col. Lyndall F. Urwick. He himself is one of the true pioneers of the management movement. He, more than any other person, has been responsible for bringing to the fore the significant contributions to management. The world of management is indebted to him for his own books and for his efforts in bringing to universal attention the work of Follett, Fayol, Graicunas, Mooney and others – and for the *Golden Book* in both its first and this, its second, appearance.

Similarly, in the preface to the whole expanded book, Harold Koontz said:

The entire management movement – and indeed, all those interested in management, whether as scholars or as practitioners – owe Col. Urwick a deep and lasting gratitude for the care and dedication he displayed in developing the original *Golden Book* nearly three decades ago. He painstakingly researched the pioneers and their respective contributions to the management field and preserved for all time bio-bibliographical summaries, photographs, and brief comments on personalities.

Even allowing for the normal eulogistic comments of preface writers, these recognitions were undoubtedly sincerely meant, while the decision of the AMA to publish the book was a further recognition of the status in which both the original book and Urwick himself were held.

NOTES ON THE THEORY OF ORGANISATION

This book was published by the AMA in 1952, derived in large part from the notes which Urwick used to lecture on the AMA Management Course, and in response to numerous requests from other teachers and students. As Urwick's foreword says, the *Notes* represent an attempt to construct a theory of the subject divorced from immediate applications. The foreword finishes by saying that he 'hopes to embody these *Notes* in a definitive study of organization at a later date', an aim he never fulfilled.

The *Notes* start by saying that it is possible to have a theory of organization on one condition, namely, that there is a distinction made between the mechanics of management, disregarding people as individuals, and the dynamics, that is, those management issues which deal with people as individuals. To go back to Fayol's six dimensions of management, forecasting, planning, and organizing can be primarily seen as the mechanics, while coordinating, commanding, and controlling are the dynamics. While dealing mainly with Fayol's six dimensions of management, Urwick added a seventh, communicating, which links all the others together, and is pure dynamics.

Having made these points, as the title implies, it is important to remember that the book was about organization. Urwick, nevertheless, argued that to build up a theory of a subject requires analysis, by identifying the different elements of an idea and examining them separately. This, according to Urwick, was how the theory of management started, with Taylor analysing the detailed movements involved in metal-cutting operations. Many managers are embarrassed by taking what they had previously regarded as 'wholes' to pieces and escape from their discomfort by telling themselves that they are 'practical' men, something that is particularly popular in Great Britain. Urwick argued, however, that

we cannot do without theory. It will always defeat practice in the end and for a quite simple reason. Practice is static ... it has no principles with what it doesn't know. ... Theory, on the other hand is light-footed. It can adapt itself to changed circumstances, think out fresh combinations and possibilities, peer into the future. That, after all, is its business.

Central to his case was putting 'organization' into the mechanics category, on the grounds that it is necessary to begin by making a technically correct structure without reference to individuals. By organization, he meant 'dividing up all the activities which are necessary to any purpose and arranging them in groups which may be assigned to individuals'. To achieve this, it is necessary to analyse the situation according to certain principles:

- The principle of the objective – the purpose of the undertaking
- The principle of specialization – the performance of specific functions
- The principle of coordination – to facilitate unity of effort
- The principle of authority – the need for a clear line of authority to every individual in the group (also known as the scalar principle by Mooney and Reiley)
- The principle of responsibility – by the superior for the acts of his subordinate
- The principle of correspondence – in every position the responsibility and the authority should correspond
- The span of control – no person should supervise more than five direct subordinates whose work interlocks
- The principle of balance – that the various units in an organization should be kept in balance
- The principle of continuity – reorganization is a continuous process and provision should be made for it
- The principle of definition – all the above should be clearly defined in writing

Two other dimensions of organization discussed in Chapter 10 are committees and 'staff'. Urwick noted the characteristics, functions, and weaknesses of committees, making it clear that he had a negative view of them as compared to the role of an individual. As the staffing issue was the topic of another book in its own right, we can devote a separate section to this subject.

STAFF IN ORGANIZATIONS

Written jointly with Ernest Dale, this book was intended to suggest how to make the best use of staff, as a means of reducing the load on top management. This had been an issue which Urwick had frequently raised, usually drawing heavily on military experience and analogies. In this particular case, however, it included in addition a good deal of empirical evidence drawn from surveys in which Urwick was directly involved. Firstly, the authors carried out a small survey of what American chief executives actually did, using administration as defined by Fayol, with the addition of communicating and two dimensions of leadership, namely, representation and initiation (Pigors 1935). Given that this was the only occasion of which we are aware when Urwick used empirical data for these various dimensions, it is worth quoting the breakdown of time for American chief executives:

Functions of Leadership (%)
Representation   35
Initiation   5
Administration   60
   Forecasting   5
   Planning 5
   Organization   5
   Directing (commanding)   10
   Coordinating   15
   Controlling   15
   Communicating 5

The authors then examined methods of reducing executive burdens: delegation, committees, and, the basis of the rest of the book, general staff. As they felt that the nature of the general staff assistant's areas of responsibility is the same as that of his chief, none of this can be delegated to him personally, making him more of an aide-de-camp and an extension of his commander's personality. The military analogy differentiates between the aide-de-camp who is an assistant to a senior officer, special staff officers who look after specific functions, and general staff officers, whose job it is to convert the ideas of the commanding officer into orders. The general staff work in an

American division at that time was broken down into four groups concerned with personnel, intelligence, operations and training, and supply.

However, it must be stressed that many businessmen experienced difficulty in understanding the general staff concept, especially that the general staff officer is not a specialist and does not have responsibility for any particular function, but is merely the agent of the commanding officer. The biggest difficulty is in the staff officer giving orders to officers who are his superior in rank; this is likely to create resentment unless the staff officer is extremely sensitive and cultivates good personal relations. The question is therefore whether business can make use of general staff officers, an issue that the authors tackled by stating that business has similar problems to armies: 'Lacking general staff assistance, it is manifestly impossible for the chief executive himself to act as the central clearinghouse for all authentic communications at the highest level in a large corporation.' They therefore argue that, returning to Fayol's six aspects of management, it is possible for the general staff (i.e. assistants) to relieve the chief executive of forecasting, planning, organizing, coordinating, and most of the controlling, leaving him to concentrate on the commanding phase and the aspects of leadership noted above, other than administration.

Before moving to the use of staff positions in business, the authors explored the US Presidency and the use of the staff system, differentiating between the executive office of the President and the White House staff, noting the increase in the latter group under Franklin Roosevelt and then Eisenhower. Meanwhile, the Cabinet acted as a group of individuals intent on their own jobs and acting as commanders in the field, rather than helping the President to plan and implement his strategy. This is all too often true in business as well.

The authors held five AMA seminars for assistants, surveying their allocation of time in the same categories as used for the chief executives above, with the following results:

Functions of Leadership   (%)
Representation   6
Initiation   19
Administration   75
  Forecasting   7
  Planning   10
  Organization   6
  Directing (commanding)   2
  Coordinating   14
  Controlling   12.5
  Communicating   23.5

As most of the assistants felt the need to clarify their roles and relationships, many found difficulties in these, so much so that the authors were obliged to devote a chapter to case studies of unsuccessful assistants. These case studies were derived from a separate survey, also carried out by the authors, of the way in which assistants to high executives in 140 organizations were operating. Most of the problems were ones of definition, although there was a wide range of difficulties.

This left a final chapter to review the practical use of general staff positions in business. It is interesting that the earliest companies to make extensive use of assistants were those such as Du Pont and General Motors, which were also the first to think seriously about their organizational structures and experiment with the M-form of organization (Chandler 1962). There were also many notable examples of assistants who ultimately became presidents themselves, clearly indicating that the system was working well. The authors then set out ten prerequisites for success, mainly concerned with the analysis and definition of roles, not least those of the chief executive's own job, and then finally examined those parts of Fayol's administrative functions where an assistant might be able to contribute. The book consequently provided an extensive expression of much of what Urwick had been advocating for many years.

MANAGEMENT AS A PROFESSION

The question 'Is management a profession?' had been a source of considerable debate since the early 1920s, starting with the writings of Sheldon and Lee. Urwick was one of the major proponents of a positive answer to this question, strongly linked as it was to several of his conceptual underpinnings of management. It was not until the debate heated up in the mid-1950s, however, that he wrote his definitive statement on the subject, a pamphlet which was published by UOP. It started with a quotation from Hutton's book reviewing the work of the Anglo-American Productivity Teams, entitled *We Too Can Prosper*:

Many teams have found that industrial management in America was not only a business or a career, but was also recognized on all sides as the mainspring of the high American productivity, as a service crucial to national well-being, as a function deserving of social respect and esteem, and as the prime contributor to the nation's strength and progress. It was *as much of a clearly marked profession as, say, that of a civil engineer, doctor, or lawyer.* (Emphasis in the original.)

From this base, Urwick argued that 'whether management is or is not regarded as a profession is not wholly academic or a matter of words' but has a 'considerable influence on . . . whether we shall be able to pay our debts or must face a falling standard of living for our people'. At the same time, he recognized that the proposition 'runs counter to quite a large array of British prejudices and patterns of thought'. What, he asked, caused this resistance, especially among businessmen? Some of it might be traced to the traditional British dislike of 'theory' and strong preference for practical solutions. In addition, 'many men in responsible positions today are wholly innocent of any formal preparation for their tasks'. This meant learning by 'experience' and 'trial and error', and by imitating others. Moreover, those who have learnt through experience are often doubtful of their ability to handle subordinates who may be their intellectual superiors. A third dimension was the concern that young men who have learnt management by study might 'become over-impressed by their own theoretical knowledge'. Another aspect was 'the British prejudice in favour of amateurishness', especially at the board level, where in spite of excellent attributes in many respects, many have no pretence to knowledge of the industry with which the company is concerned. Moreover, 'no one dreams of regarding this as any disadvantage', since the ideal of the 'gentleman of leisure' was so deeply embedded in the national consciousness. Indeed, since business activities were not associated with high status, 'being a Director' was regarded as something subtly different from 'being in business'. Thus, Urwick argued, 'the proposition that management should be treated as a profession cuts across many of these . . . habitual ways of thinking, some of them, as has been shown, with their roots deep in British history'. Moreover, the objections to regarding management as a profession considered so far are 'all of them subjective' and 'not susceptible to objective discussion'.

Urwick then moved on to discuss sources of confusion about the term 'management', identifying five in particular: those responsible for the conduct of the business, the activity of directing, a body of knowledge, those identified with employers vis-à-vis wage-earners, and a definition of status in an organization. As a result, not only could the question of management as a profession mean a number of different things, but also the answer needed to be linked to the five definitions. Clearly, there was a sufficient body of knowledge relating to management. On the other hand, those identified with employers did not provide an adequate basis for defining managers professionally, while status in an organization was dependent on that organization's characteristics. However, provided the responsibility for the conduct of the business and the coverage of activity were confined to executive aspects, Urwick saw no practical obstacle to the professional organization of those engaged in the occupation.

Having made this claim, he went on to accept that even those who were not influenced by the prejudices mentioned earlier could have doubts as to whether management should be organized professionally. This could be explained by the tradition that many managers in Britain had historically risen from the ranks through foremanship, developing mastery of their trades as they did so. If management was to be made into a profession, younger men with none of this maturity could claim managerial status. This he answered by arguing that the weakness of the old shop-floor type manager was the lack of educational qualifications, making it difficult for such people to understand or accept new ideas. Moreover, with the spread of educational opportunity, fewer first-class men would start life on the shop floor. A second reason was the assumption that passing examinations would make a manager, whereas nothing could be further from the truth. All responsible people accepted that practical experience was the most important element in the development of professional competence. What systematic study could do is to make learning by experience more reflective, and therefore more effective, thereby systematizing experience and enhancing an awareness of gaps. A third reason was that because management would be a new profession, it would be many years before any but a minority of younger entrants would have professional qualifications; meanwhile, the older managers would feel handicapped. It would consequently appear common sense, in light of the quotation from Hutton's book with which the pamphlet had started, to put management on the same plane of social approval as in the United States. Although there were still no formal professional qualifications for management in the United States, the major universities had been granting well-recognized degrees in management subjects for many years.

What Urwick did not do was to become involved in the problematic issues of what constitutes a profession, including such issues as ethics and institutional rules of behaviour. But as events have unfolded, the model Urwick suggested of following the American system has come to pass and management has been accepted as a profession, albeit a 'weak' one.

MANAGEMENT EDUCATION AND DEVELOPMENT

The education and development of managers was always one of the main concerns of Urwick's view of management, an issue that featured prominently in much of his writing and many of his talks, from his 1928 paper to the end of his career. Central to his vision was the nature of management, which was in turn closely related to his view of management as a science, which could be learnt and understood through a body of knowledge. However, he did accept that there was no one single science. In talking to the Academy of Management on 'Papers on the Science of Administration' more than three decades after its first publication, Urwick asserted:

Students of management must recognize quite clearly that the phrase 'scientific management' was coined as a convenient slogan, in connection with the Eastern Rates case in 1910. It did not affirm and was never intended to affirm that there could be a single science, a single organized body of knowledge, covering the whole art of managing, any more than there can be a single science covering the whole practice of medicine. Managing, like medicine, is a practical art, and its successful practice depends on balancing and applying to the individual case knowledge derived from a whole series of underlying sciences. . . . Many of these sciences are at very different stages of development and sophistication. . . .

Management is four groups of sciences. Management is getting things done for, with and through people. Therefore there were two broad divisions – knowledge about things and knowledge about people. But people behaved differently as (a) isolated individuals and (b) members of social groups of all kinds. So you've really got four subjects. There's the task you give to the individual – the lathe operator. Then there's the relating of tasks done by individuals in a group and this is organization. These tasks had to be related otherwise there was no accurate communication and no game could be played without communication. Then for the people there is the psychology of the individual and the sciences bearing on group behaviour. Thus management is an integrating discipline.

The simple ideas in these paragraphs can be translated firstly into the broad content of management, as depicted in Figure 9.3, and secondly, to illustrate his point about the four groups of sciences, another of his wonderfully complex diagrams provided in Figure 9.4. There is a symmetry about this diagram which, although elegant and indeed memorable in its presentation, must raise suspicions about their interactions.

Urwick had a long battle with the British universities, which he dated from the lack of a course at Oxford which would be relevant to his future career in the family business. The 1928 article was followed by various lectures and articles, one of which was 'A British Graduate School of Business', published in the *British Management Review* in July 1950. This started by looking at the Harvard Business School and the American system of both graduate MBAs and undergraduate degrees, comparing this huge framework with the almost total lack of any equivalent in Britain. It ended with a plea, stating 'the need for the immediate establishment in this country, in connection with an existing university, of a residential School of Business Administration on the American pattern'. However, rather strangely, he did not make this the centrepiece of his educational framework in the 1950s, leaving it to the Foundation for Management Education (FME) a decade or so later to pursue American-style business schools. Instead, he concentrated his attentions on defending his 1947

MANAGEMENT IS CONCERNED WITH →	A. THE INDIVIDUAL (THE 'CELL')	B. THE SOCIAL UNIT (THE 'ORGANISM')
1. WORK ('MECHANICS')	1A. THE TASK	1B. ARRANGING AND CORRELATING TASKS
2. PEOPLE ('DYNAMICS')	2A. ADJUSTING THE INDIVIDUAL TO THE TASK	2B. MOTIVATING AND INTEGRATING THE GROUP

Figure 9.3 The content of management.

management education scheme (described in Chapter 7), while frequently attacking the universities for their neglect of management studies.

A typical example of the latter was 'The Universities and Business', published in *The Manager* in August 1961, which followed an interview with Alan (later Lord) Bullock, Master of St Catherine's College, Oxford. While agreeing with Bullock's complaint that business took too little interest in what the universities were trying to do, Urwick argued that the relationship between the universities and business should start with the student and what the student needs if he/she is to develop into the kind of individual the nation requires. Bullock had maintained that it is not the purpose of a university to train managers and salesmen as such, but Urwick countered by noting that this did not prevent universities from providing a basic education whose subject matter is relevant to the student's future career. Indeed, he noted that 'it is possible to obtain a degree at Oxford today equipping a student with basic knowledge appropriate to almost any specialized profession in the alphabet. . . . But business is omitted, as, somehow or other, not "an intelligent occupation"'. Part of the reasoning behind these sentiments was based on snobbery, but in addition he stressed that while management is an integrating or catalytic discipline, university curricula were generally highly specialized. As a result, he asked: 'Is not the actual situation that the universities . . . have discarded their primary function, which is to prepare the next generation for positions of leadership. . . . And is not this fact the real basis of the lack of understanding between the universities and business leaders?' (It should be noted that while this comment puts the blame on the universities, Urwick

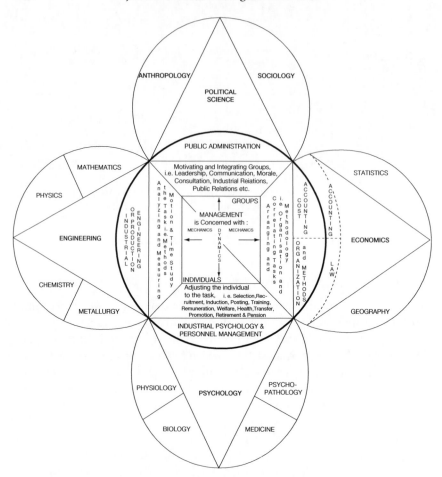

Figure 9.4 Management as a basic intellectual discipline.

elsewhere also blamed business leaders for their lack of interest in the development of their managers and workforces.)

Taking up another of Bullock's suggestions, that of continuing discussion, Urwick argued that 'the time is past for continuing discussion' and goes on to describe developments in the United States. This was written a few years before the Franks Report, leading to the start of the modern system of British management education, the outcome of which would have greatly impressed Urwick. On the other hand, it is vital to add his distinctive approach to management education: 'I wish to disclaim emphatically any intention of trying to teach anybody anything. Learning should develop a state of mind, the integration of theoretical study with practical experience.'

This highlights how in-company development was another recurring theme in his repertoire of talks. An excellent example was a chapter he provided for an anthology *Training Managers in the Public Services*, entitled 'Management Development in the USA'. This was based around the major findings of the AMA survey, specifically:

1. The corporation or company must have a clearly formulated view as to the future course of business.
2. A relevant plan of developing organization structure for delegation of executive responsibility.
3. An estimated assessment of likely forward requirements in executive positions.
4. Intentions or proposals for attaining those requirements through either promotion or recruitment.
5. A programme of intended development actions in respect of candidates, whether from promotion or through external recruitment.
6. The determination and introduction of a systematic scheme for assessment of executive performance and of personal development progress.
7. An effective system for individual counselling in association with the two foregoing procedures.
8. Adequate supervision of all the foregoing stages.

HUMAN RELATIONS AND PERSONNEL MANAGEMENT

Urwick frequently wrote or lectured on the topic of human relations or personnel management; indeed, both Guillén (1994) and Witzel (2003) emphasize his interest and significance in these areas. As an example, *Personnel Management in Relation to Factory Organization* was one of a series on various aspects of personnel management produced by the Institute of Labour Management (ILM). This book was a measure of Urwick's stature, because although he was not a leading member of the ILM, he was asked to write on this topic. His paradoxical view was that personnel management could not be isolated in a specialized department, since it permeates all aspects of management; the responsibility for dealing with people rests with all executives and supervisors. However, at the same time the function does require specialization in applying the methodology of science to its special range of problems, both in terms of the underlying disciplines of psychology, sociology, anthropology, medicine, and statistics, as well as emerging techniques such as methods of selection, training, rating and knowledge of trade union organization, unemployment and health insurance, and so on. This led him to identify three separate roles that the personnel manager can play, namely, 'staff', 'line', and 'functional', fitting once again into his military thinking. He also recognized the special difficulties associated with integrating personnel work into a business, in particular, because most executives regarded it as their distinct responsibility, to be discharged 'in the light of native wit and experience'. Indeed, they feel that 'they cannot discharge their responsibilities properly or maintain discipline unless they have unlimited initiative and authority vis-à-vis the workers in their departments or sections'.

Although Urwick had some sympathy with this position, he felt that the correct arrangement of the duties of the personnel manager was a matter of the utmost importance and delicacy. This was especially the case when it related to industrial relations, where the personnel manager clearly needed to liaise with senior management, given the need to negotiate on behalf of the employer, who is ultimately the board. Internal consultative machinery was another area where the personnel manager's role was to save the time of the chief executive. An additional area where the chief executive would rely on the personnel manager was the selection, development, and promotion of senior executives, giving them a key role in ensuring effective succession.

Interestingly, Urwick defined the personnel manager as a 'staff' role, as discussed earlier in this chapter, since ultimate responsibility for these issues must lie with the chief executive. There are also some specialized aspects of the personnel role, however, such as recruitment, training, and welfare, where he is a manager with a 'line' relationship of responsibility to the chief executive, and where there may well be specialized personnel assistants in branches or sub-departments who are directly responsible to him. In addition, there are relationships with colleagues in other departments in which the personnel manager adopts a 'functional' relationship, that is, a specialized authority concerned with a special subject. In many instances, in fact, this functional role is more common than the staff or line role, although one which can create difficulties for reasons noted earlier, namely, that line managers do not want to lose their authority over their direct workforce, even if the functional manager is expressing the policy of the whole organization of which their unit is only a part. Without some prescribed authority over issues such as pay or other conditions of employment, however, the functional personnel specialist cannot make his knowledge effective in the service of the undertaking. As in so many aspects of organization, it is the balance between functions which is of the essence.

The relationship between line, staff, and functional relationships is shown in Figure 9.5. This again reveals Urwick's proclivity for drawing up intricate diagrams that reflected the combination of roles with increasingly sophisticated organizations.

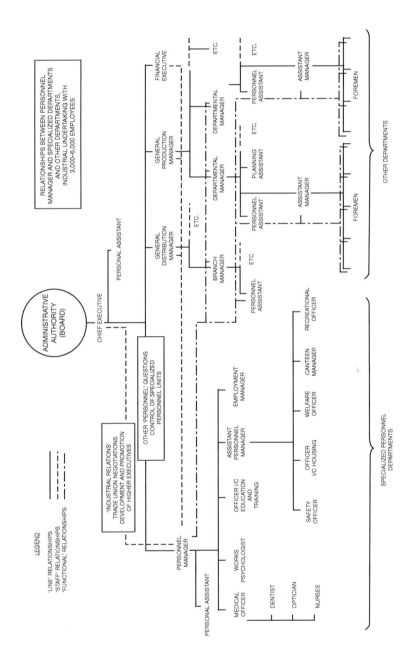

Figure 9.5 Line, staff, and functional relationships.

LEGEND

'LINE' RELATIONSHIPS
'STAFF' RELATIONSHIPS
'FUNCTIONAL' RELATIONSHIPS

RELATIONSHIPS BETWEEN PERSONNEL
MANAGER AND SPECIALIZED DEPARTMENTS
AND OTHER DEPARTMENTS,
INDUSTRIAL UNDERTAKING WITH
3,000–6,000 EMPLOYEES

ADMINISTRATIVE
AUTHORITY
(BOARD)

CHIEF EXECUTIVE

PERSONAL ASSISTANT

GENERAL
DISTRIBUTION
MANAGER

GENERAL
PRODUCTION
MANAGER

FINANCIAL
EXECUTIVE

ETC.

BRANCH
MANAGER

DEPARTMENTAL
MANAGER

DEPARTMENTAL
MANAGER

ETC.

ETC.

ETC.

PERSONNEL
ASSISTANT

PERSONNEL
ASSISTANT

PLANNING
ASSISTANT

PERSONNEL
ASSISTANT

ASSISTANT
MANAGER

ASSISTANT
MANAGER

FOREMEN

FOREMEN

ETC.

OTHER DEPARTMENTS

'INDUSTRIAL RELATIONS'
TRADE UNION NEGOTIATIONS
DEVELOPMENT AND PROMOTION
OF HIGHER EXECUTIVES

OTHER 'PERSONNEL' QUESTIONS
CONTROL OF SPECIALIZED
PERSONNEL UNITS

PERSONNEL
MANAGER

PERSONAL ASSISTANT

WORKS
PSYCHOLOGIST

OFFICER I/C
EDUCATION
AND
TRAINING

ASSISTANT
PERSONNEL
MANAGER

EMPLOYMENT
MANAGER

MEDICAL
OFFICER

DENTIST

OPTICIAN

NURSES

SAFETY
OFFICER

OFFICER
I/C HOUSING

WELFARE
OFFICER

CANTEEN
MANAGER

RECREATIONAL
OFFICER

SPECIALIZED PERSONNEL
DEPARTMENTS

SEMANTICS AND EMERGING VIEWS ON ORGANIZATIONS

Throughout his career, but especially in the latter stages, Urwick was concerned by the semantic problems arising in management, and especially the word 'organization'. He argued that the use of the term to describe an institution as a whole, as in 'the organization' or 'organizational behaviour', had diverted attention from the sense of organization as structure, that is, defining the pattern of posts and the process of allocating people to them, as used by Fayol, Mooney and Reilley, and others. As he put it: 'It is impossible to build a science on a colloquialism, only on the exact definition of terms.' This was the argument that he expressed in an article entitled 'Semantic Hay – The Word "Organization"', published in *Omega* in 1971, at the age of 80.

The editor of *Omega* then asked Professor Derek Pugh of the London Business School to respond to this article. Pugh, who had led the Aston Group in defining a new way of measuring the way in which enterprises defined their pattern of posts, professed to be 'nonplussed' at the argument that there had been any diversion away from the study of structure (Pugh 1973: 348). Moreover, he argued that 'Urwick is wrong in suggesting that a science can only be *built* on an exact definition of terms. Indeed exact definitions are a product of the scientific process, not a prerequisite for its beginning.' He also defended the use of the word 'organization', suggesting that 'organizations are collectivities where the processes of managing as defined by Fayol and Urwick take place' (1973: 349), and claiming that the use of the word in this way has been taken into general usage. Urwick, however, was not mollified, responding in a further issue of *Omega* in a highly distinctive manner:

> *Lines on D. S. Pugh's Theory of Organization*
> I have no animus
> Against the Pughsillanimous
> Nor any intention
> To handicap invention
> But D. S. Pugh's semantics
> Play such curious antics
> That it is hard for a simple mind
> Not to be left behind
>
> Thus 'organization means one thing
> And organizing' another
> The latter is the 'done thing'
> But, for the first, O brother!
> Beware the plotting varlets
> Who foil the finest theories
> Of academic starlets
> When they dance among the fairies

'A word is just a word' – deny
that wisdom if you can
And often, just a wordless sigh
Proclaims another man.
'Do not disturb my learned peace
with nonsense about meaning
But just supply the "elbow grease"
And I will do the gleaning.'

The issue of whether there was or could be a unified theory of management was one of considerable debate in the post-war period. It is perhaps best articulated in Harold Koontz's edited book (1962) *Towards a Unified Theory of Management,* the papers for which are also in the Henley Archive, indicating Urwick's awareness of this debate. Some sixty of the best-known names in American management participated in the symposium, the aim of which was to bring together eminent scholars with diverse research and analytical approaches to management, as well as experienced practitioners. The long-term goal was to make a start in clarifying some of the language of management, in integrating the study of management and its underlying disciplines, and to carve out a general theory of management. Urwick would have strongly approved of such an enterprise. In his initial paper, Koontz suggests that there were six main groups in management theory, namely:

- The management process, fathered by Fayol, and including Urwick amongst others, and known as the traditionalist or universalist school
- Empirical, that is, a study of experience
- The human behaviour school, including human relations and leadership
- The social system school, including Chester Barnard and Herbert Simon
- The decision theory school, that is, game theory
- The mathematical school, that is, those who see management as a system of mathematical models and processes

It must be admitted that the goal has not gone much further than this noble initial attempt. The classicists as a group were generally criticized by those who followed for their insufficient emphasis on the human aspects of management, including leadership, motivation, and communication. Nevertheless, as we have seen in this chapter and other parts of the book, Urwick made a point of differentiating between what he called the mechanics and dynamics of management, providing the basis for much of what would follow.

10

An Evaluation

Lyndall Urwick died peacefully at home on 5 December 1983, just three months short of his ninety-third birthday. He was buried in Longueville, Sydney, where he and his wife had been living since emigrating to Australia in 1961. A Thanksgiving Service was held in London on 24 January 1984 at St James's Church, Piccadilly, attended by a very large congregation. The main eulogists were John Marsh, the Director-General of the British Institute of Management (BIM), and Bruce Hills on behalf of Urwick Orr and Partners (UOP). Several obituaries also appeared in leading newspapers and journals, including *The Times*, the *Telegraph*, *Management Today*, and the *Newsletter of the American Academy of Management*, reflecting the esteem in which he was held as one of the leading management thinkers of his age.

In the Introduction, we noted that Urwick had many careers, many sides to his character, and that few people had been connected with such a wide variety of projects. It is now time to pick up these dimensions, amongst others, and proceed to evaluate his contribution to management. Starting with his character and abilities, the chapter deals firstly with the main influences that fashioned his outlook, beliefs, and vision. The next section assesses the various roles in his career, followed by his writing and its place in management thought. The final sections examine his impact, first in Britain, then internationally, coming finally to a summary of his place in history.

CHARACTER AND ABILITIES

Having provided Mrs Rowe's affectionate pen-portrait of Urwick in the Introduction, it is useful to recall it here as a starting point on which we can build an assessment of his attributes. Above all, it is apparent that Urwick's passion for management was unparalleled in Britain; and not just management in the abstract, but professionalism in management, derived from first reading Taylor in the trenches through to his last years. Few people have given such an abstract cause so much emphasis; passion really was the word to describe his attitude, a characteristic we have attempted to portray in this biography. At the same time, there are many other attributes: a single-minded vision which scarcely wavered throughout his life; a strong morality of almost religious dimensions; a continuing energy and commitment to hard work, indeed a workaholic; a strength and forcefulness of personality; and decisiveness in all issues. He was larger than life, with considerable charisma and what often goes with it, self-reliance, self-confidence, and self-esteem, tending on occasion towards arrogance. Beyond these attributes, he had considerable skills both as a writer, in prose and poetry, and as a speaker, as well as being a linguist of some ability.

On social and political levels, he was more tolerant and less class-conscious than many of his private school and Oxford contemporaries in the liberalism – with both a large and small 'L' – which he displayed throughout his life. He even discussed with the Webbs, the founders of the Fabian Society, the possibility of some tutoring. Nevertheless, he was patrician in other ways, not least in being able to devote considerable time to his passion for management because of what would seem to many to be extremely comfortable circumstances. If he had been concerned with making a fortune for himself, he would not have suggested shares for the consultants in UOP. Indeed, Tisdall (1982: 57) argued that Urwick was an idealist who had relatively little interest in the commercial aspects of running a consultancy. He was socially acceptable, a good networker, and maintained friendships with lots of people from different stages of his life, abroad as well as in Britain. He was an inveterate letter-writer; Roper (2001b) notes that he used draft letters, some of which were never sent, to work through his own thoughts on particular issues. He listened as well as he talked; one of his key attributes, as John Marsh noted in his eulogy at the Service of Thanksgiving, was that he never talked down to people. Both Marsh and Hills also made the point that he respected trade unions, as did Thomas (1986) in her article for the *Dictionary of Business Biography*. Although rationality was his forte, and he enjoyed a good argument, he also showed human relations skills in both the Army and the Fownes Company, and later in life retained ongoing popularity with the staff in UOP. He clearly impressed a lot of people from an early point in his life. Perhaps the most important person for his career was Seebohm Rowntree, while the Webbs presumably did not offer to provide personal tutorial service in an advanced degree to every young man to whom they were introduced. Later in life, his willingness to accept invitations to write or speak for whoever or wherever was an attractive feature – it is not known how many he turned down, but probably not many. He was especially good with younger people, whether students, managers, or especially junior consultants in UOP. Tisdall (1982: 58) notes: 'Urwick believed very strongly in both inspiration and the cultivation of the individual. His advice to young, newly qualified managers was to seek a purpose . . . and to stick to it – his own was to further the cause of management.'

Where does luck fit into an evaluation? Probably every person of significance needs some luck, often through a mentor or patron. Urwick was lucky in being able to survive the First World War when the odds were heavily against it, while in the midst of all that chaos and carnage he benefited from a huge piece of fortune in meeting Captain Walker, who was his first non-family mentor. After surviving the war, perhaps his most fortuitous development was being picked up as a promising potential manager by an excellent, indeed ideal, mentor, and patron, Seebohm Rowntree. It must be remembered, though, that Urwick positioned himself to meet Rowntree, in that his alertness to progressive movements had made him aware of the newly inaugurated 'Rowntree Lecture Conference for Supervisors', to which he sent some of the Fownes foremen in 1920. Their eulogistic presentation of Urwick's managerial style led Rowntree to invite Urwick to address the Conference in 1921, where he made a pioneering presentation of the Taylor philosophy 'Management as a Science'. In other words, he made his own luck. At the same time, Rowntree led him on to other things, notably providing him with a context in which he could flourish both intellectually and in managerial terms. In giving Urwick the effective leadership of the Management Research Groups (MRGs), this placed him in exactly the right spot when the Twentieth Century Fund was looking for a new Director of the International Management Institute (IMI), further confirming the value of his link with Rowntree. In pursuing the 'mission' side of his career, he was of course very fortunate not only that he was comfortably off in personal terms, but that UOP was willing to provide financial support for his activities.

While Urwick undoubtedly possessed a wide range of positive attributes, there were also some less positive aspects to his character that ought to be highlighted. In particular, what seemed to some as arrogance and dogmatism proved problematic, especially when he insisted on pursuing his own way to the point of a breakdown in relationships. This was certainly the case on the Administrative Staff College (ASC) working party, or at the Treasury, as well as arguably with the Twentieth Century Fund and over the issue of education within the BIM. There was also the later period at Rowntree's when he was under Arnold Rowntree, during which Quail (2009) has described him as something of 'a bull in a china shop'. He was undoubtedly obsessive about issues of management, pushing his own principles to the fore to the exclusion of other views, as the interaction with Pugh reported in Chapter 9 illustrates. He has even been accused of self-aggrandizement (Boyns 2006), although this does not fit easily with other aspects of his character. He certainly seems to have rubbed people in Whitehall up the wrong way when it came to handing out honours. Moreover, he must take a considerable amount of the blame, probably the preponderance, for the breakdown in the relationship with Orr; that was a failure in leadership, given his dominant role in the partnership. One should also add that on the domestic front he was not really a family man; his two wives must have felt lonely for considerable periods, given his propensity for travel, solitude, and hard work.

What is to be said about his use of his military title when most people who had served in the war dropped theirs as soon as they left the service? Was it a yearning for status? Or was it a desire to link himself with things military, given his interests long before actual service? He was an 'Old Contemptible', named after the Kaiser's dismissal of the six divisions which left Britain in August 1914. It is also noticeable that when he started his second attempt at an autobiography in the 1970s, he wrote about the war with such obvious emotion that readers are left in no doubt as to the power of his feelings. Interestingly, though, he also had a letterhead which did not use the title, for example, when he wrote to Stafford Cripps as Chancellor of the Exchequer about management in the civil service. Were there times when he felt that the title might be a disadvantage? As Cripps was such an ardent socialist, it might have been expected that he would never have been impressed by military titles.

The ASC issue illustrates the complexity of the man and something about his inability to work in committees. His letter of resignation from the working party provides clear evidence of how he always pursued his own principles, especially when he felt that the committee under Heyworth was being dogmatic. As he said:

But it is precisely because I believe that the cause is greater than any personal differences (or friendships) that I must, with regret, ask you to accept my disassociation from the group. For good or ill I have been associated with one cause – the promotion of more scientific methods of administration in this and other countries, throughout my adult life. I believe, though perhaps mistakenly, that I have acquired some authority and competence in this special field which is of some use to the community.

It was this position which he felt was being undermined by the committee's decisions on issues such as the length of courses and having a single executive head, given that he had advocated alternative views. Urwick was particularly aggrieved that the committee had rescinded previous decisions on the nature of the Principal's role that he had presented. What we have here is a mixture of principle, umbrage, and a desire to have his own way, which undermines the whole point of committee work. In spite of this, Henley has taken a generous line about his contribution to the formation of the college, which indicates that his role was both important and appreciated.

INFLUENCES ON HIS CAREER

Urwick was highly receptive to the views of others. In the traditions of the great liberal thinkers, he believed in the best in people, another rare thing in management at that time. Any starting point must be his upbringing in a close-knit, loving family, while his education at Repton and Oxford would have been seminal. Moreover, experiencing a highly progressive form of management at first hand helped to fashion his views, especially as this modus operandi was unusual at that time. Another uncommon feature of contemporary business families was the liberal views of his father, providing an inspirational influence at a vital time in Urwick's personal development. At the same time, a strong military orientation emerged in the young man, in large part based on his affection for an uncle, Frank Davidson Urwick, who was a professional soldier, leading to keen membership of the Officer Training Corps (OTC) at Repton, and ultimately his membership of the Territorial Army.

Indeed, Urwick could well have become a professional soldier, even without his wartime experiences. His military abilities were of an organizational as well as a fighting kind, again something uncommon in the British Army of the First World War. Quite exceptional was his chance interaction with Captain Walker and his introduction to Taylor's *Shop Management*, which determined his interest in the theory of management in a setting which must have been unique. Admiration for Taylor, however, was never so much for the details of production management for which Taylor has been remembered and criti- cized, but for his systematic and methodical approach – the 'scientific' approach. Urwick's sense of obligation to society also derived from the war, not least because he survived. In an article published in 1969 entitled 'Letter to an MBA', he vividly described his feelings:

I was a Reserve 2nd Lt and my battalion was one 2nd Lt short, so I was in the first day's fighting. Today I'm still here, with all my limbs. The chances of this happening were about one in 500. . . . We all want to 'make something' of ourselves. But how do we set about it? I was heir to a great family glove manufacturing business but I didn't merely want to make money. I wanted to make money legitimately, because I was doing something that was useful to my society.

It is perhaps easy to lose sight of this dimension of Urwick's views, and also how rare it was in his later attempts to convert British industry to scientific and systematic management.

Two years after the end of the war, Urwick went to Rowntree's in York, where he met another idealist, Seebohm Rowntree. Rowntree's was arguably the most important influence on his career, given that under Seebohm Rowntree: 'The Cocoa Works at York in those days were a kind of practical university of management.' As Child (1969: 39–40) noted: 'The Quaker employers...inclined towards the principle of employers' "duties as well as their rights", as Edward Cadbury put it.... In their opinion industry had a social function beyond that of profit-making, and production itself was a means to wider ends.' The Rowntree Group, including writers such as Seebohm Rowntree, Oliver Sheldon, C. H. Northcott, and Urwick, had a strong orientation towards the human factor in industry which contradicted the mechanistic aspects of scientific management that people such as Bedaux were introducing at that time. As these humanistic perspectives were perfectly compatible with Urwick's upbringing and latent views, they stayed with him throughout his career.

He left Rowntree's because, as he stated: 'I was offered the only international post in management worth having – the Directorship of the International Management Institute in Geneva. And I was still dreaming my dream.' The IMI also allowed him to widen and internationalize his beliefs, putting him on a different stage than that offered by his Rowntree's experience.

Apart from Rowntree and Taylor, of course, it was also during the 1920s and 1930s that he read widely on all matters relating to management and organization. This brought him into contact with some of the other great influences on his thinking, especially Mary Parker Follett and Henri Fayol. It was these pioneers that he included in his histories, especially the first book on the thirteen pioneers. In the British context, John Lee and Edward Elbourne were perhaps the most important influences on him, while in addition to Follett and Fayol internationally he made great use of Mooney and Reilley, his colleague Luther Gulick, and Peter Drucker impressed him immensely. This reveals the highly eclectic nature of his thinking, an asset that Urwick would have argued was crucial to the development of a thorough 'science of management'.

BELIEFS AND VISION

As Witzel (2002: 59) notes: 'More than any other management writer of his day...[Urwick] stressed that one of top management's key tasks was to formulate a clear vision of what lay ahead, and then to communicate that vision to all levels of the organisation.' His beliefs and vision can be expressed in the following propositions:

- Management should have a moral basis.
- Management should be based on scientific principles.
- Management, and indeed industry as a whole, should encompass both leadership and service to the community.
- Management should be a profession with ethical standards.
- Management should be about the long view, rather than a short-term perspective.
- Management requires an educational system for all managers, with industry leading, the universities providing, and the professional institutes certifying.
- Management should learn from its own history.

At the heart of Urwick's beliefs was the moral basis of management based upon personal integrity and an obligation to the wider society. These views were based on the tradition set by his father, links with others in the early management movement such as John Lee and Edward Elbourne, all significantly reinforced by his Rowntree experience. Indeed, his moral basis of management can be said to reflect Christian values as in the Quaker companies, which led British industry in this vital respect. He also took account of the views of Mary Parker Follett, using her motive of service to the community, leadership, and the use of science to make decisions (Wren 1994: 263). On the basis of these views, Urwick went on to argue in favour of a profession of management which would operate by professional standards and ethics, enlisting knowledge for the service of others. His views on leadership were also influenced by Follett, as well as his military experiences, in which 'company purposes were to be integrated with individual and group purposes, and this integration called for the highest calibre of executive leadership' (Wren 1994: 263). His approach followed what would now be considered the 'stakeholder' view, rather than the prevalent 'shareholder' view of management's obligations. It was this division which was at the heart of the philosophical divide with Filene at the time when the IMI was being dissolved.

Perhaps not surprisingly, his vision of the future was best expressed in *Management of Tomorrow*. Although Child (1969: 88) criticized *Management of Tomorrow* for 'Urwick's almost complete lack of concern for trade unionism as this might impinge upon the enterprise', this was not true in relation to his own managerial role. He was always willing to work with trade unions, even though he might not have an explicit place for them in his writings. For example, in his role on the glove-makers' JIC, in the reorganization of the sales office at Rowntree's, where the works council was represented, and in the way he set up UOP to consult with the unions before starting a project, Urwick was always anxious to involve the unions.

Taking this point further, one can quote Kransdorff's view (1984), expressed in his article 'Idealism Was Not Enough' in the *Financial Times*, written after the merger of UOP into Price Waterhouse, that Urwick was not only a visionary, but also a practising idealist, in that UOP was a bold experiment in worker participation. Indeed, Urwick's vision was a cooperative where all employees were joint owners through profit sharing. Although this vision did not encourage sufficient retention of profits when times became difficult, and a top-heavy management structure was imposed on the organization, UOP was distinctive in the way it operated. On the other hand, it is likely that Kransdorff misunderstood the concept of worker participation in this context, because in view of his military background and attitudes Urwick was never interested in sharing power with workers; consultation was as far as he would go. Nevertheless, his concept of industrial democracy was manifested elsewhere, as in his emphasis on Lilienthal's *The Tennessee Valley Authority: Democracy on the March* (1944), which assessed this bold experiment in public activism. Similarly, his participation in the Liberal Party at Oxford, and later the Liberal Party Workshop in 1926, were an expression of his views on management. Specifically, he made a particular point of the inherent role and responsibility in industrial and commercial management of service to the community, arguing that all operational activities in the business world over which management professionally presided were the lifeblood of the community.

ROLES IN HIS CAREER

One can certainly say that over the course of an extremely busy lifetime, Urwick enjoyed a range of careers that few can match. In the first instance, Urwick was involved on two levels during the First World War, as both an infantryman and on organizational work at Rouen as a staff officer. By almost any standards, he had a good war. He also did well at Fownes before the family sold its equity. On the other hand, even though he contributed effectively to certain changes at Rowntree's, he did ruffle the feathers of more senior managers, and it would not have been easy for him to continue his career there in spite of his close relationship with Seebohm Rowntree. Nevertheless, in the MRGs it was his 'hard work and management skills which enabled the programme to come to fruition' (Witzel 2003: 301).

The Directorship of the IMI was his first leadership role. Although there were some significant problems associated with that job, given the underlying political issues which had caused the departure of Urwick's predecessor, it is not surprising that Urwick was never able to resolve these. We have seen in Chapter 3 that Urwick did a good job of developing the MRGs, disseminating information through the journal and booklets, and signing up new members. However, with the onset of the Depression, it was inevitable that the deep-seated tensions would resurface between those who saw the IMI as existing only to serve the interests of large corporations on the one hand and those who wanted it to advocate business's wider social responsibilities on the other. As one of the leading advocates of the Rationalization Movement, Urwick was clearly of the latter persuasion, while Filene, the mainstay of the Twentieth Century Fund, was of the former, at least in the early 1930s. The decline in the value of the American dollar and the rise of the Nazi movement in Germany must also have been powerful pressures persuading Filene to withdraw support. In these circumstances, Urwick would have had great difficulty acting as the puppet of the Twentieth Century Fund, against his own beliefs and the views of the International Labour Organization (ILO), leading to a fundamental schism between the two and the dissolution of the IMI.

In his next role, as founder and head of UOP, however, he must take at least as much of the blame for the problems that arose as Orr, and maybe more. As Brech suggests:

Reverting to that unfortunate internal situation of conflict between the two Partners, the puzzling feature in the traumatic episode lies in Lyndall Urwick's utter failure to recognise the opportunity and the need for an input of leadership skill. Puzzling because during two decades he had been giving high significance to the 'leadership' factor within managerial responsibility, on-going from his recognition for it even earlier within the military command role. He was already moving towards his advocacy of the proposal that the military appreciation should be seen as an example and a lesson for professional management responsibility in industry and commerce.

As chairman of the company, he was naturally responsible for internal leadership in all respects, including conflict between the two founding partners. As we have already seen, Urwick had a high regard for John Leslie Orr, both as a person and manager, despite being critical of incidental deficiencies. Although he was also aware of Orr's lack of a charismatic persona, regrettably Urwick knew himself to be uneasily intolerant in dealing with lesser mortals, reducing his ability to take on a clear leadership role. Even though he possessed the knowledge necessary to be a sound leader, the circumstantial evidence points to a barrier inherent in the situation, namely, that Urwick was blinded to a solution due to his absorption of the public reputation and acclaim that his institutional educational contributions were gaining. Indeed, his external speaking and writing commitments in the late 1930s were so substantial that this must have impacted significantly on the partnership. Crucially, Urwick enjoyed this so much, compared to the relatively humdrum work of running the firm, that he distanced himself from Orr, thereby creating an enormous strain on the relationship. Urwick and Orr agreed on many things, especially when it came to policy and people, but there was a constant struggle for power. Although rivalry is perhaps inherent within management consultancy firms, at UOP this turned into a virulent form that inevitably affected morale across the organization.

Having said this, UOP was a considerable success, even if by the 1950s it was the smallest of the Big Four consultancy firms. Witzel (2003: 259) argues that UOP 'was enormously influential and was for many years the leading consultancy firm in Britain'. Its initiatives in the field of training and education, most of them stemming from Urwick's ideas, proved to be highly influential, while he made a contribution to the wider consultancy movement through his advocacy on public platforms (Tisdall 1982: 54). Management consultancy has become one of the most vibrant sectors in many Western economies, a trend that Urwick undoubtedly helped to initiate in Britain. Indeed, Lillian Gilbreth noted in her Gantt Medal citation (Thomas 1986: 601) that: 'Just as Shelley was "the Poets' Poet", he seems to be the "Consultants' Consultant"'. On the other hand, although its decline from 460 staff at its high-water mark in 1968 to 120 when it was taken over by Price Waterhouse in 1984 occurred well after Urwick had left the firm, UOP ultimately lacked the vision to change and the resources to survive when times became difficult. How far Urwick could be held to have contributed to this failure is a moot point, and while he was not involved in resisting the move away from manufacturing, certainly the organizational structure which he had designed contributed to its financial weakness.

Later roles in management were essentially as a leader in various aspects of the management movement. Ironically, though, given his knowledge of and enthusiasm for the American system, Urwick was hardly connected at all to the most influential development of that era, the creation of the first British business schools. As we have noted, although he was acquainted with John Bolton, the leading figure in the Foundation for Management Education (FME), and probably knew many of the others involved, he was not at the forefront. This may have been either because he was on the verge of moving to Australia or maybe he was getting old. Nevertheless, there is a paradox here which may not have been fully explained.

There were several different dimensions to his management movement work after 1945, none of which resolved the wider problem of British management. Indeed, one might claim that each commitment tended to fizzle out, given the lack of success with the BIM and the certificate/diploma system of management education, the small scale of the Henley ASC, and the lack of interest in the results of the Anglo-American Council on Productivity (AACP). Moreover, his pursuit of a professional framework for British management was never popular with much of the business establishment. Such was the level of disagreement on this issue that his colleague in other matters of management, Sir Charles Renold, resigned as Vice-President of the BIM when the BIM–IIA amalgamation took place in 1956, on the grounds that this gave tacit acceptance to the professionalization of management (Brech 2002–1: 802). In addition, Urwick never quite found a role in the management movement which suited his personality and capabilities, having been frustrated in his aspiration to become founding Principal of the ASC.

The final component of his career was his 'mission at large', encompassing his talks to audiences which must have totalled many thousands of people. In some respects, he can be likened to itinerant preachers such as Wesley, using not just words but style to sell his message. Since his speaking was for the most part oriented to management, rather than academic, audiences, clarity and ease of comprehension were central to the reception of the message, and for that matter his speeches were so well constructed that they easily translated into written pieces. As we have seen in Chapter 8, though, after he migrated to Australia his level of recognition in Britain fell, resulting in fewer invitations when he returned for his biannual visits. As John Marsh said at the Service of Thanksgiving, 'had he remained in Britain he would have played a special role as the professional doyen or even as an ageing master of his several crafts. As it was, for some two generations of managers he was only a name.' On the other hand, he continued to be invited to speak elsewhere, especially of course in his new homeland, as well as in other places which were happy to have him. Indeed, much of his recognition and status after 1961 was outside Britain, reiterating a point we have made elsewhere in this biography, that this says more about British industry, managers, and universities than it does about Urwick himself.

WRITING

In the long run, Urwick's significance will be judged primarily by his writings. Perhaps the first thing to note about these is their sheer scale, with some 280 books and articles over six decades amongst 998 documents of all kinds in the Henley archives. In addition to its scale, his writing was elegant and scholarly, clear and easy to read, with touches of humour and above all, reflecting his passion for management. Another important aspect of his writing was the consistency in his views, because most originated from his Rowntree years and were based on the social responsibilities of management. Crucially, though, his conceptualization was not just broad and abstract; it was rigorous, detailed, and immensely practical for those willing to implement the ideas, as the diagrams in Chapter 9 exemplify. No modern academic would dare to use such labyrinthine minutiae in a single figure. Most of his writing was not based on research in the modern vogue, but was rather inductively, philosophically, and experientially based. Nevertheless, he was strongly in favour of empirical research, as evidenced by his pursuit of surveys of the British scene while at the IMI, via the MRGs, and also with Leverhulme and the British Management Council (BMC), while we have quoted from his own survey of staff roles in Chapter 9. Frequently, his writing cited numerous sources, approximating to modern academic work, rather than much writing of his own era. Above all, he was very well read, not just in management, and had a strong feeling for history. He accumulated a considerable library of books and journals even in the 1920s (which he gave to the MRGs when he went to Geneva), which reflected his considerable intellectual interest in management as a subject, at a time when such interest was rare. In other words, he had a solid base for his writing.

As an all-round management man, his writing covered a wide range of topics; to repeat the quotation from Pugh et al. (1971: 107), 'there can be few topics in administration on which Urwick has not something to say'. Nevertheless, his particular concern was organization theory, of which Wren and Bedian (2009: 362) note that he 'worked tirelessly to develop a general theory of organization and management'. A second topic with which he will always be associated was the development of management from its original pioneers; indeed, a lot of people owe their place in the history of management to him. Moreover, as a publicist and synthesizer, he had an ability to recognize what was important; his important role in the recognition of Fayol in the English-speaking world is evidence of this, while such important figures as Graicunas and even Follett (in management anyway) owe their publications to him.

He was always generous to other authors, never claiming credit for others' work, even tending to underestimate his own contribution. We can go back to Dorothy Rowe and her statement that his favourite claim was that he had written nothing new, but only drawn the public's attention to the great writing of others. Indeed, he was a great synthesizer as a result of his interest in others and his ability to recognize their talents. He probably saw himself as a propagandist, rather than an original and theoretical writer. Urwick's writing, although his work is still recognized as path breaking, is seen as a stepping stone from one set of pioneers – Taylor, Fayol, and Follett – to another set of developments, more flexible, more American, more academic.

Nevertheless, Witzel (2003: 299) argues that he was an original thinker, even if influenced by a wide variety of others. He is the icon of classical management in Britain and a key figure, worldwide, in a school which must be recognized as an indispensable stage in the development of management thought.

To place this more firmly in context, Urwick was associated with 'The One Best Way', a concept that originated with Frank Gilbreth but was also associated with scientific management and Taylorism. Urwick argued in favour of a rationalistic systematism that would produce the same results from the same starting point, even if circumstances differed. While this led to criticism, he rejected the narrow implications of this aspect of scientific management, noting (Leadership in the Twentieth Century 1957: 1):

Much confusion has been caused by the fact that the phrase *scientific management* has been misunderstood. It has been interpreted as a claim that managing a business can be an exact science in the sense that mathematics or physics are exact sciences. Such a claim is, of course, nonsense and was never intended by those who developed the phrase. Managing a business is an art. It is an art which is concerned all the time with human beings.

He also strongly rejected another misuse of the phrase 'scientific management', quoting Taylor's famous outburst: 'Scientific Management... is not any of the devices which the average man calls to mind when it is spoken of' (Urwick and Brech 1945: 10). It was those such as Bedaux who took the idea and applied it for the single purpose of achieving greater output and managerial control, thereby giving the concept a bad name. Like other big ideas in the management world, such as business process re-engineering (BPR), its original proponents did not expect, or indeed accept, the outcomes that were imposed in its name.

A similar issue arose over his apparent lack of concern for the human dimension. This was yet another fallacy, in that he (and for that matter, Taylor) was concerned with the human factor, as he showed throughout his career. Urwick was strongly associated with what might be called the 'Rowntree School', which was strongly oriented to the human dimensions of industry, a view he held well after his Rowntree period. We have already registered Elton Mayo's recognition of him as the first person to take public notice of the Hawthorne studies. Sadler (1998) noted that he played a big part in the recognition that people matter just as much as mechanical systems, while Guillén (1994: 246) argued that: 'Lyndall Urwick was perhaps the most influential human relations management intellectual and consultant.' As Marsh noted at the Service of Thanksgiving, 'he insisted on the importance of the human factor; "man" is rightly the first concern of "*man*"agement, he used to say'.

What Urwick was trying to move away from was the tradition of rule-of-thumb-based management towards a more systematic approach to decision-making. He was not actually much concerned with the production focus, and time-and-motion study in particular, with which scientific management had become unfairly associated (in considerable part because of Bedaux's activities); his focus was rather on the higher levels of management and the need for a rational and systematic approach. It was this concept of 'rationalization' that he took up in his first foray as an author outside Rowntree's. As Urwick was more interested in the need for systematic, rather than scientific, management, he would have approved of Litterer's differentiation (1986: 20–1) between rule-of-thumb, systematic, and scientific approaches to management.

What within this barrage of writing is most important is of course a matter of opinion, creating some dispute amongst commentators. Tisdall (1982: 33) suggests that 'The best known of his books are probably *The Elements of Administration* and *Leadership in the Twentieth Century*', while Davenport-Hines in the *Dictionary of National Biography* mentions *The Meaning of Rationalisation* and *Management of Tomorrow*. The key book for George is *The Elements of Administration*, which as we saw in Chapter 9 he regarded as a milestone in the development of management, while Miner (1995), in his compendium of key writings on administrative theory, includes three from Urwick: two articles, 'The Purpose of a Business' (1955) and 'Organization and Theories about the Nature of Man' (1967), and *Papers on the Science of Administration* (1970) given to the Academy of Management some three decades after the original book was published. It is also of interest that in this compendium, Urwick's writings are referenced as frequently as any other author in the collection, providing the kind of assessment that modern academics would regard as a key measure of their influence. Thomas (1978) reserves her highest praise for his 1922 article 'Experimental Psychology and the Creative Impulse' and 'Committees in Organisation' from the late 1930s. Yet for many people, *The Making of Scientific Management* is Urwick's best-known publication, while for others *The Golden Book of Management* created a new perspective on how management developed by focusing on the individuals concerned. We for our part would suggest that in addition to *The Elements of Administration*, Urwick's most influential pieces are 'The Principles of Direction and Control' and 'Organisation as a Technical Problem', reviewed in Chapter 4. It is also worth noting that given this diversity of views on Urwick's most important writings, a substantial number were clearly influential.

In trying to assess Urwick's contribution to management through his writing, we cannot do better than to quote George (1972: 135):

Lyndall Urwick is not an innovator in the field of management in the sense that Fayol or Sheldon were. He has made a contribution, however, by his timely consolidation of the managerial principles developed by others. In fact, it sometimes happens that men who express the right theory at the right time frequently make a greater contribution than the original pioneer whose ideas were disregarded because they were decades ahead of their time. This is how Urwick has served the management continuum. His work crystallized the similar concepts that had been independently developed, thereby giving them more credence and serving to mould them into a system of managerial thought.

IMPACT ON MANAGEMENT IN BRITAIN

At the outset of the Second World War, even though management as a concept was rarely acknowledged in his home country, Urwick through his writing and his public speaking was arguably the leading figure in management in Britain. He used vehicles such as the MRGs to disseminate his views, while he had also created Britain's Management Library. In addition, in putting forward blueprints for a national management institute and an ASC, as well as starting UOP, his education-developmental work was considerable. There were consequently several ways in which Urwick could claim the leadership of the British management movement: he had written more about management than any of his contemporaries; he was the figure to whom people looked to represent management at an International Committee for Scientific Management (CIOS) conference, or as chair of a committee to set up a new system of management education in the post-war period; he was arguably the key figure in the formation of the BIM; he played an important role in setting up the ASC; and he led the deputation to study American management education for the AACP. Perhaps most of all, he was the figure who was most recognized by managers as a whole, and by the general public, as a result of his frequent appearances at conferences or public lectures. The question is whether all this amounted to much.

In the first place, it is necessary to note that the management movement was hardly a coherent entity and its leadership never formal. Indeed, we need to take a look at what the management movement represented. Child (1969: 227) argues that: 'management thought developed as the expression of an emerging would-be professional management movement. This movement was in its early stages acutely aware of the need to differentiate itself from a system of industrial control based on rights of ownership – it claimed control on the basis of professional impartiality and expertise.' Such a position, however, never won the support of industrialists on the one hand or workers on the other, and there were few managers who joined professional institutes with this perspective. Not even the BIM ever picked up the intellectual, professional, and developmental role that the management movement advocated. On the other hand, it is arguable that Urwick could have done more to make the BIM an effective body, given his role in setting it up, his status and his vice-presidential position. He was associated with the very men in the BIM who did most to make it a narrow organization concerned with recruiting only the top echelons of British management, namely, Charles Renold as the first President (Renold later became a trustee of UOP) and Leo Russell (who although backed by Urwick was never an efficient director-general). The older Institute of Industrial Administration (IIA), rather than the new BIM, was the closest to a professional institute reflecting the objectives of the management movement. In other words, the management movement, with its emphasis on professionalism through a 'scientific' approach to management, never had much of a following; indeed, if a 'movement' requires some degree of institutionalization, it never achieved that position. On education, Urwick worked through the professional institutes and the college system, rather than through the universities. Although he would very much have liked the universities to play a role, this was never a possibility up to the 1950s. He also had major disagreements over the plans for Henley, principally on the issue of the length of the programme, because while he wanted longer periods of study, akin to the American model, these were never supported by Heyworth and British business.

At another level, Urwick was also never successful as a consultant in persuading large British companies to adopt his organizational ideas; this conversion process had to wait until the 1960s when the large American consultancy operations such as McKinsey moved into the United Kingdom (McKenna 2006: 165–91). Indeed, Urwick failed to develop strong links with large British companies, through either the management movement or UOP. His most active attempt to create organizational change was during the Second World War – he always believed that management was as important in government as in industry – but this also resulted in the rejection of his recommendations both at the War Office and especially by the Treasury. While it might have been expected that Urwick would have been received better when he had been brought in by the head of Treasury, this was certainly not the case in practice.

Nor was he greatly involved with the trend that began in the late 1950s to take management into the universities, although his views were of course very much part of the groundswell of interest in this move. By the time this trend began to bear fruit in the mid-1960s, Urwick had gone to Australia. Another paradox is that in the *Dictionary* article and later, contrary to the views of many of his contemporaries Urwick had strongly urged the value of university education as the basis for a managerial career, especially mentioning economics and commerce (Brech 2002–5: 489). Yet it must also be stressed that he did not have much contact with British universities. Could he have done more to work with the universities at an earlier stage, or did his approach to professionalism need to be pursued through the professional institutes? A few universities had experimented with management education in the interwar period, but without great success or much support from industry (Keeble 1992). Having said that, British academics generally did not see management as a teachable subject, preferring to stick to the pursuit of knowledge for its own sake, rather than use it as a basis for practical subjects. Thus, there was no one in the university sector with whom Urwick could work, while the university framework failed to provide him with a position from which to launch a campaign. Things might have been different if he had become Principal of Henley. It was not until the 1970s when Aston became the first university to invite him to give a lecture series, by which time Urwick was in his eighties.

Although the inefficiency of British industry, and especially its management, was a common theme of post-war Penguin books such as *The Stagnant Society, Britain on Borrowed Time, What's Wrong with British Industry, The Rise and Fall of the British Manager*, and so on, the management movement as exemplified by Urwick was rarely identified as a key part of the solution. Nor, in the next generation, when the cultural dimensions of British industry were subject to much criticism, was this the case when writers such as Wiener (1981) and Barnett (1986) pursued similar themes. Indeed, Urwick's career can be seen as an insight into the backwardness of British management and a key dimension of the Wiener thesis. Even though the index to Wiener's book does not list the word 'management', his damning indictment of the inability of British business to adapt to change reflected the wider failure of the management movement to make much of a difference to a system that only started to adapt significantly in the 1980s.

When delving further into Urwick's approach towards management education, it is also apparent that he failed to follow up on the AACP report. Why did he not take up the MBA concept, given that he was so American in orientation? He never did pursue the MBA or the undergraduate degree in business studies, even though they were the main focus in the United States and he was always holding up this country as a paragon. So why not pursue the American degrees? There is a paradox here, because it did prove to be the way forward once the first British business schools had been established in 1965. Was it because he was too committed to the college programme of certificates and diplomas which his committee had recommended in 1948? One should also stress that he was dependent on the professional institutes and the colleges for the development of his educational plans, in spite of the 'low status of the scheme in the eyes of employers' (Brech 2002–5: 256). It was quite unrealistic to expect to be able to run a course for managers in the technical colleges, given the inherent snobbery of British business. By mid-1952, namely, before the Urwick Committee's professional 'Finals' programme had been officially initiated, the situation was reported as being complex, confusing, uncoordinated, and in need of review. Another possibility is his emphasis on management as a profession, because one might argue that this needed to be linked with the professional institutes. While one might say that any failure was as much to do with the inherent beliefs of British management, it remains a moot point whether Urwick made much of a difference on some key issues.

INTERNATIONAL STANDING

Even if he was not a man of his time in the British context – arguably, he was too far ahead of it – Urwick was one of the great internationalists of management. He was in many ways better recognized in the United States, not least because people and institutions there could appreciate his work. He also seems to have had a capacity for keeping in touch, especially with Americans, but also with developments in other countries. He was an excellent letter-writer, he had good networking skills, and was able to recognize talent in others, while he had strong friendships with people such as Mary Parker Follett and Lillian Gilbreth. These skills may be at the bottom of his undoubted ability to synthesize and publicize the talents of others. Of course, his international reputation was in large part a result of his good fortune in securing such a key position as Director of the IMI. Apart from giving him enormous opportunities both to visit and to be known in other countries, he also read more widely than most other Britons, while long after his sojourn in Geneva he was a staunch internationalist, attending almost every CIOS Conference for the rest of his life.

As a direct result of his international activities, he was given many more awards by foreign institutions, especially those in the United States, than he was in Britain, and by important institutions such as the American Management Association (AMA), the American Society for Mechanical Engineers, and the American Academy of Management. He had connections with various foreign universities, but few if any British ones. He was asked to write many more articles for foreign journals than he was in Britain, not least because there were no adequate British journals. He was also able to settle down easily in Australia, where he soon developed a highly receptive audience. Compared with his peers in Britain who lived during the management movement period, namely, those in the *Golden Book* such as Bowie, Elbourne, Lee, Myers, Renold, Rowntree, and Sheldon, Urwick stands out on the international scene. All these named were worthy people, but with the possible exception of Sheldon's sole major work *The Philosophy of Management* and Rowntree's connections with American industrialists, they were never recognized internationally in the same way that Urwick was lauded. Once again, though, this says more about the British business environment, rather than the nature of Urwick's contribution to management thinking and practice.

CONTEMPORARY RELEVANCE

While most professions recognize their origins, management struggles significantly with this exercise. This was one of the reasons why Urwick was a leading exponent of learning from the past, not only in his magisterial writing about its pioneers, but also in the way he thought and in almost every lecture that he gave. In this respect, there are four dimensions of Urwick's career that deserve closer inspection in a contemporary context.

First, as part of the Classical School, he was in no doubt that the 'classical' principles of management which he espoused, and played a key part in promoting, had an ongoing relevance, as we have seen in his review of *Papers in the Science of Administration* for the American Academy of Management in 1970. The Classicists have certainly been criticized, especially for their belief in universal principles, but neither have succeeding approaches come up with ways of analysing management activities that have been generally accepted. Indeed, universalistic principles still have a place in the management literature as a counterbalance to contingency-based approaches. Similarly, in the principles of organization problems arise when we try to move away from concepts such as hierarchy, unity of command, and the correspondence of authority and responsibility (Child 2009).

A second area where Urwick's approach strikes a modern chord is in the ethical values he associated with management, its social responsibilities to the wider community, and its role as a profession. Unhappy episodes in the twenty-first century's experience of capitalism, from Enron at the start of the century to the financial crises of 2008, have raised questions about the wider responsibilities of management, over and above narrow self-interest in the name of shareholder value. The issue of whether management is a profession has been largely ignored since Urwick's arguments with his antagonists in the BIM in the 1950s, although the Chartered Management Initiative of the 1990s made a valiant attempt to revive the British debate, followed by Khurana's controversial analysis of American failings (2007).

A third dimension of contemporary relevance lies in the operation of consultants, who have become a ubiquitous part of modern managerial decision-making. One of the strongest of Urwick's tenets about consultancy was the obligation to educate the client to operate and take responsibility for the recommendations, rather than, as often appears to be the case, for the consultants to maintain the secrets of their knowledge in the expectation of continuing contracts. UOP attempted to implement this philosophy as extensively as possible, positively influencing the strategies of other British consultancy firms from the 1940s (Ferguson 2003).

A fourth surely lies in Urwick's belief in the importance of history, not just in paying homage to those who originated ideas which are now commonplace, but in the operation of organizations in the interests of continuity, rather than on the assumption that the present and future are all that matters (Kransdorff 1998; Thomson 2001; Lamond 2005). Collins and Porras (2002) in their best-seller *Built to Last* emphasize that the strengths of their visionary companies are based on a recognition of their past for core values and purpose; although they do not quote Urwick, he would have strongly supported their perspective. And this brings us to Urwick's own place in history.

SUMMATION AND PLACE IN HISTORY

Morgen Witzel, in his *Fifty Key Figures in Management* (2003: 299) made the bold claim that: 'Lyndall Urwick is the single most important figure in the development of modern management practices and thought.' While this is certainly a strong statement, it was made in the context of evaluating many other major figures at the same time. Nor is he the only one to give such an accolade, because Kipping (1997: 71) has claimed that Urwick was 'one of the most influential British and European management thinkers of the twentieth century', and that he remains the only figure in Britain who has achieved international standing as a management intellectual. These are of course difficult issues to measure, but one way of bearing out such views is by noting the number of references to Urwick in what is still the main book on the subject, Child's *British Management Thought* (1969), in which he receives considerably more references than any other British writer. Child makes three key statements about Urwick's significance: firstly (1969: 86), that 'the major step towards the construction of a priori "principles of management"' came with Urwick's remarkable essay of 1928 on 'Principles of Direction and Control'; second (1969: 86), that 'Urwick . . . was for the next thirty years [from 1929] to become the most outstanding and prolific contributor to British management thought'; and third (1969: 87), in referring to Urwick's *Management of Tomorrow*, this was 'probably the outstanding British work of the 1930s'.

As Urwick was important in many areas, it is not enough to judge him only as a writer or as a leader in management development or as a key figure in the development of consultancy. Each area needs careful consideration. He did an enormous amount of writing – in all some 280 pieces – many of which were associated with the publication of lectures. A lot of people learnt much about management from these lectures and articles, no doubt helped by the lucidity with which they were presented. Heller, in his foreword to Urwick's *Leadership in the Twentieth Century*, notes that more than 100 people had to be turned away from the lectures which formed the basis of that book, so popular were they (1957: v). Another of his most important contributions was gaining recognition for other writers and figures in management, both in his own writing and lectures, and in his histories. While the history of management arguably awaits its own serious analyst (Wilson and Thomson 2006; Witzel 2009), Urwick's stories of the pioneers will provide an indispensable reference work for any comprehensive account. Fayol was perhaps the most important of these, although he had of course been fully recognized in his homeland of France, while in the pantheon of management thought he emerges as an important, if not dominant, figure. In the primary work in this field, Wren (1994: 303–4) notes that '[Urwick] distinguished himself by his efforts to develop a general theory of organization and management. . . . He was optimistic that a general theory of administration could be attained, and his own work represented a substantial step in that direction'. He is comparable to Peter Drucker in the US, because although he achieved a great deal of general recognition, his name is not associated in modern textbooks with the formulation of theory in detailed areas. In fact, the analogy to Drucker goes further in terms of his idealism and the breadth of his interests in management, while just like Drucker, Urwick capitalized on the past to make way for the future.

When it comes to management consultancy, while UOP may not have been the biggest of the British management consultancies, in many respects it was the most innovative, especially in its emphasis on the educative aspects of consulting, rather than merely producing reports. One might even describe the Bedford and Slough training centres as more like business schools than consultancy operations. In addition, Urwick was largely responsible for introducing a different culture than the abrasive approach taken by Bedaux in the 1920s and 1930s. Urwick, moreover, was the best-known consultant in Britain for over twenty years after founding UOP, although it must be admitted that this was in considerable part due to his standing in the management field, rather than his work as a consultant. The Lyndall Urwick Society still exists at the time of writing, which says something about the man who inspired it.

Looking more broadly, it might seem remarkable that while he was nominated for certain honours in Britain, he never received one throughout his management career. In some respects this is hardly surprising, given his aggressive and impetuous behaviour while at the Treasury, even though he was undoubtedly right in criticizing the civil service for its poor management. It must also be said that Urwick was not supported by many of the higher echelons of British business, who were for the most part quite happy with the status quo in management. In that sense, he was an irritant to those people in both government and industry who might have supported him for an honour; he was never really part of the Establishment. On the other hand, as we have just seen, he achieved substantial recognition abroad, especially in the United States. His recognition by the American management community was certainly more than any other Briton, and almost certainly more than any other foreign national who did not move permanently to the United States.

This leads us to a balance sheet of Urwick's career. There were many pluses. Amongst the major ones were: his idealistic passion for management, charismatic speaking and writing, a capacity to synthesize and conceptualize the scope and diversity of his output, his morality and professional values, crafting a vision of the future, and his place among the great Classicists. And to use a phrase of his own, he put the game above the prize. To back these up, there were also many secondary dimensions: some substantial managerial successes; his rounded, well-read intellectualism; a capacity to network and develop strong friendships, especially internationally; his role as the first great historian of management; firm support for research as well as a priori principles; linguistic skills and the entry they gave to other writers; and strong support for younger managers. Against these, however, must be set some flaws: an inability to convert ideas into durable institutions; the reluctance to accept criticism; a failure to adapt ideas to changing circumstances; and his intermittent faults of leadership, intolerance, abrasiveness, and arrogance. He was not a good committee man, not by any means always diplomatic, and not always a considerate family man. He certainly had the capacity to rub some people up the wrong way.

So, certainly a towering figure but one beset with paradoxes. Indeed, we have used the word paradox quite liberally in this final chapter, principally because while Lyndall Urwick was socially able, he had some substantial disagreements in key dimensions of his career. He looked to the future but built on the past, seeing himself as a futurist, yet becoming a Classicist. He achieved a lot of recognition in a narrow band of the management movement, but did not manage to achieve the change he wanted in the country. While the institutional changes he pursued seemed logical, they were rarely implemented. In spite of his status, he never quite led a specific movement. The change which did work out was essentially to copy the American model of management education and development, which he had surveyed and recommended as a model. Indeed, he achieved broader recognition in the United States, to the point of being something of a prophet not without honour save in his own country.

In coming to a conclusion, we should recall John Marsh's eulogy at the Service of Thanksgiving, still as true now as when he spoke the words: 'As a new economic and social era is unfolding, we need exemplars of Lyndall Urwick's integrity, his vision, his internationalism, his determination of priorities, his courage and his sense of service.' But we should finish with a suitable epitaph, for which the dedication of the second edition of *The Golden Book of Management* still seems appropriate:

> To Lt. Col. Lyndall F. Urwick
> management pioneer, eminent consultant,
> renowned scholar, and synthesizer of
> management thought

Bibliography

There is a partial descriptive bibliography of Urwick's writings up to 1958, published by Urwick Orr and Partners (1958). *L. Urwick: A Bibliography.* London.

Anglo-American Council on Productivity (AACP) (1951a). 'Education for Management'. London.

—— (1951b). 'Universities and Industry'. London.

—— (1952). 'Final Report of the Council'. London.

Barnett, C. (1986). *The Audit of War.* London. Macmillan.

Boyns, T. (2007). 'Lyndall Urwick at the International Management Institute, Geneva, 1928–1934: Right Job, Wrong Man?', Paper presented at management history workshop, Oxford.

Brech, E. (2002–1). *The Concept and Gestation of Britain's Central Management Institute, 1902–1976.* Bristol. Thoemmes Press.

—— (2002–5). *Education, Training and Development for and in Management.* Bristol. Thoemmes Press

Briggs, A. (1961). *Social Thought and Social Action: A Study of the Work of Seebohm Rowntree 1871–1954.* London. Longmans.

Chandler, A. D. (1962). *Strategy and Structure.* Harvard. Belknap Press.

Child, J. (1969). *British Management Thought.* London. George Allen and Unwin.

—— (2009). Personal Correspondence.

Clark, I. (1999). 'Institutional Stability in Management Practice and Industrial Relations: The Influence of the Anglo-American Council for Productivity, 1948–52'. *Business History,* 41/3.

Collins, J. and Porras, J. (2002). *Built to Last.* New York. Harper Business Essentials.

Coopey, R. (2003). 'The British Glove Industry, 1750–1970: The Advantages and Vulnerability of a Regional Industry', in John F. Wilson and A. Popp (eds.), *Industrial Clusters and Regional Business Networks in England, 1750–1970.* Routledge. London.

Dale, E. and Urwick, L. (1960). *Staff in Organizations.* New York. McGraw-Hill.

Davenport-Hines, R. (1990). 'Lyndall Urwick' in *Dictionary of National Biography.* London.

Drucker, P. (1954). *The Practice of Management.* New York. Harper and Row.

Elbourne, E. (1919). *The Management Problem.* London. The Library Press.

—— (1934). *The Fundamentals of Industrial Administration.* London. Macdonald and Evans.

Emerson, H. (1913). *Twelve Principles of Efficiency.* New York. *Engineering Magazine.*

Fayol, H. (1949). *General and Industrial Management.* London. Pitman.

Ferguson, M. (2001). 'Models of Management Education and Training: The Consultancy Approach'. *Journal of Industrial History,* 4/1.

Ferguson, M. (2002). *The Rise of Professional Management Consulting in Britain.* Aldershot, UK. Ashgate.

—— (2003). 'The Evolution of Education and Training in British Management Consultancy'. *Journal of Industrial History,* 6/1.

Fitzgerald, R. (1995). *Rowntree and the Marketing Revolution.* Cambridge. Cambridge University Press.

Fox, E. and Urwick, L. (eds.) (1973). *The Collected Papers of Mary Parker Follett.* London. Pitman.

Franks Report (1963). *British Business Schools.* London. British Institute of Management.

George, C. (1972). *The History of Management Thought.* Second Edition. Englewood Cliffs, NJ. Prentice-Hall.

Guillén, M. (1994). *Models of Management: Work, Authority and Organization in a Comparative Perspective.* Chicago, IL. University of Chicago Press.

Gulick, L. and Urwick, L. (eds.) (1937). *Papers on the Science of Administration.* New York. Institute of Public Administration.

Hamilton, I. (1921). *The Soul and Body of an Army.* London. Arnold Publishing.

Handy, C., Gordon, C., Gow, I., and Randlesome, C. (1988). *Making Managers.* London. Pitman.

Hutton, G. (1953). *We Too Can Prosper: The Promise of Productivity.* London. George Allen and Urwin.

Keeble, S. (1992). *The Ability to Manage: A Study of British Management, 1890–1990.* Manchester. Manchester University Press.

Khurana, R. (2007). From Higher Aims to Hired Hands: The Social Transformation of American Business Schools and the Unfulfilled Promise of Management as a Profession. Princeton. N.J. Princeton University Press.

Kipping, M. (1997). 'Consultancies, Institutions and the Diffusion of Taylorism in Britain, Germany and France, 1920s to 1950s'. *Business History,* 39/4.

Koontz, H. (ed.) (1962). *Towards a Unified Theory of Management.* New York. McGraw-Hill.

Kransdorff, A. (1984). 'Idealism Is Not Enough'. *Financial Times,* 25 June.

—— (1998). *Corporate Amnesia: Keeping Know-how in the Company.* London. Butterworth Heinemann.

Lamond, D. (2005). 'On the Value of Management History: Absorbing the Past to Understand the Present and Inform the Future'. *Management Decision,* 43/10.

Latham, F. and Sanders, G. (1980). *Urwick Orr on Management.* London. Heinemann.

Lee, J. (ed.) (1928). *Dictionary of Industrial Administration.* London. Pitman.

Light, H. (1968). *The Nature of Management.* London. Pitman.

Lilienthal, D. (1944). *The Tennessee Valley Authority: Democracy on the March.* New York. Harper Bros.

Litterer, J. (1986). *The Emergence of Systematic Management as Shown by the Literature of Management from 1870 to 1900.* New York. Garland Publishing.

Lyndall Urwick Society, The (2007). *The Urwick Orr Partnership 1934–1984.* Mimes.

McKenna, C. (2006). *The World's Newest Profession: Management Consultancy in the Twentieth Century.* Cambridge. Cambridge University Press.

Miner, J. B. (ed.) (1995). *Administrative and Management Theory.* London. Dartmouth.

Mooney, J. D. and Reilley, A. C. (1931). *Onward Industry! The Principles of Organization and their Significance to Modern Industry.* New York. Harper & Bros.

Mutch, A. (2006). 'Organizational Theory and Military Metaphor: Time for a Reappraisal?' *Organization*, 13/6.

Northcott, C. H. (ed.) (1928). *Factory Organisation.* London. Isaac Pitman and Sons.

Nyland, C. (2001). 'Critical Theorising, Taylorist Practice, and the International Labour Organization', unpublished paper presented at the Second International Critical Management Studies Conference, available at: www.mngt.waikato.ac.nz/ejrot/cmsconference/2001/papers/management%20knowledge/nyland.pdf

Parker, L. and Ritson, P. (2008). 'Lyndall Urwick: Lifetime Champion of Scientific Management and Accounting'. American Accounting Association Annual Meeting. Anaheim, CA, August.

Paterson, T. (ed.) (1964). *Monopolies and Management.* Melbourne. F. W. Cheshire.

Pigors, P. (1935). *Leadership or Domination.* Boston, MA. Houghton Mifflin Company.

Pugh, D. S. (1973). 'Colonel Urwick and Organization'. *Omega*, 1, pp. 347–52.

—— Hickson, D., and Hinings C. (1971). *Writers on Organizations.* Harmondsworth, England. Penguin Books.

Quail, J. (2008). 'Becoming Fully Functional: The Conceptual Struggle for a New Structure for the Giant Corporation in the US and UK in the First Half of the Twentieth Century', *Business History*, 50/2.

—— (2009). Personal Correspondence.

Robbins Report (1963). *Higher Education.* Cmd. 2154. London, HMSO.

Roper, M. (2001*a*). 'Masculinity and the Biographical Meanings of Management Theory: Lyndall Urwick and the Making of Scientific Management in Inter-war Britain'. *Gender, Work and Organization*, 8/2.

—— (2001*b*). 'Splitting on Unsent Letters: Writing as a Social Practice and a Psychological Activity'. *Social History*, 26/3.

Rowntree, S. (1938). *The Human Factor in Industry.* London. Longman Green.

Rundle, D. (2006). *Henley and the Unfinished Management Revolution.* Henley-on-Thames. Henley Management College.

Sadler, P. (1998). *Management Consultancy: A Handbook for Best Practice.* London. Kogan Page.

Sheldon, O. (1923). *The Philosophy of Management.* London. Isaac Pitman and Sons.

Subramaniam, V. (1966). 'The Classical Organization Theory and Its Critics'. *Public Administration*, 44, Winter.

Taylor, F. W. (1903). *Shop Management.* New York. Harper & Row.

Thomas, R. (1986). 'Lyndall Fownes Urwick' in D. J. Jeremy (ed.) *Dictionary of Business Biography.* London. Butterworth.

—— (1988). *The British Philosophy of Administration.* London. Longman.

Thomson, A. (2001). 'The Case for Management History'. *Accounting, Business and Financial History*, 11/2.

Tiratsoo, N. (2004). 'The "Americanization" of Management Education in Great Britain'. *Journal of Management Enquiry*, 13/2.

Tisdall, P. (1982). *Agents of Change: The Development and Practice of Management Consultancy.* London. Heinemann.

Urwick, L. (1922). 'Experimental Psychology and the Creative Impulse'. *Psyche*, III/1.

Urwick, L. (1928). *Organising a Sales Office*. London. Gollancz.

—— (1929). *The Meaning of Rationalisation*. London. Nisbet and Co.

—— (1933). *Management of Tomorrow*. London. Nisbet and Co.

—— (1937). 'Committees in Organisation'. *British Management Review*, Spring.

—— (1943). *Personnel Management in Relation to Factory Organization*. London. Institute of Labour Management.

—— (1944). *Elements of Administration*. London. Pitman.

—— (1952). *Notes on the Theory of Organization*. New York. American Management Association.

—— (1954*a*). *Is Management a Profession?* London. Urwick Orr and Partners.

—— (1954*b*). *Management Education in American Business: General Summary*. New York. American Management Association.

—— (1954*c*). *The Load on Top Management: Can it be Reduced?* London. Urwick Orr and Partners.

—— (1957). *Leadership in the Twentieth Century*. London. Sir Isaac Pitman and Sons.

—— (1962). 'The Father of British Management'. *The Manager*, February 1962.

—— (1967). 'Organisation and Theories about the Nature of Man'. *Academy of Management Review*, 3(2).

—— (1969). 'Letter to an MBA'. *The MBA*, IV/1, October.

—— and Brech, E, (2002). *The Making of Scientific Management* (3 vols. *Thirteen Pioneers(I)*, *Management in British Industry(II)*, and *The Hawthorne Investigations (III)*). Bristol. Thoemmes Press.

—— and Wolf, W. (eds) (1984). *The Golden Book of Management*. New Expanded Edition, in Two Parts. New York. American Management Association.

Walter-Busch, E. (2006). 'Albert Thomas and Scientific Management in War and Peace, 1914–1932'. *Journal of Management History*, 12(2), 212–31.

Wiener, M. (1981). *English Culture and the Decline of the Industrial Spirit*. Harmondsworth. Penguin.

Wilson, J. F. (1995). *British Business History, 1720–1994*. Manchester. Manchester University Press.

—— and Thomson, A. (2006). *The Making of Modern Management: British Management in Historical Perspective*. Oxford. Oxford University Press.

Witzel, M. (2002). *Builders and Dreamers*. FT-Prentice Hall.

—— (2003). *Fifty Key Figures in Management*. London. Routledge.

—— (2009). *Management History: Text and Cases*. London. Routledge.

Wrege, C., Greenwood, R., and Hata, S. (1987). 'The International Management Institute and Political Opposition to its Efforts in Europe, 1925–1934'. *Business and Economic History*, 16, Second Series.

Wren, D. (1994). *The Evolution of Management Thought*. Fourth Edition. New York. John Wiley & Sons.

—— and Bedian, A. (2009). *The Evolution of Management Thought*. Fifth Edition. New York. John Wiley & Sons.

Young, E. (1990). 'Lyndall Urwick (1891–1983) British Management Authority and His Engineering Management Connection'. *Engineering Management Journal*, 2/1.

Index

Printed and bound by CPI Group (UK) Ltd, Croydon, CR0 4YY